ECONOMICS
AS SOCIAL SCIENCE

An Evolutionary Approach

Wendell Gordon
John Adams

WITHDRAWN

The Riverdale Company

Library of Congress Cataloging in Publication Data

Library of Congress Card No. 88 61799

ISBN 0-913215-38-4

CASE ISBN 0-913215-44-9

© The Riverdale Company 1989

Published in the United States of America by
The Riverdale Company, Publishers
5506 Kenilworth Avenue, Suite 102
Riverdale, Maryland 20737

Table of Contents

Figures and Tables   v

Preface   vii

**Part I: THE EVOLUTIONARY OR
           INSTITUTIONAL APPROACH   1**
Chapter 1   The Setting   3
Chapter 2   Theory of Change: Technical Knowledge   7
Chapter 3   Theory of Change: Institutions, Biology, and Resources . . .   17
Chapter 4   Theory of Change: Interaction   41
Chapter 5   Theory of Change: Induced Technological Change   55
Chapter 6   Philosophy of Science   69
Chapter 7   Theory of Valuation (Value Theory)   83
Chapter 8   Currently Held Value Judgments   101

**Part II: IMPLICATIONS FOR
           ALTERNATIVE APPROACHES   119**
Chapter 9   Maximization and General Equilibrium   121
Chapter 10   Implications for Microeconomics   143
Chapter 11   Implications for Macroeconomics   161
Chapter 12   Implications for Marxism   177

Part III: APPLICATIONS   193
Chapter 13   Research Methods   195
Chapter 14   Policy Making, Choice, and Planning   209
Chapter 15   Policies   229

Part IV: THE LARGER PICTURE   243
Chapter 16   The Larger Picture   245

Bibliography   247

Index   251

Figures and Tables

9-1   General Equilibrium 125

9-2   Maximization: The Income Distribution and Change
in Taste Cases 127

9-3   Best-Practice Technique 129

9-4   The Edgeworth Box and the Gross National Product 130

9-5   Industry Demand and Supply: Consumer and
Producer Surplus 132

9-6   Increase in Production Capability: General Case 134

9-7   Increase in Production Capability: Special Case 135

9-8   Maximization of the Rate of Growth 136

10-1   Demand and Supply 145

10-2   Quantities Bought and Sold: Scatter Diagram 146

10-3   Supply Elasticities 147

10-4   Short-Run Equilibrium of the Firm under Competition 149

10-5   Monopoly Pricing 151

11-1   Effect of New Investment on Income, Consumption,
and Saving 162

11-2   Devaluations and Trade Balances 166

11-3   Average and Marginal Propensities to Consume:
The United States 171

11-4   Import Propensities and Elasticities: the United States 173

12-1   Yield on British Consols/Long-Term Government Bonds 183

12-2   Percent Return on Net Assets (Worth) after Taxes
for United States Manufacturing 184

Preface

Microeconomics (price theory), macroeconomics (national income theory or Keynesian economics), and Marxism are what the typical economics department offers to its students as economics. Yet, somehow all too frequently, they impress the student as descriptions of never-never lands. There is considerable awareness of this situation on the part of the faculties of economics departments. Nonetheless, the professors are driven to offer microeconomics and macroeconomics, embellished with mathematical models, as the basic approach and Marxism as the foil, the inclusion of which in the curriculum demonstrates that the department is broad-minded in presenting alternatives to orthodoxy.

There surely are meaningful alternatives to the present economic orthodoxy and its foil: Marxism. This book represents an effort to identify and present such an alternative. It attempts to be constructive rather than merely critical of the prevailing orthodoxy. It centers on ongoing process, not equilibrium, and on society as a whole, not just "the market." It asks: What influences guide or control the economy as it evolves from a vaguely known past to an uncertain future in a process where ideas as to what is desirable are continually changing?

In the biased view of the approach presented here, economics departments should make sure that their students are aware of alternatives to economic orthodoxy. Probably, in the junior or senior year, they should offer at least one course that displays an alternative to the present orthodoxy and to Marxism.

The problems to which economics ought to address itself are important. They involve the availability of jobs, the handling of production, the standard of living, the meaning of welfare, the distribution of wealth, and the understanding of the process in which we are all caught up.

Orthodox economics generally assumes that value norms—our ideas as to good and bad, right and wrong—are given from outside economics. Economists take values and goals as given data and, in their role as economists, do not presume to question their validity or how they are arrived at. For confirmation of this, check the first chapter or two of almost any elementary economics text. The profit motive and the pattern of consumer tastes and preferences are taken as given. Values are taken as given. The possibility that the workings of the economic system, including advertising for example, may influence value judgments is assumed away. The possibility that economists might well concern themselves with the role of valuation formation in the economic process is disregarded. And, although economists using this approach generally claim that they are "value-free" or "positive" economists, the approach has the by-product of sanctifying the status quo as a value. This attitude itself is a valuation. It makes the role of the economist that of a high priest describing and defending how a hypothetical market works, a market that really does not exist.

Evolutionary or institutional economics, in contrast with orthodox economics, involves looking at social order as ongoing process. Conditions change, human biology changes, technology evolves, new knowledge about resource availability is acquired, and institutionalized behavior norms change. Individuals observe all these processes and are part of them. They change their valuations as an aspect of the ongoing process. And the value judgments which they modify or self-correct as the process goes on also influence the process itself. There is no identifiable utopia which people now can characterize and know that it represents the ultimately desirable goal, some teleologically determined final state. Life is an ongoing challenge. There will always be good works (and bad works and new works and new understandings) to be participated in by later generations. One generation cannot establish the norms for utopia with assurance that future generations will feel the same. One Congress cannot set a debt limit which the next Congress must observe. One generation cannot predetermine the values of the next, although it may powerfully influence those values. The most useful legacy that one generation can give to the next is not knowledge as to how to solve the welfare maximization problem or how to draft a blueprint for the Garden of Eden. The most important legacy is understanding the nature of social process.

This evolutionary frame of reference is the only one of the prevalent economics paradigms which comes to grips with growth, change, and progress in terms that might be called post-Darwinian. It is open-ended and non-teleological in a sense not true of Marxism, it is not tied to equilibrium in the manner of neoclassical growth theory, and, it does not rely on comparative statics in the manner of national income theory.

The philosophy of evolutionary economics is pragmatic in the tradition of Charles Sanders Peirce, William James, John Dewey, and Clarence Ayres. In fact this is what economic theory in the American tradition ought to be about because change and the pragmatic handling of change come nearer to representing the behavior patterns that have prevailed as America has developed than does the utopian market equilibrium.

Countless people over the years have contributed to the ideas presented in this book and to the final preparation of the work in this form. We hardly know where to begin recognizing our debts, but must explicitly thank like-minded colleagues of long standing at the University of Texas at Austin and at the University of Maryland, College Park.

Wendell Gordon
Professor Emeritus of Economics
The University of Texas at Austin

John Adams
Professor of Economics
The University of Maryland, College Park

September 1988

Part I

The Evolutionary Or Institutional Approach

Chapter I

The Setting

One may be reluctant to subscribe to the present orthodoxy (the market solution, the quest for profits, the competitive system, supply-side economics, rational expectations) for any one of several reasons. It is difficult to believe that the best possible results for society are gained when personal selfishness is allowed to control the process of growth and change. Another ground for misgiving may be that the present orthodoxy is oriented to static equilibrium situations that are epitomized by the law of supply and demand. The market is supposed to settle into a position where demand equals supply, or supply in the aggregate creates its own demand. These are supposed to be automatic, self–regulating processes. But one needs only to look around with an open mind to be aware that something more than this is going on. Price theory (microeconomics) is not working.

Also, national income theory (macroeconomics) is not working to provide full employment and eliminate inflation. And Marxism is no more likely to conjure up a desirable world as a result of the process described by Karl Marx than Thomas More's *Utopia* was likely to be conjured up by reason.

In Part I an alternative approach to economics is offered. This approach has been called, not too satisfactorily, evolutionary economics. It has also been called institutionalism or institutional economics and we will use these three terms interchangeably.

THE EVOLUTIONARY APPROACH TO ECONOMICS

There are two chief elements in this approach: a theory of change and a theory of valuation (value). According to the theory of change:

1. The basic dynamic influence is the accumulation of knowledge, especially technical knowledge. The process of accumulation of knowledge, of all knowledge, has an internal dynamic of its own,

3

and this process is not primarily controlled by such outside motivation as the profit motive or by outside need (such as desire for a cure for the common cold).

2. The institutions into which society is organized adjust slowly and reluctantly to assimilate and use new knowledge and to accommodate and adjust their own behavior norms in the process of utilizing this new knowledge.

3. How and where production will actually occur, or where use of new knowledge will occur, is conditioned also by the availability of the natural resources appropriate to the state of knowledge.

4. Monitoring all these interrelations are individuals, who are what they are in terms of physique and behavior as a result of their evolving biology and the impact of the evolving interaction of knowledge, institutions, and resources upon them. Also, the institutions of society are monitoring the individuals and constraining their behavior. Technology and resources, and individual biology, are evolving and interacting and conditioning individual attitudes and behavior. All this involves an ongoing, mixed-up process.

In addition to the foregoing explanation of change, the other chief element in the institutional approach is a theory of valuation, which is also dynamic rather than static. It is dynamic in the manner of the pragmatism and instrumentalism of C.S. Peirce, William James, John Dewey, and Clarence Ayres. This concept holds that what is valued or desired by people changes with the passage of time as conditions are altered and technology (knowledge) accumulates. Self-correcting value judgments are made by individuals and by institutions, and re-evaluations of the appropriateness of value judgments are made.[1]

BASIC INGREDIENTS IN ECONOMIC PROCESS

It is alleged here that a useful classification of basic ingredients in the economic process consists of technology, institutions, resources, and people. This is a more useful classification than the traditional four factors of production of orthodox economics: land, labor, capital, and enterprise. Orthodox economics has gone further and has attempted to identify a type of return going to each of the factors: land (rent), labor (wage), capital (interest), and enterprise (profit). Institutional economics does not attempt a similar sharp distinction in terms of the return going to the ingredients. In view of the difficulties involved in distinguishing interest from profit and wage from profit and in identifying rent at all, it might have been better if orthodox economics had been equally circumspect.

POSITIVE VERSUS NORMATIVE

It has become customary in the first or second chapter in elementary economics texts to contrast positive and normative economics. Positive economics is supposed to deal with what "is." Normative economics involves the making of value judgments. The (value) judgment is then made by the positive economist that the proper sphere of economics is positive economics and that normative economics, involving the making of value judgments, is not a proper sphere of activity for economists. Institutional economics, if it is mentioned at all in this context, is castigated for involving the proliferation of value judgments.

One might demur as to the accuracy of this distinction by pointing out that competitive price theory is not notoriously dealing with what "is," since it involves an elaborate description of a system that does not exist.

One might also demur on the ground that the essence of institutionalism is not the proliferation of unsubstantiated value judgments and irresponsible do-goodism. More accurately stated, institutionalism involves effort to understand the process by which value judgments are made. Economists should not take as unquestioned the demand for baggy pants or tight-fitting pants, female preference for shorter or longer skirts. Economics should concern itself with the source of these preferences, especially so since advertising, which is a cost to business, has a lot to do with influencing behavior patterns.

It is important to try to understand why we behave the way we do. Economists should not dodge this responsibility.

BEGINNINGS OF INSTITUTIONALISM

Thorstein Veblen, who did his writing between the 1890s and the 1930s, was the principal originating figure in the approach which has come to be called institutionalism, for lack of a better designation.[2] John R. Commons, based at the University of Wisconsin, was another major figure in the early history of institutionalism.[3] In developing the instrumentalist aspect of institutionalism the principal figures were Charles Sanders Peirce, William James, and John Dewey, whose active careers covered the period from the 1870s to the 1940s. Institutionalism and institutionalists came to have considerable influence during the 1920s and also during the New Deal days of the 1930s.

Individuals involved with institutionalism, but not necessarily so labeling themselves, have included Wesley C. Mitchell, Morris Copeland, Gardiner C. Means, Walton Hamilton, John Maurice Clark, Edwin G. Nourse, Thurman Arnold, Adolf Berle, and Rexford Guy Tugwell. After World War II the approach was continued by Clarence Ayres, Allan Gruchy, Gunnar Myrdal, C. Wright Mills, and Marc Tool.[4] The works of Kenneth Boulding and John Kenneth Galbraith are largely in the institutionalist frame of reference; however, they do not seem to have associated themselves with the label. The Brookings Institution, at least in its early years, mostly identified itself with institutionalism, as has been indicated by Edwin G. Nourse in his preface to R.A. Gordon's *Business Leadership in the Large Corporation*.[5] To belabor some terms, perhaps unduly, it may be mentioned that neoinstitutionalism is Allan Gruchy's term for the particular slant institutionalism has taken since World War II. Also, some orthodox economists have used "institutional" to describe their ideas. One example is the term "new institutionalism," which has appeared under the auspices of Oliver Williamson and others, and has very little in common with institutionalism in the Veblen-Commons-Dewey-Ayres-Gruchy tradition.

THE NATURE OF THE ASSUMPTIONS

The nature of the economics presented in this book is evolutionary not static; it is oriented to ongoing process not equilibrium; it is concerned with valuations and how people make them and change them rather than with merely assuming a profit or gain maximization motive and the logical exercises which that assumption implies.

The ongoing process that is assumed has no fixed goal; it is not teleological; and it follows no rigorous pattern such as the thesis, antithesis, synthesis route.

Beings are living out their lives in an uncertain process which they themselves can influence in directions that they, in their own (changing) frame of reference, can be proud of or perhaps not so proud of.

NOTES

[1]A bibliography of relevant works is presented at the close of this book.

[2]Joseph Dorfman, *Thorstein Veblen and his America* (New York: Viking Press, 1934); Thorstein Veblen, *The Theory of the Leisure Class* (New York: B.W. Huebsch, 1899).

[3]John R. Commons, *Institutional Economics* (Madison: University of Wisconsin Press, 1959 [1934]).

[4]Clarence E. Ayres, *The Theory of Economic Progress* (Chapel Hill: University of North Carolina Press, 1944): Allan G. Gruchy, *Modern Economic Thought* (New York: Prentice-Hall, 1947); see also the quarterly journal of the Association for Evolutionary Economics: *The Journal of Economic Issues*; and the bibliography at the end of this book.

[5]Robert Aaron Gordon, *Business Leadership in the Large Corporation* (Washington: Brookings, 1945).

Chapter II

Theory of Change:
Technical Knowledge

The institutional theory alleges that the accumulation of knowledge or technical knowledge or technology (defined in a very broad sense as involving all tools and all mental skills) is a dynamic process that controls in major degree what people do with the state of the world and that influences the nature of human progress and change.[1] Knowledge or technical knowledge thus represents the capabilities that people possess for improving their material welfare and for performing tasks in ways that involve less effort or are more effective.

A distinction between science and technology is sometimes made. Using such a distinction, one might view Einstein's theory of relativity as a scientific advance and the discovery of the best way to arrange one's hands on an ax handle as a technical advance. Asking whether the discovery, made some thousands of years ago, that soap is useful in dealing with dirt, was a scientific invention or a technological advance only raises a question that indicates the science-technology distinction is not of fundamental importance.

Ayres wrote: "Furthermore, as regards the nature of the process there is no difference between 'mechanical' invention and 'scientific' discovery."[2]

Concerning technology, the basic difference between institutional and orthodox economic theory is the difference between a theory which alleges that the economy gets its primary impetus from the dynamics involved in ongoing technological change and an economic theory that alleges that the economy gets its drive or direction as a by-product of the desire of individuals for monetary gain. Institutional theory recognizes the existence and importance of profit and gain considerations. It does, however, say that profit seeking is merely one institutionalized behavior norm, not the only influencing force in society.

7

CHARACTERISTICS OF THE TECHNOLOGY ACCUMULATION PROCESS

Characteristics of the technology accumulation process are (1) its cumulative nature and (2) its dynamism. Sometimes also mentioned as characteristics are (3) its continuity and (4) its accelerating rate. Basically involved is an evolutionary process with its own built-in dynamism. Many works on science and technology illustrate the process.[3]

The proposition that the process of accumulating scientific knowledge is inexorably leading to the discovery of definitive, certain *truth* is not one of the characteristics of the technology accumulation process presented here.[4] The position taken by institutionalism, rather, is that the process of accumulating knowledge *may* be leading to definitive knowledge as to what the universe is all about. But neither logic nor experience gives assurance of this.

Cumulative Nature

The first characteristic of the technological process is its cumulative nature. Certain discoveries are possible because other discoveries have been previously made. Roast pork followed the discovery of fire according to Charles Lamb. The making of iron weapons followed the discovery of processes for making iron. The horseless carriage followed the internal combustion engine. This process is not, however, what has come to be called technological determinism. It is not being said that, because knowledge about fire had been obtained, roast pork necessarily followed.

The possibility of smelting copper was probably discovered by accident about 5000 B.C. in the Middle East. It may be that some rock containing copper ore accidentally fell into a fire and the copper melted, flowed out, and then hardened, offering some intriguing possibilities to an observant Stone Age cave dweller. The process was observed or discovered and a use was found, not the other way around, as the profit motive approach implies when it alleges that the offer of the reward calls forth the discovery.

Fire was a precondition for the development of copper smelting. Then with the passage of time it was discovered that the same technique could isolate other metals (tin, lead, zinc, and ultimately iron), metals that had higher melting points than copper. Some of these discoveries were probably accidental, some not. An inquiring mind, aware of what happened to copper, would be stimulated to experiment with other rocks. (This inherent dynamism of the process is the second characteristic discussed below.) Then it was further discovered that alloying or mixing these metals with each other produced new substances with additional useful properties, for example copper and tin or lead and zinc to make bronze and brass. Harder metals and sharper cutting edges were obtained as knowledge of other alloys accumulated. It was no accident that iron was not developed first in this process. Iron required a hotter fire. Just so, it is no surprise that paleolithic people did not fabricate ball point pens.

Much later, James Watt's steam engine led to the railroad and the steamboat. Algebra preceded calculus in mathematics and with good reason. The telegraph (and the Morse code) needed as a preliminary the electromagnetic relay. The fire in the prehistoric cave generated other results than metals and cooked food. It generated pottery and bricks. If the cave wall close to the fire was of clay, it would become hard and resistant to the weather. Fire, thus, was an important step in the cumulative processes leading to many discoveries.

The discovery by Marcello Malpighi about 1660 of the movement of blood from the arteries, through the capillaries, to the veins was a logical next step following William Harvey's discovery (1628) that the heart served to pump the blood in a circular flow through the lungs, back to the heart, and thence out through the rest of the body. But Harvey had had no explanation as to how the blood got from the arteries to the veins.

Clarence Ayres has cited several examples of the cumulative nature of the technological process. Writing of the two bases for Gutenberg's development of printing in the fifteenth century, he stated: ". . . these were the art of block-printing practiced for centuries by the Chinese and the system of writing by use of alphabetical-sound-symbols practiced in the West for thousands of years."[5]

Abbott Payson Usher has reported on the background of the revolution in textile machinery that was a feature of the inception of the Industrial Revolution: "The mechanical achievements of the eighteenth century in textile manufacturing were dependent on the great advances in light engineering at a craft level in clock-and-watch-making, in lathe work in wood, and in the various crafts working with non-ferrous metals. All the problems of the construction and control of geared mechanisms were involved."[6] The lathe, invented in the sixteenth century, was necessary for making screws, a humble but important feature in much production, and for developing the metal cutting capability required for producing the textile machinery and steam engines of the eighteenth and nineteenth centuries.

If ever there were a cumulative process, it involved the evolution of inoculation and vaccination from the work of Robert Sutton and Edward Jenner on smallpox vaccination in eighteenth century England. The idea of building up resistance to a disease by exposing the individual to the germs in weakened form had tremendous implications extending to Louis Pasteur's development of an inoculation against rabies in the mid-nineteenth century, to the work of Jonas Salk and Albert Bruce Sabin in developing a vaccine for poliomyelitis in the 1950s and down to the development of a vaccine for hepatitis in 1982. Along the way, similar methods were used to develop immunity against cholera, typhoid fever, and tetanus. Now we have influenza shots every year, and they are continually modified to deal with new strains of the disease.

Knowledge in astrophysics and microphysics has cumulated in a fairly orderly way from Copernicus (circa 1500), to Galileo (circa 1610), to Isaac Newton (1643-

1727), to Albert Einstein and Niels Bohr. Knowledge about the cosmology of the universe grows.

The discovery shortly after World War II of the role of deoxyribonucleic acid (DNA) by Francis Crick and James D. Watson and the consequent proliferation of work in genetic engineering is engendering the prospects for mind boggling developments in the ability to create new forms of life, including major modifications of human biology. Some have gone so far as to call this "playing God." The United States Patent and Trademark Office has authorized the issuance of patents to cover some of these new forms of life (but not yet including green people). Such changes and the prospects of more are underway and with momentum. The implications are not trivial. And some of the nontrivial implications have nothing to do with the profit motive.

One should grant and emphasize that these cumulative processes have not necessarily followed rigidly predetermined sequences or orders. In many circumstances chance may determine which development occurs first. In the evolution of agriculture, Charles Townshend (1674-1738) fostered turnip production and the use of turnips as cattle feed and the use of clover in crop rotation to avoid letting land lie fallow for extended periods of time. Jethro Tull (1674-1741) developed a drill for sowing grain (1701), an improvement over throwing the seed broadcast, and he encouraged the hoeing out of weeds. Robert Bakewell (1725-1795) developed selective cattle breeding. Humphrey Davy (1778-1829) and Justus Liebig (1803-1873) developed artificial organic fertilizer. One of these developments was not a necessary preliminary to the others. And some of these developments may have occurred when they did under the influence of some version of the profit motive or because the desirability of such a development was conceived first and motivated or induced the discovery.

Evidence of the role of appropriate antecedents in leading to specific new discoveries can be found in the circumstance that frequently major new discoveries are made separately by different inventors at about the same time. Newton and Baron Leibniz developed calculus at roughly the same time. Charles Darwin and Alfred Russel Wallace developed the concept of evolution at about the same time; similarly for Alexander Graham Bell and Elisha Gray and the telephone. In economics, the idea of imperfect or monopolistic competition was developed at about the same time in the 1930s by Joan Robinson and Edward H. Chamberlin. Robert Merton has called this phenomenon "multiple independent discoveries."[7]

To a major degree one discovery waits on another. A new scientific discovery occurs because it is the next natural step in a technological sequence and not necessarily because people want to solve such and such a problem and go out and do it, or because the profit motive calls forth such and such a product. The cures for the common cold and for cancer will come at the appropriate stage in the evolution of technology and not because we are desperate for cures for these ailments and a squad of scientists has been generously subsidized to find those cures. If wishing and conscious diverting of resources to the task could do the job, we would have had a cure for cancer long ago. Edison could not have invented the electric light globe in 5000 B.C., or even in 1800 A.D., merely because people were clamoring for artificial light and profits could be made by providing it.

Dynamism and the Nature of Thought Processes

To say that the process of accumulating technical knowledge is dynamic is to say that the process has an internal drive that is not primarily dependent for motivation on influences from outside the process, such as the profit motive or the desire for a solution to a certain problem. What is involved is a process by which individuals acquire new understandings. Perhaps a thought or a speculation is present in the mind. One is wondering what to do about the cockroaches. One hears Mohammed Ali speak favorably of D-Con Roach Powder. At first one pays no attention. But then an impulse jumps a synapse in the brain. And one says; Maybe D-Con Roach Powder is what I need.

Or one is puzzling with a homework problem in algebra. One is stumped. One tries different possibilities. One looks out the window. One thinks about something else. Then suddenly the idea that will solve the problem comes to one. Again, *an impulse jumps a synapse in the nerve system in the brain and one is aware of a relationship of which one had been unaware the moment before.*

Issac Newton was speculating about the nature of gravity, or Albert Einstein about the nature of time and space, or Benjamin Franklin during a storm is intrigued by the nature of lightning. Perhaps they received an additional suggestive idea from somewhere or even from another cubicle in their own minds. Their brains put the two considerations together. One's conscious mind has no awareness of the logic by which the connection was made. A nervous impulse passed from one neuron to another in the mind of Newton or Einstein or Franklin. Perhaps at the moment they were a bit discouraged as to their ability to solve the problem. They might temporarily daydream, with their minds halfway on the problem and halfway not, and some capability in the brain (perhaps on the right-hand side) took over and, without a by-your-leave, where one moment frustration existed, the next moment an impulse has bridged a synapse gap. "Eureka," and Archimedes goes running naked through the streets of Syracuse proclaiming he can check the purity of gold. A person may get the insight after receiving or coming to understand some new discovery which one juxtaposes in the mind's eye with problems and processes that had been puzzling. All of a sudden there is a connection made. Society has new knowledge. Individual desire for profit or gain may stimulate this process or one may be induced by felt interest or need, but such influences need not be present for the process to go on. Nothing more than Veblen's idle curiosity may be motivating.[8]

In some cases society may envisage, ahead of time, the new technology that it desires and call on inventors, with suitable promises of reward, and then get the technology that is desired. This is the basic conception of the modern theory of induced technical change. But no such mechanism can call forth inventions "whose time has not yet come." This follows from the cumulative nature of the knowledge-acquiring process.

To some extent we control what we are thinking about and the results of our thoughts. But also we have to be aware that frequently we are thinking about certain things without any conscious decision or desire to do so. We are caught up in an ongoing process over which we have some control, but also which in some sense controls us. And occasionally, if we pause to think about it, we are quite surprised at the turn our thinking and conclusions have taken. But this does not keep us from continuing to participate in ongoing mental processes, idle and not so idle speculations (idle and not so idle curiosity), daydreaming, reverie, analysis.

Indicating the possible and frequent independence of this dynamic process from the constraints of the profit motive and the call for a new product or method is the tendency for inventors to discover something different from whatever they were initially looking for, if indeed they were initially looking for anything in particular. William Henry Perkins discovered aniline mauve dye while trying to synthesize quinine. Henry Bessemer discovered his steel-making process while trying to find a way to make iron cheaper. Charles Goodyear discovered rubber vulcanization by accidentally spilling some rubber on a hot stove, or so it is said.

According to the Charles Lamb story, roast pork was discovered because a farmer's house burned down with a pig still inside. Alexander Fleming discovered the germ killing property of penicillin as a result of noticing that some "penicillin" mold, that blew in his laboratory window, killed some bacteria with which he was working in a petri dish.

Much research in chemistry involves concocting a new compound (and there are infinite possibilities) and then engaging in endless checks to see what the stuff could possibly be good for. Quite a few years ago there was a cartoon (possibly by Lichty) that showed a laboratory manager saying to a young scientist, who is holding a test tube out of which a dancing girl is emerging: "Creating life in a test tube is all very well, Figby, but you were hired to find a new dandruff shampoo."

This is not an unimportant quibble. Orthodox economics is attempting to explain the structure and functioning of the economy by alleging that the profit motive or the desire to maximize welfare is the basic influence. In fact, the hard core neoclassical economic theory orients itself to gain maximization as *the* factor explaining the behavior of the economy and the consequent look of the world.[9]

None of these comments is intended to deny the possibility that a scientist may set out to find a product that will perform a certain function and find it. Or a scientist may go looking for a process that will cut some labor cost relative to capital cost, or vice versa, and succeed. Institutionalists argue that such behavior is only part of the story and that economics is off base in modeling the economic process as though the profit motive or the desire for gain is the whole story in explaining causation.

The more likely prevailing causal influence is that a given discovery occurs when it is "ripe" in the context of the ongoing process of technological accumulation. The nature of new technical discoveries is essentially dependent on the nature of previous discoveries.

Veblen says that the picture of "need calling forth invention" may have the story backwards: "And here and now, as always and everywhere, invention is the mother of necessity."[10]

Continuous and Accelerated Growth

A third characteristic of the technological process is its continuity. In general, knowledge once acquired is not lost. And one can observe over the great sweep of history the process by which knowledge generates other knowledge in an ongoing, continuous process. With regard to the controversial issue as to whether an item of knowledge, once acquired, can possibly be lost, we must default. Influential institutional economists (Ayres among them) have argued that in a sense knowledge, once acquired, cannot be lost. A steam engine was developed in Egypt by Hero of Alexandria about the time of Christ. Similarly, weaving machinery was invented but not exploited in Poland in the twelfth century. Much the same type of machinery, five centuries later, was basic to the Industrial Revolution. Was the knowledge found and lost or was it merely dormant or was it really never found? The issue does not really seem worth arguing.

A fourth item in the list of characteristics of the technological process is that knowledge is being accumulated at an accelerated rate over time. It is unclear, however, how the concept of an accelerated rate of accumulation can be quantified for purposes of statistical testing. And a process that involves, say, merely doubling knowledge every twenty or forty years (a constant, not an accelerated, rate of accumulation) could certainly generate a major increase without necessarily involving an accelerated *rate* of accumulation. Again, here is an issue that is hardly worth arguing.

It is discreet to grant the possibilities that the rate of accumulation may decelerate or the accumulation process come to an end. Possibly, even, all that is knowable might be known. This is conceivable. In any event, it is probably best not to allege the existence of any natural law to the effect that knowledge in general will accumulate indefinitely at an increasing rate. There is too much involved that we simply do not understand.

PARADIGM SHIFT

Thomas Kuhn has placed the technology accumulation process in a different perspective.[11] He argues that, during a given period in a given discipline, the nature of the research going on is controlled by a prevailing paradigm or model, or frame of reference. He argues that, during a given period in a given discipline, the nature of the research going on is controlled by a prevailing paradigm or model, or frame of reference. Scientific revolutions are "those non–cumulative developmental episodes in which an older paradigm is replaced in whole or in part by an incompatible new one."[12] A lot of ongoing minuscule advances in the theory covered by the paradigm are swept aside. During the sixteenth century, Copernicus and Galileo revolutionized astronomy with the idea that the earth rotates around the sun instead of the other way round. The theory of evolution in the nineteenth century revolutionized thinking about how people came into being. Shortly after 1900, Einstein upset Newtonian physics. In consequence of such changes, the prevailing approach ("normal science") in a discipline comes to change drastically its orientation. For Kuhn, "normal science," during any given period, is little more than a mopping-up exercise. "Few people who are not actual practitioners of a mature science realize how much mop-up work of this sort a paradigm leaves to be done or quite how fascinating such work can prove in the execution. And these points need to be understood. Mopping-up operations are what engage most scientists throughout their careers. They constitute what we are here calling normal science."[13]   This is a pretty accurate description of what most economists have been doing for the past three decades or so as they have elaborated the mathematical models of microeconomics and macroeconomics.

To what extent is Kuhn's scientific-revolution or paradigm-shift concept compatible with institutionalism? Perhaps it is and, at the same time, it is not. If institutionalism thinks that technical knowledge is being accumulated at a rapid, even an accelerating, rate, then institutionalism has a problem with the implications of the sort of stagnation that Kuhn claims characterizes a "normal science" paradigm. Yet at the same time there is an awful lot of sophisticated, trivial research going on, perhaps more so in economics than in physics or biology.

More generally, there is probably not the clear-cut distinction between paradigms that the Kuhn approach implies. There have been only a few dramatic, Kuhnian-type episodes. But also there has been a lot of alternating speeding up and slowing down in the knowledge accumulation process.

So, it seems, Kuhn's "scientific revolution" concept is, at the same time, not all that dramatic a paradigm shift itself relative to institutionalism.

TYPES OF TECHNOLOGIES

Some effort at classification of technologies is helpful to clarify what is involved, even though there is probably no classification that will be satisfactory for all purposes. Types of technologies may be identified as (1) specific to an individual plant or firm (firm specific), such as the arrangement of machinery in a given plant building of a certain shape. Or a technology may be (2) specific to an industry (industry specific), a new process for making a known product, such as a procedure for making steel or for making aluminum pots. Or a technology may have (3) a general application in different firms or industries to common types of problems (function specific), as for example a new system of bookkeeping that is usable in many industries. (4) Most obvious of all would seem to be the invention of a new product. (5) Somewhat less clear-cut is a fifth type of possibility (factor specific technology), involving a situation where a given product may be produced by different possible processes which use the factors of production in different proportions. A change in the relative cost of different materials or types of labor may make it desirable to shift to a new technology that uses the factors of production in those different proportions.

In some cases technology may not be separable in any meaningful sense from the form and substance of the capital equipment in which it is embodied. The technology *is* the structure of the machine, lathe, or bulldozer. In other cases technology may be almost entirely in the mind of the worker; it may be a way of doing things. It can be the knowledge that a little soap on the threads of a screw may facilitate turning the screw. "Instinctive" knowledge as to which way to turn the steering wheel of a car when it begins to skid is technical knowledge. This distinction depends on the location of the technology or knowledge. It may be in the mind (disembodied) or it may be embodied in the structure of the equipment. (This may not be quite the same disembodied-embodied distinction as that made in the production function literature.)

For the moment, so much for the role of technology.

NOTES

[1] C. E. Ayres, *The Industrial Economy* (Boston: Houghton Mifflin, 1952), p. 52. This is a broad definition of technical knowledge which includes as technology phenomena sometimes classified separately as science or technology (or techniques). The concept might be defined even more broadly as including all "rational knowledge," and in fact the expressions knowledge and technical knowledge are here indicated as synonyms. The activity called innovation by Schumpeter is, however, not included. Some of the terminological differences and problems are discussed in: Francis R. Allen, *Social-Cultural Dynamics* (New York: Macmillan, 1971) and in Francis R. Allen et al., *Technology and Social Change* (New York: Appleton-Century-Crofts, 1957).

[2] C. E. Ayres, *The Theory of Economic Progress* (New York: Schocken Books, 1962 [1944]), p. 113.

[3] A sample of history of science and technology books might well include: Melvin Kranzberg and Carroll W. Pursell, Jr., eds., *Technology in Western Civilization* (2 vols.; New York: Oxford University Press, 1967); David S. Landes, *The Unbound Prometheus* (Cambridge, Eng.: Cambridge University Press, 1969); John Jewkes, David Sawers, Richard Stillerman, *The Sources of Invention* (2nd ed.; New York: Norton, 1969 [1958]); J. Bronowski, *The Ascent of Man* (Boston: Little, Brown, 1973); Daniel J. Boorstin, *The Discoverers* (New York: Random House, 1983); Thomas R. DeGregori, *A Theory of Technology* (Ames, Iowa: Iowa State University Press, 1985); Maurice Daumas, ed., *A History of Technology and Invention* (New York: Crown Publishers, 1969). See any edition of *The World Almanac* for long tables of inventions and discoveries. And in a similar vein there is: Michael Hart, *The 100: A Ranking of the Most Influential Persons in History* (New York: Hart Publishing Co., c1978). Many of the "hundred" turn out to be scientists and inventors. Biographies of inventors and works describing particular inventions abound in the literature. By way of example there are: James D. Watson, *Double Helix* (New York: New American Library, 1968); Michael Bliss, *Discovery of Insulin* (Chicago: University of Chicago Press, 1982). *Technology*

and Culture is the journal of the Society for the History of Technology. Also see: Emilio Segrè, *From X-Rays to Quarks* (San Francisco: W. H. Freeman, 1980 [1976]).

[4] Larry Laudan, *Science and Hypothesis* (Dordrecht: Reidel, 1981), pp. 226-245.

[5] C. E. Ayres, *The Problem of Economic Order* (New York: Farrar and Rinehart, 1938), pp. 13-14.

[6] Kranzberg and Pursell, vol. I, p. 232.

[7] Robert K. Merton, *The Sociology of Science* (Chicago: University of Chicago Press, 1973).

[8] Thorstein Veblen, *The Instinct of Workmanship* (New York: Kelley, 1964 [1914]), p. 85.

[9] Milton Friedman, *Essays in Positive Economics* (Chicago: University of Chicago Press, 1953), pp. 21-23; Hal R. Varian, *Microeconomic Analysis* (New York: Norton, 1978), pp. 1, 80.

[10] Veblen, p. 314.

[11] Thomas S. Kuhn, *The Structure of Scientific Revolutions* (2nd ed.; Chicago: University of Chicago Press, 1970[1962]).

[12] Ibid., p. 92.

[13] Ibid., p. 24.

Chapter III

Theory of Change: Institutions, Biology, and Resources

The basic ingredients in the economic process are technology, institutions, the biology of people, and resources. This chapter concerns itself with defining and explaining the roles of the last three of these four ingredients.

PART I.   INSTITUTIONS

To turn, then, to institutions and the implications of institutionalized or customary behavior. An institution involves groupings of people with common behavior patterns, the members having an awareness of the grouping. In this definition the emphasis is on the institutionalized behavior patterns. It is not especially helpful to reify institutions in the sense of thinking of them as either buildings or as groups of people without regard to the nature of the influence that links them together. It may be noted that people, as individuals, play the role of custodians of the technical knowledge which society possesses. So they are also involved with technology. At any rate the essence of the institution is the behavior pattern which is observed by the group of people. And, thinking in these terms, John R. Commons has defined an institution as "Collective Action in Control of Individual Action."[1]

EXAMPLES OF INSTITUTIONALIZED BEHAVIOR NORMS

Examples of institutions and behavior norms include: the nuclear family in western civilization and the father's role as head of the family; primogeniture in controlling kingly succession; in the Islamic religion, the practice of facing toward Mecca while praying; the corporation under capitalism and limited liability of the stockholders; labor unions and group solidarity; the Latin American hacienda in

17

the nineteenth century and the system of debt peonage. In the tradition of Anglo-Saxon law, lawyers keep silent as to the misdeeds of their clients.[2] The steel industry typically, since 1900, has reacted to falling demand by raising prices—in order to maintain profit levels. Other industries frequently do the same, in spite of the law of supply and demand and its presumption that falling demand means lower prices.

Farmers demand government price supports during periods of low farm prices and denounce government interference with the marketing of farm products during periods of high farm prices without apparent awareness of the inconsistency. But then, people in the oil industry and the automobile industry and the steel industry, and so on, commonly do the same.

Another interesting behavior norm in the automobile industry was the belief, which was especially prevalent at General Motors, that it was possible consistently to make more money by making heavier, faster, more gadget-laden (more gadgets in the base sticker price so that the buyer had no real option but to take all the gadgets) cars.[3] And maybe they had a certain logic on their side. The American people love gadgets.

Many years ago, William Graham Sumner said of institutionalized behavior norms or folkways:

> The folkways are habits of the individual and customs of the society which arise from efforts to satisfy needs; they are intertwined with goblinism and demonism and primitive notions of luck . . ., and so they win traditional authority. Then they become regulative for succeeding generations and take on the character of a social force. They arise no one knows whence or how. They grow as if by the play of internal life energy. They can be modified, but only to a limited extent, by the purposeful efforts of men. In time they lose power, decline, and die, or are transformed. While they are in vigor they very largely control individual and social undertakings, and they produce and nourish ideas of world philosophy and life policy. Yet they are not organic or material. They belong to a superorganic system of relations, conventions, and institutional arrangements.[4]

Institutional theory does try to explain whence and how institutionalized behavior norms arise. But, aside from that, there is in the Sumner view much that is basic in the institutional theory regarding the nature of institutions.

CHARACTERISTICS OF INSTITUTIONS

Characteristics of institutions and their institutionalized behavior norms are that they are (1) static, and (2) inherited from the past. (3) They are eternally obsolescent. They need to be (4) psychologically defensible. And they are (5) dictatorial. (6) Also, they are difficult to change.

Static Nature of Institutions

A prime characteristic of institutions and their behavior norms is that they are static. There is nothing inherent in the institution, viewed as a set of behavior patterns, that causes those behavior patterns to change. This does not deny the possibility that individuals, who are members of an institution, may be influenced to try to change some or all of the behavior norms of the institution. But the institution as such has no built-in tendency to change and, in fact, tends to inhibit the individual participants from fostering change.

John Maynard Keynes, not generally thought of as an institutionalist, observed the phenomenon: "The difficulty lies, not in the new ideas, but in escaping from the old ones, which ramify, for those brought up as most of us have been, into every corner of our minds."[5]

Daniel Boorstin mentions an example from Herodotus. He says that Herodotus "observed dispassionately the variety of local customs, noting that men naturally preferred the customs into which they had been born. When Darius asked his Greek subjects what he would have to pay them to eat the bodies of their fathers instead of burning them on funeral pyres, no sum could tempt them. He then sent for some Indians, who customarily ate the bodies of their deceased fathers, and asked what would induce them to burn those bodies. But not for any price would they tolerate such sacrilege. Everywhere, Herodotus said, custom is king."[6]

Inherited from the Past

An institution's behavior norms, its patterns of ways of doing things, are inherited from the past. This has to be so because the setting involves ongoing process. And, in the nature of things, any behavior norm currently being applied has to have come into being at an earlier time, whether it be the practice observed in some places of having prayer before football games or whether it is the banker's practice of checking credit ratings before making loans. An institution is, then, any agency endorsing a complex of standardized behavior norms that continue to prevail until an outside influence comes along and forces change. The typical example of such outside influence is new technology, but other examples may involve other institutions that have contradictory or inconsistent behavior norms.

Perhaps knowledge of the origin of some behavior norm is lost in the past or confused in mythology. There is the rain dance, the practice of shaking hands, bowing, using assorted gestures to indicate approval or disdain or stop or go. What are the origins of the practices?

Or the origin of the behavior pattern may be known. The limited liability features of corporate stock came into being at the time of the Industrial Revolution to facilitate the mobilization of large blocs of capital from many people.

Appreciation of the inherited nature of behavior norms is found not only in the minds of institutional economists. It is a relation amply appreciated by those right-wing Austrian libertarians Friedrich von Hayek and Ludwig von Mises. For example, Hayek wrote:

Man is as much a rule-following animal as a purpose-seeking one. And
he is successful not because he knows why he ought to observe the
rules which he does observe, or is even capable of stating all these
rules in words, but because his thinking and acting are governed by
rules which have by a process of selection been evolved in the society
in which he lives, and which are thus the product of the experience
of generations.[7]

What Hayek says and what he does not say are both interesting. What Hayek
does not emphasize is the inhibitory role of these inherited practices. But it is of
some interest to note that von Hayek and von Mises have been far less committed,
than has been the case with most right-wing economists, to the rationality or
economic man assumption of orthodox economics.

Obsolescent or Obsolete

Even if the behavior norm still has a useful aspect, it will almost certainly be
a bit dated and not as appropriate for dealing with current problems as it might
be. Since it came into being at some earlier time, it is likely that the behavior
norm will have been more appropriate to the conditions of the time when it came
into being than to present conditions; and it would be something of an accident if
the norms were thoroughly appropriate for dealing with present day conditions.
The divine right of kings may have been a concept that helped bring some order
out of chaos in the seventeenth century, but it is not a concept with which many
people have much empathy in the twentieth century. Their dated nature, sometimes called past-binding ceremonialism, is an important characteristic of institutions and their behavior norms. Prevailing behavior norms are more appropriate
to the past than to the present. They can generally stand some change to advantage. And yet they prove very difficult to change. This does not matter much in
most situations but may be fantastically important in other cases, such as the
difficulty involved in reducing discrimination against blacks and other minorities.

Behavior norms are dated, more appropriate to the time they came into being
than to the present. Contrast this presumption of inappropriateness with the
orthodox economic assumption that the standard situation is a static equilibrium
characterized by efficiency. The economy settles into an optimum situation as a
result of the workings of competition, and somehow these workings produce the
best possible results for society, or so says orthodox economics. By contrast
institutionalism has it that our behavior patterns always leave something to be
desired even in terms of our own needs and desires. There are changes that may
be made that should generate results more in our interest if we can just bring
ourselves to make those changes.

Psychological Defensibility

The individual has a psychological need to be proud of one's own behavior. This
is the psychological defensibility consideration. Being proud of one's own behavior

involves being proud of the historical origins of that behavior. This is the *past glorifying* aspect of behavior. One is not likely to live a genuinely satisfying life if one is eternally ashamed of one's roots.

The glorification of our past involves a lot of ceremony and ritual. We are likely to be much concerned that the ceremonies commemorating our past are properly conducted. This is the *ceremonial adequacy* consideration.

One needs to participate in such activities with relish and pride. The labor union member must really be edified by union activities: picketing, parading, speech making. The same is true for the members of the Moral Majority or the KKK and their rituals.

Also, for a coherent, satisfactory society as a whole, there must not be major, bitter cleavages among important groups such as the labor unions, the Moral Majority, and the young upward-mobile professionals. There must be substantial agreement on general social institutionalized behavior norms. If there is not, and major groups have increasingly the feeling of being left out and individuals have the feeling of lack of harmony with institutions and between the institutions with which they are intimately associated, then there is social trouble in that society.

Social discord was prevalent in the United States in the 1960s and 1970s, in considerable measure as a by-product of the war in Southeast Asia and the Watergate scandals involving President Richard Nixon. Despite the very substantial economic prosperity of an unprecedentedly large percentage of the population, there was major, general discontent with society. Youth vociferously expressed lack of confidence in anyone over thirty. Family relations were in turmoil. Draft evasion was prevalent. Young people were migrating to Canada and Sweden to avoid military service. Crime rates were up. Drug use was up. The divorce rate was up. Academic performance in the schools was down. Policemen were "pigs." There was general dissatisfaction, although to considerable degree it was "a rebellion without a cause," at least in terms of economic conditions. And racial integration was progressing faster than it had for a hundred years, although it can hardly be alleged that the process was easy. Women and various minority groups were improving their relative positions. And yet everybody was unhappy about everything. The middle class was rebelling against the property tax in particular and taxes in general. Inflation meant that, although one was better off in a real sense than the year before, one was not as much better off as one thought one was going to be when one got a salary increase.

If one becomes disillusioned with the behavior norms of the institutions in which one has been brought up and has failed to find a place in a compatible institution, one is disoriented. Words for the condition are alienation and anomie. And if a significant segment of the population is thus disoriented the society itself is in trouble—the condition of United States society in the 1960s and 1970s.

John Locke anticipated the understanding of the necessity for psychological defensibility: ". . . who is there almost that dare shake the foundations of his past thoughts and actions, and endure to bring upon himself the shame of having been a long time wholly in mistake and error?"[8]

Dictatorial (Locke's Three Types of Laws)

Institutions are dictatorial, which is to say people are constrained to observe the institutionalized behavior norms whether they like it or not. The individual who may be tempted not to conform is likely to find that non-conformity is a behavior that exacts a high price. So, what are the sources of authority in connection with the enforcement of such norms?

John Locke had something to say about these matters in connection with his famous identification of Three Types of Laws:

The Divine Law: "which God has set to the actions of men,—whether promulgated to them by the light of nature, or the voice of revelation." And God has powerful sanction: "He has power to enforce it by rewards and punishments of infinite weight and duration in another life; for none can take us out of his hands."

The Civil Law: "the rule set by the commonwealth to the actions of those who belong to it . . . [which] has power to take away life, liberty, or goods, from him who disobeys. . . ."

The Law of Opinion or Reputation: "Virtue and vice are names pretended and supposed everywhere to stand for actions in their own nature right and wrong. . . . [M]en everywhere . . . give the name of virtue to those actions which among themselves are judged praiseworthy; and call that vice, which they account blamable. . . . [T]hough that passes for vice in one country which is counted a virtue, or at least not vice, in another, yet everywhere virtue and praise, vice and blame go together. . . . If any one shall imagine that I have forgot my own notion of a law, when I make the law, whereby men judge of virtue and vice, to be nothing else but the consent of private men, who have not authority enough to make a law: especially wanting that which is so necessary and essential to a law, a power to enforce it: I think I may say, that he who imagines commendation and disgrace not to be strong motives to men to accommodate themselves to the opinions and rules of those with whom they converse, seems little skilled in the nature or history of mankind. . . . [N]o man escapes the punishment of their censure and dislike, who offends against the fashion and opinion of the company he keeps, and would recommend himself to. Nor is there one in ten thousand, who is stiff and insensible enough, to bear up under the constant dislike and condemnation of his own club. He must be of a strange and unusual constitution, who can content himself to live in constant disgrace and disrepute with his own particular society."[9]

Any member of a fraternity or sorority or of a radical group, whether Communist, KKK, or neighborhood gang, can appreciate what is involved here.

The leaders, those with most status, in an institution have a very real stake in maintaining and enforcing respect for the traditions of the institution. Change in behavior norms is likely to carry with it change in leadership as well. And leaders generally have an interest in maintaining their status, and their traditional perquisites. They have, beyond the prestige of their status, which is no small factor, readier access to the police than do the rank and file members of an institution. They have control of the administrative and organizational machinery. It is difficult to fight those who dominate the channels of communication. Frequently, but not in all situations, they have the power to hire and fire the run-of-the-mill members. Many, or even most, people would rather cultivate power than fight it.

Before leaving the matter of dictatorial constraint, some further qualifications as to the nature of the constraint may clear the air. We may do what we are constrained to do, and do it with relish. We resist conforming in connection with some of our constrained behavior and conform with a will in other circumstances. Or our attitudes may change with time. The rebellious youth of twenty may, as a man of forty-five, be quite sure of the justification for imposing on one's own children much the same constraints one indignantly resisted earlier. C. Wright Mills has indicated one setting where a similar phenomenon occurs.[10] A youth who was scornful of Rotary-Club-type behavior may somewhat cynically join the Rotary Club on becoming a junior executive because it is the judicious thing to do and then later come genuinely to endorse the activities of the Rotary Club with enthusiasm. "The long acting out of a role, with its appropriate motives, will often induce a man to become what at first he merely sought to appear."

In any event, behavior is in general highly constrained, rather than representing a "freedom of choice" which reflects an individual's inmost sacred psyche. This inmost sacred psyche, the revealing of which is the "revealed preference" that economists qua economists believe we cannot or should not try to look behind, may well be nothing more than institutionalized behavior norms.

Difficult to Change

Institutionalized behavior norms are difficult to change. It is not enough that there be a reasonably obvious, pretty good reason for changing a behavior pattern to insure that it will be done. And of course the difficulty is compounded if anyone has even a small genuine interest in maintaining the status quo.

Since time immemorial new members of the University of Texas Board of Regents have been appointed by the outgoing governor a week or two before leaving office. It would seem preferable for the incoming governor to make such appointments. And yet changing the procedure requires the approval of the outgoing administration which does not favor the change. And, once installed, the incumbent governor will not want to make the change because if the change is made he or she will never appoint anybody.

Most of us are aware of the difficulties in effecting a transfer to the metric system in the United States. And how about the problem involved in changing the location of the letters on the typewriter keyboard? The arrangement that has prevailed for many years can be improved upon. But a lot of us have a vested interest in fingers trained to use the keyboard the way it has been.

Then there is the sort of difficulty involved in the effort to reduce smoking or heavy drinking. At the level of the individual there are the well known psychological problems. At the level of society as a whole there are questions as to how to enforce or encourage such abstinence in a society that prides itself on "the freedom to choose" of the individual. Enforcement by law, using the police power, is not necessarily a good way to get things done, and yet how does society deal with the individual who will not listen to sweet reason?

By comparison with these problems the issue as to whether "rain dances" on the part of various Indian tribes are very useful becomes a fairly trivial issue. So the people have some time on their hands while they stand around hoping for rain. Why not dance a little? And occasionally, rain does follow rain dances. An individual has to see that happen only once in a lifetime to become impressed and converted. Partial reinforcement of a behavior pattern may foster a tenacious habit. Or maybe the noise really does make it a little more likely that it will rain? At any rate nothing much is gained by cancelling the dances.

The difficulties of the United States automobile industry vis-à-vis Japan especially in the 1970s and 1980s are an example of unwillingness on the part of Detroit to adopt new techniques of production such as the Japanese have been using (for example a much higher degree of automation in Japanese automobile production in spite of the fact Japanese labor has been paid less than United States labor) and foot dragging by both the American companies and the motoring public in changing their orientation from the big, heavy, gadget-loaded gas guzzlers to the smaller more-miles-to-the-gallon car.

One may question whether it is so difficult to make changes since there are large numbers of people who are devotees of rule trashing, who are unhappy with The Establishment, and relish letting their dissatisfaction be known. Where is their devotion to institutionalized behavior norms? Are not they really free souls? But if one takes a deeper look at the circumstances of such people, one is likely to find that they are members of groups of dissenters and the form in which they express their dissent is likely to be very rigorously controlled by the institutionalized behavior norms of their dissenting group. The Establishment is merely an institution of which the people in question are not members. Dissidents, whether KKKers, or anarchists, Brown Berets, or Gray Panthers, are likely to be under very strong constraints to follow the behavior norms of their dissident group. Even the teenager demanding use of the family car for the evening and denouncing parental authority in the process may well be saying almost what one has been encouraged to say by others in the clique or gang. In fact overt dissenters may well have less real freedom of action than do many nominal cooperators with The Establishment, who frequently go off quietly and do what they please. Typically, dissident groups have to enforce strong discipline on their members if they are to survive.

If one is bemused by examples of unusual situations involving resistence to change, one may observe the family dog expressing disapproval of odd or unusual behavior by the dog's "master."

CIVILIZATION AND THE NEED FOR INSTITUTIONS

Thorstein Veblen spoke of imbecile institutions: "But history records more frequent and more spectacular instances of the triumph of imbecile institutions over life and culture than of peoples who have by force of instinctive insight saved themselves alive out of a desperately precarious institutional situation, such as now (1913) faces the people of Christendom."[11]

It is tempting to observe the uselessness, the merely ceremonial role, or even the reprehensibility (on some criterion or other) of certain practices and come to the conclusion that all institutions, all institutionalized behavior norms, represent undesirable limitation on our freedom to choose. On the political right, the Libertarians (but certainly not the Moral Majority or Right to Life groups) come close to taking this position, as also do Milton and Rose Friedman in their *Free to Choose.*[12] On the political left, various groups under such labels as radical, hippie, and what not, seem to condemn institutionalized behavior norms (while other groups on the left are frequently castigated for their apparent desire to plan the lives of everybody). Concern for freedom is not a monopoly of either the left or the right, nor is the urge to hold other people to one's own behavior norms. Those thoroughly dictatorial institutions, college fraternities, enforce behavior norms on the members that very closely resemble communism with a small "c." Uninhibited borrowing of each other's clothing is standard behavior. But, ask the fraternity members what they think of Russian "communism."

It is not a technology versus ceremonialism dichotomy, alleging that technology is good and ceremonialism is bad, that is being presented here.

Much of what has been said, and will be said in this book, with regard to institutions and their role may sound derogatory. That is regrettable. A society, to operate at all, has to have organization and, therefore, it has to have behavior norms. The alternative is chaos. It is highly desirable that cars observe the red and green lights at intersections. As life gets technically more complicated it will be increasingly important to have reasonable rules to control behavior, for example, to prevent electronic whizzes from destroying the monetary system. The necessity for standardization and simplification (in a setting where things are tending to get all too complicated) means, in certain contexts, an arbitrariness that, to a bright young person with a 140 I.Q., seems unreasonable or repressive. For example, you had better just sit there waiting for that light to change even though you see no traffic coming from any direction, whether you are driving a car or riding a bicycle. And so far as "keep off the grass" is concerned, it is true that the grass will not be killed if you are the only one who walks on it. But the advantaged, the intelligent, and the attractive have a special obligation to set a good example in the observance of reasonable rules. The "beautiful people" and the brilliant should not ipso facto be above the rules. They have more going for them than most people anyway; they should be especially conscientious to set a good example instead of being insistent on exploiting their initial advantage and almost fanatical in their defense of personal license.

Civilization, as an alternative to chaos and bestiality, is possible only on the basis of social understandings that constrain people to act in a decent and consistent and predictable manner toward each other. These social understandings constitute those institutions, that institutional order, which we call civilization.

The need for social institutions was recognized by the chief revolutionary of them all, Karl Marx, who wrote in "On the Jewish Question" (1843):

All emancipation is bringing back man's world and his relationships to
man himself. Political emancipation is the reduction of man, on the
one hand to a member of civil society, an egoistic and independent
individual, on the other hand to a citizen, a moral person. The actual
individual man must take the abstract citizen back into himself and, as
an individual man in his empirical life, in his individual work and
individual relationships become a species-being; man must recognize
his own forces as social forces, organize them and thus no longer
separate social forces from himself in the form of political forces. Only
when this has been achieved will human emancipation be completed. [13]

Civilization has gotten where it is by imposing behavior patterns which permit
society to operate as a coordinated entity. The behavior of the maturing individual
is conditioned by society as the infant becomes the child, the youth, and the adult.
By the time individuals reach maturity, they have learned that there are some
things society simply does not allow. And they will get along better if they conform.
Even if the individual has a naturally rebellious instinct, he or she will have found
out that it is better judgment to rebel in some ways rather than in other ways.

Individuals may have either of two quite different reactions when asked to
behave in the institutionally prescribed manner. They may conform (and generally
do) or they may rebel. Frequently they will rebel briefly and then conform. Or
they may rebel against their own parents, but, upon becoming parents, may try
to force their own children to follow the precepts which they themselves had
resisted. Make your bed; pick up your litter; speak civilly to others; help with
the dishes; get off the couch or at least get your shoes off the couch or off the
edge of the coffee table or off the table in the school library; get home from your
date at a reasonable hour (you are a lot less likely to have an undesired pregnancy
to contend with); do not make quite such a din with your rock'n'roll music; wipe
your feet; wipe your nose; practice a little courtesy. Making a half-way civilized
citizen out of a baby *homo sapiens* is an activity that takes a considerable amount
of doing, and quite a period of time, and is sometimes less than successful. The
process is not helped by "manly" fathers who take pride in the cavalier exploits
of their sons. "Oh that is really all right; I did the same thing when I was young,"
he says and smiles as junior throws a rock at a car and fortunately misses.

Some friction between children and parents is a natural part of the growing-up
process. Major rebellion is something else. Rebellion may reflect little more than
a concern for self, or may involve a reaction to a legitimate serious grievance.
This makes a good deal of difference. Society improves as a result of successful
rebellion in a good cause. It is in trouble if too many of its members spend too
much of their time rebelling as an expression of self-indulgent insistence on having
one's own way in trivial matters. One type of rebellion may be the making of a
society or culture. The other type, if there is a considerable amount of it, may
well be the society's undoing.

Also there is the problem of the moderately worthy cause which is overexploited by moderately aggrieved people with aggressive instincts or a compulsion to muscle their way into positions of leadership. A good deal of the present rebellion against The Establishment (whatever that is) probably, if implemented, would involve little more than a substitution of the New Establishment (meaning new institutions) for the old one without any real change in conditions. Repeated revolutions in underdeveloped countries are a tragic example. The positive merit of change depends on the character of the New Establishment (institutions) which is replacing the old. It is not enough to be told that the Old Establishment must go, simply because it is the Old Establishment, without regard to the desirability of the new institutional order and the ability of the leaders of the new order to behave responsibly instead of their making the new order into an ego gratification trip.

If we conform to the little rules that are half-way reasonable, we are going to be in a lot better position for protecting the greater freedom that matters and for protesting the important unreasonable rules. Persons interested in being genuinely effective in changing some undesirable feature of society may be well advised to be pretty much conformist in most other aspects of their behavior. They will get a better reception when they present their arguments for changing what really needs changing.

We do have to have institutions (social organization and rules) in order to avoid chaos and in order to have civilization. The problem is to manage so that we are masters of the rules instead of the rules (tradition and force of habit) being our masters. The society that is flexibly, continually, objectively, and intelligently reevaluating its rules and norms is going to assimilate technology more readily, offer a higher standard of living to its members, and be a more pleasant place in which to live, than is the society which is rigidly frozen in its ways or given to violent, irresponsible change.

The objectionable institutional practice is the one which gets its sanction from habitual thought, mores, and customs, without being revalidated currently in terms of whether or not it facilitates the constructive use of worthwhile new technology. This is the test as to whether the practice is instrumental. If, however, the habitual practice plays no significant inhibitory role, there is no particular harm in its continuance. And if people enjoy it, get some emotional satisfaction out of it, why not?

All this may seem almost trivially obvious, but the economist may be well advised not to make that charge too scornfully. We are here talking about the influences that control a great deal of human behavior which the economist with singleminded determination tries to explain with the assumptions of rationality, economic man, the profit motive, and the desire to maximize gain. And that approach may also be viewed as inadequate and as capable in many cases of generating error, or undesirable results, or high standard of living for a relatively few people who are adept at exploiting the market system, the particular pattern of economic institutionalized behavior norms that prevails in Western society.

MEMBERSHIP IN MANY INSTITUTIONS
(REFERENCE GROUPS)

It is perhaps self-evident—but, then again, maybe it is not—that one person may play roles in various institutions: church, home, trade union, place of employment. In responding in one setting to the norms of one institution and in another setting to the norms of another, the nature of one's behavior (in response to the same issue) may be rather different in these different settings. One may be genuinely full of concern for fellowpeople while in church on Sunday, and genuinely concerned to increase profits at the expense of fellowpeople the other six days of the week.

Muzafer and Carolyn Sherif have worried with the implications of this phenomenon. In describing some of the influences at work on a Spanish-speaking boy they have written:

> For example, he may be an American boy attending a certain school
> with other boys and girls in his neighborhood, but belong to a Spanish-
> speaking family whose members have encountered social and economic
> obstacles to improving their lot. He goes to church, spends his leisure
> with other Spanish-speaking boys in his neighborhood, and belongs to
> an athletic club run by the city. Whose appraisals count for him? Those
> of his schoolmates? His teachers? His parents? Those who discriminate
> against his kind? The church authorities? His neighborhood friends?
> The athletic staff? Fellow team members? Or are his sights set beyond
> the present toward images of successful, more prosperous persons
> he sees on the printed page, television, and movie screen? These are
> all identifiable sets of people whose appraisals we can ascertain. But
> which are his *reference groups*—which are the sets to which he feels
> he belongs, wants to belong, relates himself, psychologically?[14]

In discussing the implications of the relation between groups of different ages, they wrote: "During the adolescent period—the transition betwixt and between childhood and adulthood—agemates in general and one's own associates in particular become major reference groups for the individual. Being in the same boat, they appear more capable of understanding him. They are the ones whose opinions *matter* and whose actions *count*. The 'inner voice' which prompts and regulates his social actions (and decides what he will spend money on) is likely to tell him what *they* will think."[15]

This is the reference group phenomenon. On a particular issue, one, consciously or unconsciously, may have to make a choice as to which institution's behavior norms one will adhere to, and which of the institutions of which one is a member is one's dominant "reference group" on a particular issue. Understanding this and reconciling these differences in a way that is satisfactory to oneself and to society is one of the most difficult problems confronting the individual.

PART II. INDIVIDUALS AND THEIR BIOLOGY AND PSYCHOLOGY

THE PLACE OF BIOLOGY

People take a people's eye view of the Universe, just like rats would seem to have a rat's eye view of the Universe. People are important, not because the Lord made them important, but because we are people and we are important to ourselves, while probably not especially so to the rats or the cockroaches. The ongoing social process determines who is included in and who is left out so far as influence on the process itself is concerned, and whether people believe a person begins to exist in a meaningful sense at conception or at birth, is determined by the institutionalized behavior norm with regard to this matter. There is probably no "provable" scientific basis for saying one thing or the other. And, be all this as it may be, as matters stand on Planet Earth, people, subject to vicissitudes of wind, weather, and cosmology (technology, resources, and institutionalized behavior norms) dominate the beings on the earth, at least to some degree, if not as effectively as they might wish in some cases. Test this by trying to housebreak a dog or get rid of cutworms in the garden.

These human individuals, with their evolving biology, are the custodians of the evolving technical knowledge and the creatures of the evolving institutionalized behavior norms subject to the constraint imposed by evolving resource availability. The individuals are playing a many faceted role as they are influenced and influence while playing out the role that they have the leverage to play. The little green beings from outer space might arrive and change the scenario, or we might change it all by ourselves by injudicious detonation of atom bombs or use of germ warfare; or the penguins, assisted by climatic change, might take over (or the rats, or the cockroaches, or the elephants).

Meanwhile, here we are. Maybe there is a Lord that cares about us and maybe not.

We have a rather remarkable ability, that is to say: people in contrast with other animals, to take into account our own circumstances, anticipate old age and death, and plan improvement. We have been endowed with a hand and a brain that have more capabilities than have been bestowed by nature on most other creatures, up to this time on this planet. Conceivably the porpoises have more intelligence, but they are handicapped by not having a five-fingered hand. So we observe our technology and resources and participate in creating, subject to our institutionalized behavior norms, changing conditions.

As beings we have a changing biological make-up. Historically, the influences controlling biological evolution have been beyond our control, but even that may be changing thanks to biotechnology and understanding of DNA.

Both heredity and environment influence the manner in which an individual responds to social or cultural pressures. There is interaction between biological and social influences. But the actual content of much behavior that is attributed to biological drives derives its particular form of expression from custom, habit, and institutionalized norms. LaPiere and Farnsworth have commented: "If motivational terms (such as organic hunger) are to be used to explain some complex patterns (as entering a restaurant to order dinner), it must be clearly recognized that they do not refer to biological drives, but rather to complex social developments upon the original organic bases." [16]

Muzafer Sherif has written: "Like other organisms, man is born with certain needs, such as the needs for nutrition, shelter, and later, mating. . . . Along with this, we note another fact. When we observe people in the search of food, shelter, or mates, we conclude that these activities run in certain prescribed channels. People do eat, mate, and enjoy the security of shelter; but how and under what circumstances they will eat, mate, and enjoy shelter are, to a great extent, regulated by customs, traditions, laws, and social standards. This is true for every individual, living in every society we know, primitive or developed. If an individual does not come under this category to any important degree, he cannot be said to be a member of society." [17] The need for food is biological. A taste for oysters is cultivated. Taking a cracker and grape juice last Sunday at Communion is an institutionalized behavior norm.

Much or most behavior is what it is because of the influence of habit or custom, which does not gainsay that in some sense much or most is due to the influence of biological evolution or that there is a type of overlap and no precise measure of relative importance in the process is feasible.

INSTINCT PSYCHOLOGY

Thorstein Veblen titles one of his books, published in 1914: *The Instinct of Workmanship*. [18] The question was later raised whether he was using the term instinct in a manner professionally acceptable to psychologists or biologists. Is there such a thing as "instinct," professionally defined, so far as people are concerned? After Veblen wrote, one of the standard complaints against institutionalism has involved this use of the concept of instinct.

According to Veblen, instincts are not reflexes (tropismatic actions) like the knee jerk, they are biologically determined reactions, of some sort, to a stimulus. The nature of the instinctive reaction is determined by heredity. Thus, Veblen was saying that workmanship, the tendency to work with care and to take pride in the product of one's work, is an hereditary attitude; also, it is an instinct in the sense that the individual with this instinct will automatically be workmanlike when confronted with a task.

Is this Veblenian position an expression of the instinct psychology of William McDougall which enjoyed a vogue in psychology in the early years of the twentieth century and then fell under a cloud during the 1920s? According to McDougall:

> [An instinct is] an inherited or innate psycho-physical disposition which
> determines its possessor to perceive, and to pay attention to, objects

of a certain class, to experience an emotional excitement of a particular quality upon perceiving such an object, and to act in regard to it in a particular manner, or, at least, to experience an impulse to such action.[19]

For McDougall, an instinct was not a purely mechanical reaction. It was thus not a tropism or a reflex, nor was it a conditioned reflex. But it was physiological in nature in the sense of involving the psycho–physical system. McDougall provided a list, in fact various lists, of instincts: the parental (protective) instinct, the instinct of combat, and the instincts of curiosity, food seeking, repulsion (disgust), escape, gregariousness, self-assertion and submission, mating, acquisitiveness, and self-actualization (the instinct of workmanship). Then there was the instinct to appeal against unfavorable rulings, as for example: poor grades. Would McDougall have called Veblen's concept of idle curiosity an instinct? It is not clear. McDougall did deny the role of instinct to playfulness and to imitation.

A criticism of McDougall expressed in 1919 ran as follows: "McDougall's theory was vitiated because it contained the notion of subjective purposiveness and hence involved recourse to unobservable phenomena."[20] So instinct psychology was, at least temporarily, discredited by the behaviorism vogue, which tried to limit the coverage of psychology to "the observable evidences of organismic activity to the exclusion of introspective data or references to consciousness and mind."[21]

Behaviorism is the psychology of J. B. Watson and B. F. Skinner. For better or worse, and whether or not Veblen was guilty of expressing the McDougall position, he was discredited, at least in some circles, by his espousal of instinct psychology. In the larger picture, however, Veblen was in some pretty good company: Sigmund Freud, Karl Marx, Konrad Lorenz, and Abraham Maslow. In retrospect this issue may appear as a bit of a tempest in a teapot, and maybe that is just about what it was. In any event, concern about workmanship is an important concern, whether, or in what sense, it may be an instinct.

EVOLUTIONARY PROCESSES

Human biology could have gotten where it is via several different routes: (1) (scientific) creationism, (2) Darwinian evolution, or (3) punctuated equilibria, and (4) there are no doubt other possibilities.

Scientific Creationism

Scientific creationism is a doctrine that people (Adam or Eve or whoever) and the rest of the universe as well were created by some Lord or some superior power (acting according to its lights) in a process that may or may not have been over a period of six days or so, after which strenuous process everybody needed a rest on the seventh day, except the wife, all of this happening about 4000 B.C. And this is the crux of the matter. People were created in their present form by a superior being rather than evolving from more primitive forms. Creationism, thus described, enjoys little credibility in biology departments, but it exercises a very considerable influence on the content of the texts used in biology courses in high schools and perhaps also in colleges: Texas fundamentalists have been especially influential, nationwide, in this process because of the early timing of textbook selection for the public schools of that state and because there is statewide selection of textbooks which are then provided en masse to the schools of the state.

Darwinian Evolution

Evolution is a concept developed in the mid-nineteenth century by Charles Darwin and, independently, at virtually the same time by another Englishman, Alfred Wallace. It involves the proposition that human biology evolved to its present state via a process of mutation and natural selection that has lasted over hundreds of thousands of years. Biological changes occur in people occasionally by accident (the process of mutation); the changes that become permanently incorporated in later generations are those that are relatively useful (the process of natural selection, involving the survival of the fittest). And the poor devils born with the undesirable traits are more likely to die off early without passing them on (the failure to survive of the less fit). It has been said that both Darwin and Wallace arrived at this insight after reading Thomas Malthus's *Essay on Population.*[22] So the development of the theory of biological evolution might be said to be an example of the cumulative process in acquiring technical and scientific knowledge.

Punctuated Equilibria

The concept of punctuated equilibria is a reaction to the observation that slow Darwinian evolution is a process that simply could not have worked fast enough to evolve the biology of people to the stage it has reached in the twentieth century. The punctuated equilibria concept runs to the effect that there have been brief chaotic eras, perhaps the beginning or the end of an ice age or as a result of some other major climatic disturbance, when there has occurred a tremendous acceleration in the pace at which mutations are going on, and new species have emerged rapidly. Then the biological form is likely to remain virtually unchanged for thousands of years. Recent proponents of this view include Stephen Jay Gould and Niles Eldridge.

At present there is a lot we do not know about the origin of life, the origin of the universe, and the possible existence of either a personal god or some other power or force "out there," the nature of which we do not comprehend.

SOCIOBIOLOGY

During the past couple of decades a type of biological determinism, sociobiology, has been advocated by Edward O. Wilson.

The principal goal of a general theory of sociobiology should be an ability to predict features of social organization from a knowledge of these population parameters combined with information on the behavioral constraints imposed by the genetic constitutions of the species. It will be a chief task of evolutionary ecology, in turn, to derive the population parameters from a knowledge of the evolutionary history of the species and of the environment in which the most recent segment of that history unfolded. The most important feature of the prolegomenon, then, is the sequential relation between evolutionary studies, ecology, population biology, and sociobiology . . . . The species lacks any goal external to its own biological nature.[23]

Aside from, possibly, overdoing the emphasis on the role of genes in the argument over the relative roles of genes and culture in influencing behavior, Wilson might be said to have "shot himself in the foot" by somewhat gratuitously alleging some implications on the touchy racism subject. He seems to say that the white race is superior in terms of intelligence and in terms of survival value. In *On Human Nature* he tries to mollify hurt feelings on this score.[24] But Wilson remains under a shadow on the racism issue, at least in the impression of some.

The more important criticism of Wilson is that he is either merely repeating the obvious point that biology and culture interact or he is overselling biological determinism by claiming too much for the power of biology to predict changes in social organization.

DNA AND BIOTECHNOLOGY

More interesting than the pros and cons of sociobiology are the possibilities, opportunities, and dangers placed in prospect by biotechnology—by the possibility of "human engineering." Following conscious policy the human race can now change the nature of its own biology. Without too much ability to foretell just what the implications of the result may be, science is developing the ability to modify the genes and change the biological nature of people.

Herman Muller, as a consequence of his work on fruit flies in the 1920s and 1930s, was among the first to extol the possibilities for improving the human being by controlled modification of the genes: ". . . man is the first being yet evolved on earth which has the power to note this changefulness, and, if he will, to turn it to his own advantage."[25]

Then came Francis Crick and James D. Watson in the 1950s, with fuller knowledge as to how the process might work as a result of their identification of the protein substance recombinant DNA (deoxyribonucleic acid) molecules which control heredity and the physiology of living organisms.[26]

People can influence the biology of people and the future form and look of individuals without knowing what exactly may be the effect of any given mutation that they manage to bring about. Is it "ethical" for people, or for some people (either biologists or politicians), to dabble around in this business? This is a value judgment. And what may be said about value judgments is the subject of chapter 7.

PART III. RESOURCES

One more ingredient beside technology, institutions, and individual biology, is involved in the economic process: resources. What is required is a broad definition of resources. The concern involves the whole physical and energy content of the Universe. It is the evolving physical setting in which technology, institutions, and people are playing out their roles. At issue are the processes by which neutral stuff evolves into resources, the influence of the location of resources on the location of production, and the question of the exhaustibility of resources.

NEUTRAL STUFF AND RESOURCES

In the terminology of Erich Zimmermann, the individual is "submerged in an ocean of 'neutral stuff,' i.e., matter, energy, conditions, relationships, etc., of which he is unaware and which affect him neither favorably nor unfavorably."[27] Then some of this neutral stuff may become a valuable resource "in response to increased knowledge, improved arts, expanding science, but also in response to changing individual wants and social objectives . . . . Resources *are* not, they *become*, they are not static but expand and contract in response to human wants and human actions." The raw materials of the earth, neutral stuff, become valuable resources because the given state of technology so decrees. And, as technology evolves, the relative usefulness of different raw materials changes. In the early 1700s the substitution of coal for wood in steelmaking by Abraham Darby at Coalbrookdale in Shropshire, "thanks to Britain's exceptional resource endowment (in coal) . . . changed a high cost industry (in Britain) into the most efficient in the world,"[28] and made Britain the dominant industrial power of the world.

The process for making aluminum out of bauxite, developed in the 1880s by Charles Hall and Paul Louis Toussaint Héroult, made a fairly useless type of clay into a valuable resource.

Also, the advance of science and technology and changes in behavior norms may leave some resources behind as transportation has left the horse and agriculture has left the turnip. So, the process of creating and destroying resources is a dynamic process. It is not useful or particularly meaningful to try, at a given time, to quantify the resources available to a society with the implication that this quantification will have validity at future dates. Trying to take an inventory of resources has been a common procedure in geography and planning. The procedure is useful, desirable, even necessary, at a given time in connection with a given bit of planning and at a given stage. But the implication that an inventory of resources has continuing validity in long-range planning can be misleading.

LOCATION

Frequently the neutral stuff that will be a useful resource in the context of some newly developed technology is located in fairly clearly defined geographical areas. Petroleum deposits are where they are, the same for copper, lead, and zinc, gold and silver, and bauxite. They can only be drilled for or mined where the deposits are. But, somewhat more subtly, the juxtaposition of Lake Superior iron ore and Ohio and Pennsylvania coal, and utilizing Great Lakes transportation, dictated that the United States would have an important steel industry and that it would be centered in Ohio and Pennsylvania. The iron ore came to the coal because, among other reasons, the weight of iron ore used in the industry was less than the weight of coal. Also, Ohio and Pennsylvania were handier to the consuming markets than was northern Minnesota.

One does not want to overemphasize this influence. The Swiss watch industry did not develop because Switzerland produced the relevant raw materials. So, as Zimmermann emphasized, the location of a given industry is influenced not only by the presence of the appropriate physical resources but also by the whole range of institutional influences, including the initial location of the labor supply with the most appropriate skills.

The vision involved in integrating these diverse conditions into an enterprise located at a given place is the essence of entrepreneurship which mixes a little arithmetic with a little intuition, but probably does not include the ability to solve maximization problems in the calculus of variations.

FINITENESS AND EXHAUSTIBILITY

As to the exhaustibility of resources, it is clear that a country, or the world as a whole, can literally exhaust the supply of a given resource. The world could run out of petroleum or whale oil or wood, although the eventuality of running out of petroleum may not be as close as some of the cries of alarm of the 1970s implied. More of a threat to petroleum and gasoline supplies, in a practical sense, is political trouble in the Middle East. Put that consideration into an econometric model if you can.

The world could run out of whale oil and did in the nineteenth century in the sense that it became obvious that there was insufficient whale oil to continue providing a major source of fuel for lighting. It ran out of Peruvian guano in the same sense. And England ran out of wood (for purposes of fueling industry with charcoal) in the seventeenth century. If industry were to develop, as it did with the Industrial Revolution, a major source of energy had to become available. Coal, first, played the role then petroleum, then now perhaps coal again or the heat from the sun.

The question as to whether exhaustion of resources in general is a threat to the survival of the human race or to its standard of living, in the sense alleged by the Club of Rome, the Hudson Institute, and various governmental studies such as the Paley Report of the early 1950s, is a different matter. The studies that are the basis for this sort of concern about exhaustion and survival generally compare the rate of use of various resources with the known supplies or reserves of those resources and observing, for example, that the world's oil will only last, say 28 years (the world's copper only so long, the world's zinc only so long) at the current rate of production of known reserves. Then a table of all the minerals is constructed in these terms and it looks as though by the year 2000, or some date, the world will genuinely be in desperate straits with regard to resources in general.

This traditional way of analyzing the resource problem disregards the manner in which, as ongoing process, new resources are created out of neutral stuff in response to the needs of industry. The cyclical manner in which concern for raw material availability gyrates should warn groups like the Club of Rome that it is possible to misunderstand the nature of the general resource availability situation. We move through cycles in which, for a while, we are concerned about raw material availability and raw commodity prices rise. Then there is a period of raw commodity surplus and prices fall.

Anyone who has checked the history of agricultural prices in the United States over the past hundred years knows that more often than not the farmers are bewailing surpluses and low prices, and the same for the mining companies. But then there comes a period of scarcity and high prices when the raw commodity producers call for the cessation of governmental interference with the market (an interference that they had demanded during the periods of surplus). What is involved is hardly a precise twenty-year cycle between extremes of gloom and doom because we are about to run out and gloom and doom because we have too much. But it does involve an interesting ability to blow hot and cold on the matter without much recollection of what one's attitude was the year before.

It remains true that there may be crop failures and desperate hardship in some parts of the world (perhaps the Sahel region of Africa, or Ethiopia) while there are surpluses in Iowa. The structural and adjustment problems are eternally with us, not having been worked out either by the free market or by governmental regulation.

We do have problems in the raw commodity area. But a simplistic belief that we are "about to run out" is hardly even a first approximation of a reasonable understanding of the problem.

Around us is all the bulk of earth and air and universe, and especially the sun. In any given state of the technical arts, that area of the world will tend to develop most rapidly which is well endowed with the raw materials appropriate to the prevailing state of knowledge. And individuals will migrate there if they can.

Particular types of neutral stuff come and go as valuable resources. There is not much point in speaking of the danger of exhausting resources. The chemicals of which the Earth is made are transformed, and they change in relative value, but they are not exhausted, although the process of entropy may diffuse them.

It may be at some time in the indefinite future the improvement in welfare on planet Earth will be held back by the lack of some particular resource or by the presence of too many people in relation to the area of the earth. One can hardly prove the contrary, but there is every reason to believe that this will not be the essence of our problems for the next hundred years.

We may want to limit the population because in our opinion people are cluttering up the place, or are polluting it unduly, or are hard to live with, but it simply is not true that lack of raw materials in any overall sense is at present a significant factor holding down welfare. The possibility, however, does exist that the institutional hindrances, which make difficult the increase in welfare in a country like India, may make population control a desirable development policy in such a country. Thus, population control may be opted for on the ground that it is easier to implement such a policy than it is to change certain other institutions. But that is a judgment which will be made by those in a society in a position to make it (as part of the ongoing self-correcting value judgment process).

In addition, it should certainly be granted that at any given time particular shortages may create structural problems, or force institutional change, and may be a considerable cause of inconvenience until the appropriate adjustments are made. In fact, the availability of resources plays a twofold role concerning which it is desirable to be explicit. (1) New technology creates new resources out of neutral stuff. And the location of the chief deposits of the new resources influences the location of the new industry. (2) Any particular resource may become exhausted. And the exhaustion of particular resources may lead to a shift to other raw materials, for example, as sources of fuel, or to abandonment of some particular industry, or to a shift in the geographical location of an industry and a change in institutionalized norms in particular industries. The structural and geographical changes may cause great inconvenience to large numbers of people. And the difficulties will be enhanced because bureaucrats, industrialists, politicians, labor unions, and people in general will resist making the appropriate changes.

In the long-run the world is not going to run out of resources in general or energy in particular. There are oil shale, coal, atomic power (fission and fusion), solar energy, thermal power (underground hot water), the wind, and even the tides, especially in the Bay of Fundy and the Bay of Mont St. Michel. The energy problem can be dealt with in a manner that will provide more than adequate energy over the long haul. But short-run complacency about the energy problem may lead to trouble. And the same is true for any resource. Short-run adjustment and bottleneck problems can be serious.

All these possibilities plead for thoughtful planning not for worry and distress.

NOTES

[1]John R. Commons, *Institutional Economics* (Madison: University of Wisconsin Press, 1961 [1934]), p. 69; see also: F. Stuart Chapin, *Cultural Change* (New York: Century, 1928), pp. 45, 48.

[2]See an article by Stephen Gillers entitled "Lawyers' Silence: Wrong . . .?" in the *New York Times,* February 14, 1983; also an editorial on the subject: "Lawyers for Hire for Anything?" in the *New York Times,* February 11, 1983.

[3]John McDonald, *The Game of Business* (Garden City, N.Y.: Doubleday, 1975), pp. 28-61.

[4]William Graham Sumner, *Folkways* (Boston: Ginn, 1906), p. iv.

[5]John Maynard Keynes, *The General Theory of Employment, Interest, and Money* (New York: Harcourt, Brace, 1936), p. viii.

[6]Daniel J. Boorstin, *The Discoverers* (New York: Random House, 1983), p. 564.

[7]Friedrich A. von Hayek, *Law, Legislation, and Liberty,* vol. 1, *Rules and Order* (Chicago: University of Chicago Press, 1973), p. 11; see also Ludwig von Mises, *Theory and History* (New Haven: Yale University Press, 1957), p. 159.

[8]John Locke, "Concerning Human Understanding," in *Great Books of the Western World,* vol. 35: *Locke, Berkeley, Hume* (Chicago: Encyclopedia Britannica, 1952 [1690]), p. 111.

[9]Locke, pp. 229-231.

[10]C. Wright Mills, *The Power Elite* (New York: Oxford University Press, 1956), p. 439.

[11]Thorstein Veblen, *The Instinct of Workmanship* (New York: Augustus M. Kelley, 1964 [1914]), p. 25.

[12]Milton and Rose Friedman, *Free to Choose: A Personal Statement* (New York: Harcourt Brace Jovanovich, 1979).

[13]Karl Marx, *Early Texts,* ed. David McLellan (Oxford: Basil Blackwell, 1971), p. 108.

[14]Muzafer Sherif and Carolyn W. Sherif, *Reference Groups: Exploration into Conformity and Deviation of Adolescents* (Chicago: Regnery, 1964), p. 6.

[15]Ibid., p. 164.

[16]Richard T. LaPiere and Paul R. Farnsworth, *Social Psychology* (New York: McGraw-Hill, 1949), p. 39.

[17]Muzafer Sherif, *The Psychology of Social Norms* (New York: Harper and Row, 1966 [1936]), p. 1.

[18]Veblen, pp. 4, 13, 27-28.

[19]William McDougall, *Introduction to Social Psychology* (London: Methuen, 1936 [1908]), p. 25.

[20]Knight Dunlap, "Are There Any Instincts?," *Journal of Abnormal Psychology* 14 (1919), pp. 307-311.

[21]*Webster's Seventh New Collegiate Dictionary.*

[22]J. Bronowski, *The Ascent of Man* (Boston: Little, Brown, 1973), pp. 305, 306.

[23]Edward O. Wilson, *On Human Nature* (Cambridge: Harvard University Press, 1978), p. 3; Edward O. Wilson, *Sociobiology* (Cambridge: Harvard University Press, 1975), pp. 5-6.

[24]Wilson, *On Human Nature,* pp. 47-51.

[25]Herman J. Muller, *Out of the Night* (New York: Vanguard Press, 1935), pp. 113, 126.

[26]James D. Watson, *Double Helix* (New York: New American Library, 1968).

[27]W. N. Peach and James A. Constantin, *Zimmermann's World Resources and Industries* (3rd ed.: New York: Harper, 1972 [1933]), pp. 8-15; or Erich W. Zimmermann, *World Resources and Industries* (2nd ed.; New York: Harper, 1951 [1933]).

[28]David S. Landes, *The Unbound Prometheus* (Cambridge, Eng.: Cambridge University Press, 1970), p. 95.

Chapter IV

Theory of Change: Interaction

The institutional or evolutionary theory of change views the accumulation of new technical knowledge as the primary, dynamic element in the economic process. Then the effective use of the new technology will probably call for changes in institutionalized behavior norms. Institutions, tending to be static, will resist making the appropriate changes. So, the effectiveness in introducing new technology is greatest where the institutional resistances are weakest.[1]

William Ogburn described this process:

> A very common pattern is for the technological change to affect, first, an economic organization which, second, causes a change in some social institution, such as the family or government, and which finally causes a change in the social philosophy of a people. Thus technology brings the factors which take occupation away from the home; which cause a loss of other functions of the family, such as caring for the old; which causes the government to provide old-age pensions; which in turn tends to weaken the social philosophy of laissez faire.

> As the hoe evolved into the plough, food was raised from seeds of grasses—notably barley, oats, wheat, and rice—all of which could be preserved longer than fruits; and animal food, particularly milk, was produced from tamed animals. This increased food supply, based upon technology, made possible communities much larger than were possible in the hoe, or digging-stick culture.

> Thus the first direct adjustment to the technology that increases the food supply and makes it more assured from season to season and from year to year is a larger population. But the adjustment in turn to a larger population may be a greater division of labor, a specialization of occupation, different religious ceremonies . . . or the creation of

41

social classes. These are derivative adaptations to the original or direct adaptation to the technological innovation.

Men adjust to the steam engine by letting it drive their tools for them. Consequently, they work away from home in factories. Then the family, a social institution, adjusts to the absence of workers and to the new production and to the additional source of income. The adjustments in the family are the decline in the authority of the husband and father, the removal of economic production from the home, and separation of husband and wife, and the different type of education for the children. These are not the direct adaptations to the steam engine but are adaptations to the uses of steam-driven tools away from the homestead.[2]

TECHNOLOGY AS INSTIGATOR

New technology, to be effectively used, is going to require institutional change. The invention of the cotton gin by Eli Whitney about 1793 revived the institution of slavery, which was moribund at the time, at least in the American South. The discovery of the New World by Columbus in 1492 rendered a similar disservice in reviving slavery and the slave trade on a world scale in the sixteenth century. African slaves were wanted in the American tropics because of the (institutionalized?) unwillingness of the Indians to adapt to the plantation way of life. The Indians died in preference to participating in the plantation culture. The Las Casas effort to abort the use of Indians as slaves on the plantations and in the mines of the New World was a frustrating struggle in sixteenth century America.

In an even earlier time ploughshares brought society out of the hunting and fishing stage of development and into the institutional setting of sedentary agriculture with its very different implications for the nature of family life.

The automobile encourages the middle-income American family (an institution) to move to the suburbs. The presence of large numbers of people (with automobiles) in the suburbs creates that remarkable institution, the suburban shopping center. It is easy to take interrelations like this much as a matter of course. We were brought up with them. And yet the mental effort involved in backing away and taking a second look may generate the impression that here are interrelations that dominate our lives, and which have economic as well as sociological content. They have made suburbia, for good or ill, what it is. They are the essence of the lives of many of us.

James N. Danziger has cited examples of the effect of computer technology on institutions. "Computing tends to increase the importance for decision and action of quantitative, technical criteria . . . . Computing use tends to isolate individuals, reducing their interaction with other people in both work and leisure settings . . . . Computing increases social control and monitoring, reducing the privacy of individuals and small groups . . . . The current impacts of computing tend primarily to serve the interests of the more dominant groups in a given setting, thus reinforcing existing power distributions."[3]

In an infinite regression, all the norms of all the institutions had to come from somewhere else, not just from other institutions. And the chief candidate for the role of major influence has to be evolving technological or scientific knowledge.

In important degree, it is going to be and has been the nature of the evolving technology that has dictated the essential features of the behavior norms—not exactly, but substantially. Technology qua technology probably does not much care whether drivers hold to the left or the right. Whatever, they had better get organized and all act consistently; they had all better drive on one side of the road or the other.

Each corporation is an institution with some unique characteristics. In many cases one can almost see the invention calling forth the particular corporation: the Bonsack cigarette machine and the American Tobacco Company, centrifuges and the American Sugar Refining Company, refrigerated railroad cars and Swift and Company.

An interesting argument has been developed by Lynn White, Jr., to explain the emphasis on the importance of the individual in western society: "During the ninth century the chimney and mantled fireplace appear, first at the abbey of St. Gall in Switzerland. A well-designed chimney flue drew the smoke out through the wall while radiating considerable heat into the room . . . . The lord and lady began to spend less time in the great hall and to seek privacy in their withdrawing rooms . . . . By implementing privacy it provided an essential milieu for the growth of the western ideal of the idiosyncratic individual."[4]

In the early 1950s C. Wright Mills offered a sophisticated argument explaining the new importance of the middle class in his book *White Collar:* "The proliferation of new professional skills has been a result of the technological revolution and the involvement of science in wider areas of economic life; it has been a result of the demand for specialists to handle the complicated institutional machinery developed to cope with the complication of the technical environment."[5] Mills viewed "the new middle class" as the technocrats needed to run the system because of its complexity. Owners and executives are dependent on them because they cannot learn all they need to know to manage the system.

So, it is the complexity of the new technology that calls forth this new middle class. These circumstances give the new middle class the leverage to extract quite attractive rewards from the system without the necessity of unionizing to do it, a significant change in the structure of the labor market. But this is not to say that the new middle class is unorganized. It organizes itself most effectively to protect certain freedoms and a certain mystique that it is protecting a freedom to choose, which on closer inspection turns out to be a highly constrained "freedom to choose." Whether they like it or not they cannot escape from the complicated and coordinated management that is necessary, and to which they must conform, if this most intricate society is to be operational. Nevertheless, they want both the freedom to generate garbage and the freedom to see to it that the garbage disposal dump is not in their neighborhood.

The phenomenon of the role of the technocrat has also been noticed in underdeveloped countries. Helio Jaguaribe, a Brazilian, writes: "What is coming into being is an immense new middle class of technician-managers which is forming at the center of contemporary society. It will be this new middle class, and not the vanishing proletariat, which will take charge of the formation of a new society."[6] The chief struggle going on is one for relative position among technicians, managers, bureaucracy, and executives. The power struggle among these groups is the really important economic conflict in society, not the traditional capitalist-proletariat so-called class struggle.

At the time of the Meiji Restoration in Japan about 1868, leadership in that country decided to do what was necessary to acquire the ability to confront Western power effectively. It was the understanding of this leadership that the assimilation of Western technology was essential in this process. But the leaders did not want meddling foreign investment to be the channel by which the technology came in. Japanese people traveled the world and brought back knowledge of the Western technology. Incidentally, they thus avoided a heavy interest rate burden for the next hundred years such as they would have incurred had they resorted to the foreign investment process.

It is one thing to acquire knowledge about foreign technological practices. It is quite another matter to implement the use of that technology in industry. There needed to be institutional changes if the newly acquired knowledge was to be used effectively in Japan. The changes did not need to duplicate Western institutions, but they did need to be such as would permit the effective use of the new technology. Japan did a miraculous job of fostering the creation of workable institutions. The old aristocracy was soundly defeated by the forces seeking to establish the power of the Emperor and this institutional shock contributed to reducing the resistance to change of the old institutions. At any rate, the Samurai warrior class was co-opted into the new business and industrial groups. Their resistance to change was circumvented by thus giving them a leading position in the new order. Highly integrated government-business cooperation then expedited the industrialization process.

The workers were conciliated with employment practices that came close to ensuring a lifetime job guarantee in the firm where one worked. All this facilitated industrialization. But it should be noted that these institutional changes did not involve an effort to copy the American or British institutional systems.

Latin American countries can learn a good deal from the Japanese experience. What they should learn is not the desirability of copying Japanese institutions, but the importance of practicing the sort of self-reliance the Japanese practiced. An equally important lesson would be to avoid significant reliance on foreign investment.

Thorstein Veblen had an expression for this sort of thing: "the cultural incidence of the machine process."[7]

The implication is that technology and new technological possibilities are the prime instigators of social or institutional change. And, since the process of accumulating technical knowledge has its own internal dynamic, one is visualizing a process that may be influenced by the profit motive but is not primarily guided by the profit motive.

RESISTANCE OF INSTITUTIONS

Initial Resistance and Strength of Resistance

Institutions resist the changes in their behavior norms that are indicated if effective use is to be made of new technology.

The Eastern Roman Empire with its capital in Constantinople survived in a more or less moribund state for a thousand years from the fifth to the fifteenth century. The Holy Inquisition, which was especially dominant in southern Europe in the seventeenth century, was dedicated to suppressing the changes fostered by Martin Luther and the Reformation. China in the nineteenth century tried to defend itself against the West by protecting the old cultural ways. More recently, as examples, there were: the resistance of the United States automobile industry to the production of small cars and to the use of lead-free gasoline and other environmental protection measures, the general resistance to the assimilation of the metric system in the United States, and the resistance of the United States steel industry after World War II to the introduction of basic oxygen furnaces and other new technologies.

During the 1970s and 1980s the fear of safety-related litigation held back technical innovation in many areas and the Food and Drug Administration became more and more reluctant to grant quick approval for the use of new drugs. Fear of multimillion-dollar legal judgments and high insurance premiums made doctors more and more reluctant to perform even moderately risky operations. The reluctance has extended even to the willingness to practice obstetrics, the delivery of babies.

"Reasonable" (whatever that is) control of the innovation process is surely desirable. Individual entrepreneurs left free to operate in an unregulated market process are quite capable of introducing processes or products which will have an injurious effect on the human race. The production of aerosol sprays, which have turned out to be a threat to the ozone layer around the earth, is an example. Impact studies (that do not take forever), conducted by competent professional scientists under instructions to take the long-run general welfare into account, are desirable. But at this stage it becomes a decision for society (not for the individual entrepreneur) to make as to whether the new process should be used or the new product adopted. For better or worse, the judgment will be ad hoc. Each case will be different. Each industry will involve different considerations. And there is no mathematical model that will permit a computer to grind out an answer solving the problem, QED, as to whether the development should occur. Certain aspects of the decision-making process may usefully be computer aided. But that is rather different from obtaining a neat final solution from the computer.

After 1986 a new Russian leader, Mikhail Gorbachev, attempted to open up somewhat the Soviet society and economy to unconventional information and artistic works. The nuclear disaster at Chernobyl was discussed with a frankness unusual in the Soviet press. The phenomenon came to be called "glasnost" (openness) in the American press. By the summer of 1987, more traditionally minded Russian leaders, including Yegor K. Ligachev, the second-ranking Communist

Party leader, were beginning to bemoan this relaxation of controls. One may surmise that these major institutional changes will be, at best, implemented slowly against great resistance. But since these changes should make the Soviet Union "easier to live with" from the viewpoint of the United States, it might behoove the United States to be less overtly hostile to that country while the efforts are going on.

Workers quite frequently resist, including by violent means, the introduction of new types of machinery, under the impression that unemployment will result, as it very likely may in that particular line of activity. Cotton-picking machinery does reduce the need for cotton pickers. And the cotton pickers resist, even though picking cotton has never been considered one of the more pleasant employments and there may be more and better jobs available as a result of higher production. One of the more famous examples of this phenomenon was the Luddite movement in England during the 1810 decade. It involved major resistance to the introduction of the machinery that constituted the essence of the Industrial Revolution. One surely is justified in saying that the Industrial Revolution was desirable and that it made higher standards of living possible. But also, more considerate and humane *planning* could have avoided a lot of suffering along the way.

Workers are not alone in resisting change. This is an area where they frequently have a common interest with their employers and with the capitalists who have financed the industry in which they have been working. The capitalists do not relish the introduction of new machinery that will hurt the relative productivity of machinery from which profits could otherwise still be made, if somehow the introduction of the new equipment could be prevented or postponed. Again, the United States steel industry after World War II is a prime example of this phenomenon.

The Collapse of Resistance,
the Concept of Threshhold Resistance,
and the "Usefulness" of Forecasting

As an historical fact, the institutionalized resistance to the use of new technical knowledge frequently does collapse and the look of the world is modified and some behavior norms are changed.

Sometimes there is not much resistance and change occurs in a fairly tranquil and orderly way. In other cases violence and violent revolution occur to implement the change process. There are two aspects of the problem: (1) the timing of the crumbling, and (2) the identification of the direction in which various components of the crumbling structure will jump. Quantifying the jump would be desirable, but efforts along that line are secondary to the understanding of timing and direction. And accurate quantifying is probably, in general, not possible anyway.

It is generally true that institutions do not change behavior patterns perceptibly during long periods in spite of minor pressures. During this period those standard parameters of orthodox economics, the elasticities and marginal propensities really are constants, or at least sufficiently close to being constant to justify econometric methodology and the claim that such and such a relation will probably hold: for example, that a spurt in investment will increase output by roughly such and such an amount. Then, one fine day, a somewhat stronger pressure (perhaps not a much stronger pressure) topples the house of cards and completely changes the nature of the behavior patterns of the institution. The Bastille falls, the Winter Palace is stormed, the Mongols breach the Great Wall, Henry VIII decides he wants a divorce. A whole economic and social order (or something less) collapses—an order that only the day before had been thought to be impregnable, like the Diaz order in Mexico in 1910. The behavior patterns are suddenly and drastically changed. Major new decisions need to be made. Yet the parameters, elasticities, and marginal propensities laboriously computed during the period of stability are now useless as guides in planning how to deal with the new situation.

The analysis of institutional change has some analogy with the role of the critical mass in nuclear physics and with sensitivity testing in statistics. "A test item will *respond* or *not respond* to a certain level of test stimulus (e.g., a shell will explode or not explode when subjected to a certain shock)."[8] This is the problem of measuring threshold resistance.

It would be nice if a formula could be developed to measure the amount of pressure it would take to break down the threshold resistance that a given economic institution presents to the assimilation of a given bit of a new technical knowledge. Unfortunately what is involved is frequently more qualitative than quantitative. At a given time, most politicians have the same rules of thumb regarding what it takes to win elections. For example, advocacy of segregation was a standard rule of thumb in the South for many years and the "separate but equal" principle was supposed to provide equity to the blacks. Anyone who suggested that a politician proceed counter to that rule of thumb needed to have the head examined. Then some particularly striking contrariwise development occurs; and a lot of rules of thumb get changed. Even George Wallace "got the message."

There may be a useful analogy with the contraction of disease. Persons may live for many years as carriers of germs of a certain type without ever, themselves, catching the disease in question. Then, one not-so-fine day a slightly increased concentration of the germs may bring one down with the ailment. Or some outside event may activate the germs and change their role from endemic in the carriers to epidemic in other people. The foot-and-mouth disease may be endemic among cattle herds in Argentina that have built up some resistance and then may become epidemic when fortuitous circumstances move the disease to a different setting, such as Mexico or Texas.

A particular institution may change its ways drastically (or collapse) when technical change acquires sufficient force to compel the modification. The modification of behavior patterns then occurs in spite of institutional resistances, which are stronger the longer the institution has been set in its ways and the more isolated it has been from the forces of change. Francis Stuart Chapin has described a "societal reaction pattern" (in response to pressure or disturbance) that works something like this:[9] In phase I the group reacts against the change which seems to be called for by the pressure or disturbance. The group's reaction takes the form of an effort to enforce its mores on those trying to implement change. In phase II the significance of the inadequate adjustment is fairly generally felt. The group then reacts by expressing a willingness to experiment with some possible changes, by trying different expedients. During this period, the general feeling is of chaos and unsatisfactory conditions. Then in phase III "the group integrates its trial and error efforts into a stable plan," and the result is one with which the group is reasonably well satisfied.

In all this, the crucial stage is reached when the institution under pressure is still quite determined to defend its norms. Toward the end, collapse may be substantially speeded or delayed by whether the patient happens to go out on a cold, rainy night, or whether a politician picks up a dog by its ears at just the wrong time and place. Fate, and external forces, and human will can play an important role in influencing the timing of institutional change. But this does not mean that it is possible to quantify the resistance of institutional thresholds or to forecast the timing of major change by using statistical techniques.

An attempt to quantify threshold resistance is the wrong way to approach the problem. Using such an approach, one might try to develop methods for jolting undesirable institutions with shocks of increasing force until the desired change occurs, but that makes the process sound too orderly. It is probably not desirable to overwhelm an institution with far more force than necessary. Yet starting with shocks that are too mild may help build up the institution's resistance so that it takes, later, a much more disruptive shock than would have otherwise been necessary. The South was not hit hard enough in 1954, and it built up its resistance to desegregation. Perhaps President Eisenhower should have acted with more authority (an easy thing for someone else to say). His personal presence in Little Rock might have had a calming influence and prevented the occurrence of many similar incidents that followed. But he went on with his golf game.

David Landes has tried to explain why French development lagged behind the German in the period 1850 to 1914. In so doing he points out that France had been ahead of Germany earlier for a long period, from perhaps 1780 to 1850, but was making progress slowly. This slow progress, he indicated, perhaps allowed French institutions to build up resistance to change. It permitted "the development within her body social of psychological and institutional antibodies to the virus of modernization."[10]

Probably not much can be, or should be, tried along the line of forecasting the timing of the collapse of institutions. But maybe an inability to time catastrophe or to read the future is not of major importance. It would certainly be no favor to the family dog to tell it two weeks ahead of time that the family is going on a vacation and it is going to be boarded out at the veterinarian. Probably most of us would not care for the picture if we could see into the future. We would probably not care to anticipate either the gladness or the sorrow. Most of us, if we had a choice, would really not like to know ahead of time when we are going to become ill or when we are going to die. "Oh blindness to the future! kindly given," as Alexander Pope wrote in "An Essay on Man."

Forecasting is not, or rather should not be, the most important job of economics.

But the role of forecasting is even more dubious than this. As John Dewey has said: ". . . the assumption is generally made that we must be able to predict before we can plan and control. Here again the reverse is the case. We can predict the occurrence of an eclipse precisely because we cannot control it."[11] If the fact of the forecast influences the likelihood of the event, forecasts are either self-fulfilling or self-defeating.

As John Jewkes has commented: "Peering into the future is a popular and agreeable pastime which, so long as it is not taken seriously, is comparatively innocuous."[12]

The chief duties of the economist should involve studying conditions, identifying possible problems and policies, and working for the changes which society deems desirable. Much can be done along these lines without the ability accurately to quantify in forecasts.

We should not weep over our inability to forecast the future. Instead, we should relish the chance to use our judgment in an effort to shape the nature of that future. What we desire of our policy tools is, modestly, that we know something about which way they are likely to work if we use them discreetly, not precisely by how much. Investment creates productive capacity and, very likely, jobs. Increased production generates higher income. More progressive taxes redistribute income, probably increase total spending, and make for a society which is kinder to relatively more people. By how much? Do we really need to know? And, for better or worse, we must do the best we can without being entirely sure that these relations will always work, even in the desired direction.

We probably do need to think more about the likely nature of the impact of new technology and make thoughtful assessments as to these effects. Is the new invention likely to be just a flash in the pan? Is it likely to have adverse ecological effects? Will it involve major institutional changes which can be guessed at; and can likely transitional difficulties be anticipated? Have we a tiger by the tail? How do we want to react to DNA and the possibility that we can reorganize human biology?

Intransigence in resistance to change makes the ultimate change far more drastic than would have been the case if moderate change had been accepted with a good grace by the institution in the first place. During the 1980s, the overdone resistance of President Reagan and Governor Clements of Texas to tax increases severely handicapped efforts to deal with problems in a reasonable way. As a result, will the change be more drastic when it comes?

Institutional change that permits the effective use of new technology will not necessarily destroy a whole social and economic order. The chaos that goes with the destruction of whole social and economic orders is hardly desirable if it can be avoided. In fact the construction of a better order may be a lot easier if we use much of the order that we already have as a base, rather than insisting on starting again from scratch.

It is worth looking at a few of the institutional change problems in this more modest and, perhaps, more important setting.

Change may be rough on people. Perhaps fashion renders obsolete the women's fur-felt hat, or technology bypasses the horse and buggy. Jobs in the fur-felt hat industry and in the smithies are threatened. At first the afflicted industry is likely to attempt to obtain higher tariffs to help solve its problem. Next it may, reluctantly, try a little innovation. Detroit might actually manufacture a small car—but not before offering strong resistance, trying the Edsel first, and letting several decades go by. Perhaps adapting to new technology will save the situation. It did not hurt the Singer Sewing Machine Company, after World War II, to start making sewing machines that would do fancier stitching, as a way to deal with the Japanese competition, after they failed to get the tariff protection they pleaded for first.

Maybe an industry is really dying instead of just being afflicted with the sniffles. Shifting workers, capital (where feasible), and entrepreneurs is then called for. The workers really need society's help. The entrepreneurs should be able to look after themselves. They are supposed to be a self-reliant breed. Ayn Rand said so and would not have approved of Lee Iacocca running to the government for aid.

Although change may be hard on us, it may also represent an interesting reorientation of life, depending on our personal reaction and on how much thoughtful help we get in making the transition. It may be the lack of thoughtful help on the part of the government and our fellows, and the lack of a job guarantee, that sends the neurotic or the disappointed into a state of mind that they cannot handle psychologically, while the adaptable person makes a pleasant experience out of the changeover.

After institutional resistances break down, what happens next? The manner in which people have tried to analyze economic problems in the past may lead them to seek answers of the wrong type and to be frustrated when such answers are not readily forthcoming.

Human will and judgment in times of great institutional flux can play a powerful role in influencing the direction that the new pattern of behavior will take. In fact, it is at such times that individuals can exert a significant influence on the course of history. During the period that a static institutional order prevails, individuals, regardless of ability, can have little effect on the course of events. But energetic and aggressive individuals may have profound influence during a period of institutional commotion and exert influence out of all relation to the individual's abilities or the real merit of one's ideas. In Russia in 1917, Lenin seized a country which was in institutional turmoil, and he and a small number of associates effectively influenced the nature of the new order. For better or worse?

A similar situation existed in the United States during the 1930s. Leadership at such times can accomplish more in ninety days than could have been accomplished in fifty years of ordinary conditions. The circumstances that permit some change will likely permit a great deal, once institutional resistance is finally broken.

Gunnar Myrdal has observed that: "Often it is not more difficult, but easier, to cause a big change rapidly than a small change gradually."[13] What is involved is to seize the opportunity presented by a state of flux. And society must just hope that the fates will put men of good judgment and compassion at the helm in such times. Most of the rest of the time, the effort to exercise thoughtful leadership is just an exercise in frustration.

For reasons that are not entirely clear the revolutionary leaders in Cuba, Iran, Northern Ireland, Nicaragua, Libya, and many other places in recent years, have not shown a knack for using their opportunities constructively. The new leaders, temporarily, have unprecedented opportunities for constructive reworking of the institutional arrangements of the society, for feathering their own nests, or for botching up and creating a new repressive regime. Mostly the post World War II period has seen macho, charismatic leaders of revolutions and founders of new countries taking advantage of the situation to entrench themselves in power permanently. The tough, successful leader of a revolution or an independence movement does not seem generally to have the understanding, the tolerance, or the willingness to make the effort to engage in the give and take and conciliation necessary if a society is to be open, free, genuinely democratic, and effective at raising the average standard of living. Instead the successful revolutionary reacts to criticism with a revival of repression.

The founding fathers of the United States were unusual revolutionaries because they were willing to let power move out of their hands. They believed in the procedures of the new Constitution, not the cult of personality.

The Issue of Technological Determinism

The process of innovating the use of new technology calls forth new institutionalized behavior norms. Is this technological determinism? To some degree the issue involved is rather trivial semantics. But there is enough substance to the charge that this is technological determinism, and to the fact that institutionalism has been chided on this score, so that the issue is worth attention.

Technological determinism, at least in the strong statement of the concept, alleges that the nature of the new technique being implemented precisely determines the nature of the change in institutionalized behavior norms that will result. If this is technological determinism, the concept should not be endorsed.

The better concept surely is that the innovation will call forth new institutionalized behavior norms more appropriate to the effective use of the new technology than were the old behavior norms. But there may be assorted possibilities as to what those new norms will be. And it may be fairly fortuitous which change in fact occurs; for example, which law with what legal provisions Congress will actually pass in an effort to deal with the situation.

In the setting of the implications of the new technology being made available by the Industrial Revolution, the guild system was scarcely appropriate. But either the type of capitalism which actually emerged in the West, or some type of state socialism such as emerged in the Soviet Union, or something similar to the Japanese approach could provide a sufficiently hospitable setting for large-scale, capital-intensive industry. The nature of the technology did not preordain capitalism, whatever that is.

INDIRECT ADAPTATION (INTERACTION OF INSTITUTIONS WITH INSTITUTIONS)

Especially because there has been some confusion on this score, it is worth emphasizing that the whole interaction story is not told by a simple allegation that the utilization of new technology works directly to involve change in the behavior norms of certain affected institutions. The story may well be more complicated and more subtle. The norms of a certain institution may be affected directly by some new technology and the changed comportment of that institution may be a subsequent influence forcing a change in the behavior norms of yet another institution.

Many mothers have been freed for commercial employment because such household appliances as the vacuum cleaner and the washing machine and such food processing practices as commercial canning and freezing made the maintenance of the home a less time-consuming task. Many mothers then found it possible and desirable to work away from the home. As a result of more mothers working (an institutional change in one area occasioned by the vacuum cleaner, etc.), the institution of the day nursery increased in importance and exposed many young children to a rather different type of rearing. Even some fathers (but certainly not all) have assumed greater responsibility for the daytime care of their children.

Another important example involves the origin of labor unions. The new technology being brought into use by the Industrial Revolution in the early nineteenth century gestated giant corporations. The individual worker was in a weak bargaining position vis-à-vis these corporate giants. The existence of this bargaining strength in the hands of the corporations motivated the workers to form unions so as to bargain more effectively against corporate management. In consequence there came into being a new type of organization, the labor union, with its behavior norms, as a result of a two-step process: technology bringing on the corporation, and the corporate institution bringing on the labor union institution.

William Ogburn has gone so far as to say: "The most numerous adjustments to a technological environment are the derivative ones; for any one direct adaptation to a technological element creates a change in a custom or an institution to which several other customs or institutions will adjust. But commonly these derivative adjustments are not seen as adjustments to the technological element in the first instance."[14]

NOTES

[1]The relevant bibliography is that at the end of this book.

[2]William F. Ogburn, *On Culture and Social Change* (Chicago: University of Chicago Press, 1964), pp. 82-84, 134. In one of the essays Ogburn indicates that he had this conception of the technology-institutions relation as early as about 1914.

[3]James N. Danziger, "Social Science and the Social Impacts of Computer Technology," *Social Science Quarterly* 66 (March 1985), pp. 3-21, esp. pp. 13-16.

[4]Gerald Holton and Robert S. Morison, eds., *Limits of Scientific Inquiry* (New York: Norton, 1979), p. 55.

[5]C. Wright Mills, *White Collar* (New York: Oxford University Press, 1951), p. 113.

[6]Helio Jaguaribe, "El Pensamiento Social y Político de Marx," *Trimestre Económico* XLVI (October 1979), p. 828.

[7]C. E. Ayres, *The Industrial Economy* (Boston: Houghton-Mifflin, 1952), p. 58.

[8]Mary Gibbons Natrella, *Experimental Statistics* (Washington, D.C.: Government Printing Office [for the National Bureau of Standards], 1963), pp. 10-11.

[9]F. Stuart Chapin, *Cultural Change* (New York: Century, 1928), p. 228.

[10]David S. Landes, *The Unbound Prometheus* (Cambridge, Eng.: Cambridge University Press, 1970) [1969]), p. 236.

[11]John Dewey, *Intelligence in the Modern World: John Dewey's Philosophy* (New York: The Modern Library, 1939), pp. 952-3.

[12]John Jewkes, David Sawers, and Richard Stillerman, *The Sources of Invention* (2nd ed.; London: Macmillan, 1969 [1958]), p. 170.

[13]Gunnar Myrdal, *Asian Drama* (New York: Random House/Pantheon [for the Twentieth Century Fund], 1968), p. 115.

[14]Ogburn, p. 84.

Chapter V

Theory of Change: Induced Technological Change

Technological change may be facilitated or induced by outside (independent) influences or the process may have its own internal dynamic. Outside influences tending to induce new discoveries might include the profit motive (the desire for gain) or some other inducing factor such as individual, social, or governmental effort to obtain knowledge as to how to do something thought desirable, such as obtaining a cure for cancer, or for the common cold, or for cockroach infestation, or for a drought, or for AIDS . . . . This latter group of "other inducing factors" embraces the influences involved in the scientific method to be discussed at the beginning of chapter 6.

First, or next, what of the profit motive as an influence motivating technological change—and a lot of other things also, such as buying and selling and production?

THE PROFIT MOTIVE

Orthodox economics works with the presumption that it is the profit motive that propels the system. The profit motive is supposed to involve a homogeneous phenomenon which can be represented in a mathematical formula as a number. And the nature of the behavior of the participants in the economic process can be explained by their efforts to maximize such a number.

But the profit motive cannot be the simple, homogeneous concept envisaged by microeconomic price theory.[1] Is one speaking of maximizing a quantity of money? Or is one talking about maximizing a percentage rate? Is one talking about next week, this week, this year, the next ten years, eternity, or the life span of the capital equipment? During the 1970s and 1980s American business has been much criticized for overemphasizing annual profits, the short-run (so-called) "bottom line." It has been pointed out that the reason for this is that the formula used for determining the bonuses of corporate executives is likely to be computed on the basis of annual profits, the short-run "bottom line." A platitude explaining

55

business behavior has been the importance of this "bottom line." It is sometimes said that a factor in the relative success of the Japanese in recent years has been their taking a longer run perspective.

In *The New York Times,* Steve Lohr has quoted Reginald H. Jones, former head of General Electric, as saying (in answer to the question: "What evidence is there that managers are overly concerned with short-term profitability?"): "I think that the most damning thing is that nearly two-thirds of the inventory of U.S. industry is still accounted for on a FIFO (first-in, first-out) basis, which increases both reported earnings and tax payments. The reason for that is the unwillingness of management to face up to the lower reported earnings that would result under LIFO (last-in, first-out)—perhaps because most top executive contracts are tied to reported earnings. For G.E., the net effect of LIFO is roughly $1 billion that is not taxed and can be used for internal investment."[2] It may be noted that this explanation of behavior is loaded with institutionalized behavior norms that complicate the meaning of profit maximization, and with the interplay of conflicting interests among decision-makers in relation to the profits of the entity being considered.

In various circumstances profits are visualized as a percentage rate to be maximized. In accounting, there are automatic distinctions between interest rates on bonds and profit rates or net earnings rates related to net worth. But even here there is question: net worth, original investment, total assets, or sales, or reproduction cost? In economics, much of what accountants call net earnings is visualized as interest on capital. In the setting of pure economic theory there is a question as to the meaningfulness of speaking of a profit rate because of the difficulty in identifying: percentage of what? But if one can identify "percentage of what" there would still be the question as to the appropriate time period: month, year, or ten years.

The Marxists make the profit rate [$p = s/(c + v)$: p, profit rate; s, surplus value; c, constant capital; v, variable capital] a function of capital. But that definition cannot allow for a distinction between profit rates and interest rates.

In many situations, for example, frequently in connection with public utility rate regulation, it is said that it takes a rate of return (probably here speaking of all capital whether derived from bonds or from net worth) of such and such a figure, say 14 percent, or there will be inadequate investment. How can such a figure be arrived at or justified? In a given situation, a given company may be compared to the industry average. But where did the industry average come from if all the companies in the industry are similarly regulated? The average then is some sort of a self-fulfilling prophecy. Is 14 percent the profit rate necessary to stimulate new investment as long as the company presumably can get the regulatory commission to approve 14 percent? There is circular reasoning there. Perhaps executives will try to get 14 percent as long as they believe they can get it, but, once they are convinced 14 percent is not possible, they will settle for 10 percent or 6 percent. In a sense, anything over zero is gratuitous if we are really talking about profit as distinct from interest.

Some say that entrepreneurs have to get such and such a rate of return or they will not "enterprise." What is the importance of their not functioning as entrepreneurs? If their profits are a return for their pure genius (flashes of inspiration) as distinct from labor time (which earns a wage), and capital (which earns interest), and land (which earns rent), what are the implications? As long as profits exceed zero, there is gain from enterprising. Businessmen have 24 hours a day like other people. If the choice is between obtaining something and obtaining nothing as a reward for a stroke of inspiration, how can it be meaningful to speak of a "reservation price," as it were. Something is preferable to nothing, or if not why not? And one then may or may not in addition choose to work as a chief executive, for a salary, for some number of hours per week. A much observed fact in connection with small-scale businesspeople is that many seem to net (profit plus salary) less than they would net as salary if they worked for someone else. Preference for the independence of being self-employed is a factor, as is hope that the situation will get better, as it does for some and not for others.

Is there a meaningful distinction between profits and interest? If profit does involve something different from a return on capital, what is it? Joseph Schumpeter argued that (1) profits under pure competition would be a temporary reward for the innovating entrepreneur, which that individual gains until competitors, attracted by those gains, enter the market and drive profits to zero. Or (2) it might be a reward for managing somehow to obtain a degree of monopoly or oligopoly or monopolistic competition-type leverage.

Some economists cannot bring themselves to say the profit rate under competition is really zero (especially when they are confronted with the lack of belief on the part of those budding entrepreneurs, their students) and prefer to speak of a normal profit that the entrepreneur will obtain even under pure competition. But it remains unclear just what the influences are that will control the amount of this normal profit, however, except for some unsatisfactory platitude such as that it will be comparable to what other entrepreneurs are making. But what will determine that? And one is caught in an infinite regress.

What about risk (or uncertainty) as a basis for profit? Frank Knight had some things to say about that.[3] Risk, he says, cannot be a basis for profit because one can insure against risk and risk then can be reduced to being a recognizable element in cost. Uncertainty, however, is another matter. Knight says: "All true profit is linked to uncertainty." It may, unpredictably, create a situation where one may lose and another gain. This distinction between risk and uncertainty is predicated on a distinction in the meaning of words. An intelligent, risk-taking businessman can use actuarial techniques to establish what the degree of risk is and compensate for it. Uncertainty is the ingredient that nobody can anticipate, and therefore the intelligent rational businessman has no basis for estimating its implications. But, put this way, one might well wonder why the system should reward anyone for being the beneficiary of accident. The profit-making entrepreneur is supposed to be contributing something important to the process.

Arguing in these terms, it might seem that there is a place in the system for a premium for risk-taking, but it would seem that it is a premium (or loss) in relation to the normal interest rate and would be earned by the capitalist, as distinct from the entrepreneur.

In the mystique describing how capitalism is supposed to work there is assumed to be an identity between the owner and the decision maker. The individual owner, who has an interest in obtaining profit, makes the decisions which will affect profit. But in the typical corporation today, especially the typical large corporation, it is corporate employees (the president, assorted vice-presidents, chief executive officers, and such like) who make the decisions. Stockholder-owners have virtually no meaningful role in the process. This is the phenomenon of the divorcement of ownership from control.[4]

There has been a bit of literature designed to sweep this problem under the rug. It may be argued that corporate officers are likely to own some stock and thus have an interest in the profits of ownership. Or it may be argued that corporate officers view their role as that of trustees for owners and in consequence they work for profits because it is their ethical duty to do so. But these arguments leave doubts. Maybe corporate officers fancy themselves as empire builders, and they get their satisfaction from controlling ever larger corporations. Or they are more interested in higher salaries, higher bonuses, more generous expense accounts. And these are cost items that decrease profits. So, there is a significant gray area.

There is ambiguity as to what motivates decision makers in corporations. And the economist's assumption of the profit motive may be missing a whole other world of considerations involved in the decision-making process.

When one gets down to the nitty-gritty, the corporate manager's publicly expressed interest in profits is a façade, an attitude executives had better express (and in some sense convince themselves that they believe) to the effect that corporate profits are the name of the game. If they do not speak this language with convincing sincerity, the anonymous stockholders just might rise in righteous wrath and evict them from office. But all the executives really have to do is to speak the language and seem to believe it, and the stockholders will leave them alone and continue to sing the praises of the free enterprise system. But also, by this time, the executives are likely to have convinced themselves that they believe what they are saying.

Another possibility is that, in some cases, the corporate executives may be a little old and a little tired and quite content for the corporation to rock along protected in its share of the market by a network of restrictive practices. During the 1930s such a behavior pattern was called "rationalization."

Corporate executives also may make decisions on patriotic or "good citizenship" grounds that will have the effect of reducing profits. In fact, corporate executives on the average may be about as likely to be patriotic as the next fellow. German corporate executives were notoriously patriotic in this sense during the 1930s. Perhaps they had no choice.

Yet another type of approach involves questioning the view that there is homogeneity in the behavior patterns of decision makers even when they are profit motivated. This issue has been studied by Michael Maccoby, a psychologist.[5] He interviewed many corporate executives and analyzed their attitudes. As a result he found four chief psychological types: the craftsman, who has a genuine interest in workmanship and in the quality of the product; the jungle fighter, who relishes power, competition, and playing the game tough and no-holds-barred; the company man, who submerges personal interest into an emphasis on company loyalty and doing everything possible to further the interest of the company in the setting of some sort of vision of what is good for the company; and the gamesman, who relishes knowing the rules and then playing skillfully in order to win, again in terms of some sort of vision as to what is meant by winning. It seems probable that even if the executive is trying to maximize money profit, one will behave in very different ways depending on what sort of a person one is. Standard economic theory fails to get hold of the complications involved in these considerations.

Yet another perspective: Economic theory assumes that competition, in the effort to make profit, results in a trend toward better and cheaper products and increased efficiency. Such behavior results in the profit payoff for the rational businessman under competition. But what if profits for a number of years into the future will be increased if the industry continues to use obsolete machinery and somehow manages to prevent the introduction of technological improvement. Is behavior of this sort a significant aspect of what has been going on, for example in the United States steel industry after World War II? In any event there is considerable evidence that such behavior is common.[6]

Economists have tried to analyze the phenomenon of technological innovation using standard price theory analysis. It may help to make the point as to the difficulty involved in doing this to indicate the process by which an underdeveloped country may obtain new technical knowledge from a more developed country. Presumably the competitive market would work and the underdeveloped country people would pay an appropriate price for the desired technology. But there is a hitch which Kenneth Arrow has called "a fundamental paradox in the determination of the demand for information." Arrow pointed out that the "value for the purchaser is not known until he has the information."[7] And if the potential purchaser already has the information, why should one pay for it? And where has the monetary profit motive gone in handling this situation?

Of course much knowledge transfer occurs via channels quite apart from those involved in ordinary marketing. Students from underdeveloped countries obtain knowledge at universities in developed countries in pricing arrangements involving tuition and scholarships that are pretty much divorced from standard competitive influences.

In the world of business there certainly are myriads of situations where the entrepreneur is basing a decision on profit-making considerations of some sort. And the entrepreneur in a particular industry is likely to be pretty well indoctrinated with the desirability of particular business practices. There are standard or customary mark-ups, and that sort of thing, which simplify life but are not being continually changed to accommodate profit maximization. The industry may well see to it that its members believe they will fare better in some meaningful sense if each adheres to these behavior norms and abstains from "rocking the boat." It does seem clear that very few business people formalize a marginal cost equals marginal

revenue concept to determine their level of production. By and large the information is just not there to do it, for one thing. But one does make decisions on the
basis of a perception that this will work better than that, it seems to one, and
more profit will probably result if I do this rather than that. Various versions of
the profit motive are important and influential.

So, any idea that there is a general equilibrium world out there where welfare
is being maximized for all as a result of each business person rationally pursuing
profit and each consumer rationally maximizing one's welfare is purest hogwash.
Even von Mises and von Hayek have said so.

The underlying relation in developing the implications of the profit motive in
price theory is probably that "marginal cost equals marginal revenue" controls
the quantity of production. But it is difficult to identify a legitimate role for the
concept. It does not seem legitimate to assume that the concept can be used as
a basis for justifying the unique, long-run solution allegedly generated by general
equilibrium analysis. The concept simply cannot handle technical change and
decision making over time. It therefore has little use for analyzing the long-run
behavior of large corporations. Conceivably "marginal cost equals marginal revenue" might be argued to provide a satisfactory criterion for the behavior of small
firms in the short run. But even here, the well known fact that the profits of small
firms, especially in the short run, are likely to deviate wildly from average profit
rates raises questions as to the meaningfulness of applying the criterion even
here. It is notorious that economics has very little that is helpful to say to the
small-scale businessperson, apart from providing some clichés about demand and
supply and how wonderful the market system is.

With respect to the role of profit in influencing the invention process in particular,
two questions may be asked. Are inventors primarily motivated by the desire for
profits? Do inventors in fact reap substantial profit from important, successful
inventions? One might think that, given the importance of the questions and the
amount of opinion on the subject that has been vouchsafed, there would exist
substantial factual studies and authoritative answers to these questions. We stand
to be corrected by anyone aware of such work.

Anecdotal-type comments with some relevance may be made, but they hardly
settle the matter. Thomas Alva Edison frequently said that he identified inventions
that were needed and went out and produced the invention. Edison certainly was
also a successful profit-making businessman, at least some of the time. In 1877
he founded the company that became General Electric. Ultimately he lost influence
in General Electric to the investment banker J. Pierpont Morgan.[8] Edison's chief
rival in developing electric lighting, Nikola Tesla, died destitute.

Writing about the major inventors of the period of the Industrial Revolution,
Harry Elmer Barnes says: "Not one of the real inventors (involved in the Industrial
Revolution) was adequately rewarded for his invention."[9] Kenneth Arrow has
generalized to the effect that: "Basic research, the output of which is only used
as an informational input into other inventive activities, is especially unlikely to
be rewarded."[10] Christopher Freeman, in speculating as to whether knowledgeable people have even a rough idea as to what the "payoff" on a particular invention

will be, wrote: "Early estimates of future markets have been wildly inaccurate."[11] How would one have predicted the implications of the internal combustion motor in 1880? How could the economic system have operated appropriately to reward the inventor of the internal combustion motor?

One of the more interesting "put downs" of the economics model (that has it that the economy is run by millions of rational, think-alike, economic men busily pursuing a commonly held concept of the meaning of profit) is the contrary impression, also widely held, that entrepreneurial success rarely involves doing things in conformity with the generally held views as to appropriate procedure. Economics tries to have its cake and eat it too while fostering the concept of the rational economic man and the concept of imaginative iconoclast at the same time. In one concept everyone gets the same profit rate. In the other concept it is only the trail-blazer who profits.

Paul Samuelson says that the maximization-of-profit syndrome is a hypothesis involving a "Mixture of truism, truth, and untruth."[12]

All in all, it is not at all clear that the typical corporation, as an entity, is working essentially to maximize profits (a good deal of neoclassical and Marxist theory to the contrary notwithstanding). And, if it is not, a lot of price theory becomes a pretty bootless logical exercise and a lot of the paeans of praise for the "enterprise system" lose their underlying rationale, as does the logical structure of price theory and general equilibrium analysis. And the logical difficulties with general equilibrium theory which are discussed in chapter 9 become of mere academic interest. The relevant frame of reference does not exist.

INVENTION, INNOVATION, AND SCHUMPETER

Joseph Schumpeter's concept of innovation includes a distinction that may be helpful in identifying the meaningful role of the profit motive in economic process.[13] Innovation is the commercial application for the first time of unused, but known, technology. At any given stage, the process of invention and technological accumulation has produced a store of knowledge available for use but which has not yet been used. This knowledge may be said to be stored, perhaps in a "cookbook" (much of it in patents in the patent office). The innovator, or entrepreneur, with knowledge of market conditions may thumb through this cookbook and say: "Ah, ha, I can make a profit by manufacturing and marketing such and such a product" and proceed to do so, and perhaps be rewarded with profits for playing this role of innovator. But the innovator did not discover the invention. The distinction between innovator and inventor is a useful, meaningful distinction. But it should not be taken too literally.

Even the picture of the imaginative innovator thumbing through a cookbook of recipes available to all is hardly an accurate description of how things really are in a "high-tech" world, where it takes a major amount of knowledge in a field to be able to identify and understand the information that is available.[14] Just any high-school drop-out who is street-wise, tough, and intelligent is not going to be able to "go it alone" in this world, a certain amount of loose talk to the contrary notwithstanding.

There may well be some tendency for innovation, as well as invention, to occur only when "its time has come." This view is given credibility by the great variability in the length of the time periods between invention and innovation, 79 years in the case of the fluorescent lamp, one year in the case of freon refrigerators;[15] however, the strong implication of these differences is lessened by realization that many inventions may require considerable modification before they are ready for commercial production or innovation. And when innovation finally occurs there may well be mistakes in judgment as to the best process to innovate. A case apparently can be made, involving the innovation of the vaccine against poliomyelitis in the 1950s, that it might have been better to have used the Salk vaccine (involving the use of dead virus) rather than the Sabin vaccine (involving the use of live virus).

John Dewey has written of the role of the innovator:

> No amount of desire to make money, or to enjoy new commodities, no amount of mere practical energy and enterprise, would have effected the economic transformation of the last few centuries and generations. Improvements in mathematical, physical, chemical, and biological sciences were prerequisites. Businessmen through engineers of different sorts, have laid hold of the new insights gained by scientific men into the hidden energies of nature, and have turned them to account (the innovation process).[16]

Schumpeter for his part believed that innovators during the early period after they introduced their new products or processes gained pure profits. Later, after other not so innovative enterpreneurs copied their success, the profit (rates) of all would fall to zero, or to some normal rate, and there would no longer be any pure profit in that particular branch of activity.

BIAS IN INVENTION (INNOVATION)

The expression generally used in the literature on this subject is bias in innovation. In the context of the distinction made in this book between invention and innovation, what is involved is actually likely to be bias in invention. The argument was developed by J. R. Hicks in relation to the roles of labor-saving and capital-saving technical progress.[17] The idea was that if the cost of one factor, say labor, is rising relative to the cost of another factor, say capital, there will be a tendency of new inventions (innovations) to make relatively less use of the factor rising in relative cost (labor).

Various economic historians, for example, Nathan Rosenberg, Paul A. David, H. J. Habakkuk, and David S. Landes, have made use of this concept.

Along the same line, the induced technical change model of Charles Kennedy alleges that new technical knowledge is discovered in a pattern that makes relatively less use of the factor of production that is rising in relative cost.[18] Kennedy's concept of the innovation possibility frontier (a curve relating the proportion in which a technical improvement will reduce the amount of labor required to produce a unit of product with the proportion in which a technical improvement will reduce the amount of capital required to produce a unit of product) has become a fairly famous concept in this sort of analysis in which the goal is to maximize the proportionate reduction in unit costs, as a result of using alternative technologies that are relatively more or less capital- or labor-intensive, subject to the constraint imposed by the innovation possibility frontier.

Contrary to this viewpoint, in the early days of the Industrial Revolution there was no such pronounced pattern. Labor- or capital-saving discoveries were not bunched according to which factor was falling in relative price, despite the fact that, if this concept is meaningful, there should have been such a pattern. Alan Milward writes:

> Many of the early innovations of the industrial revolution appear to
> have been labor-saving but by no means all of them. The speeding up
> of textile machinery was capital-saving: the steam engine required
> less capital than the water wheel for a given output of power and
> improvements in the steam engine concentrated on saving fuel. Some
> of the process developments in the later years of the nineteenth
> century, requiring the use of hydro-electric power, were extremely
> capital intensive but in general, as the century wore on, more and
> more innovations saved on both factors though to different degrees
> in each case.
>
> Railways . . . were capital intensive in themselves but the reduction
> in the time taken to transport goods allowed businessmen so to reduce
> stocks that railways brought down the capital:output ratio of the
> economy as a whole in spectacular fashion. [19]

It is true that in some cultures the institutional order is such that labor-saving inventions are resisted (even when labor is in fairly short supply) because of worker fear of unemployment. Such behavior has been observed not only in western Europe and the United States in recent times but also in ancient Rome. In contrast, in the China of a thousand years ago, where labor was more abundant by comparison with the West, a common attitude was to encourage labor-saving innovation on the common sense grounds that it is better to work less. [20]

Kenneth Arrow has made the point:

> . . . the stability of the invention (innovation) possibility frontier in any
> form has neither rationale nor empirical support. A gross reading of
> history suggests the bias is apt to vary from time to time due much
> more to changes in the state of knowledge than to changes in capital-
> labor ratios. . . . Columbus may have been impelled by a desire for
> spices, but it was the supply of corn which was increased. [21]

Paul Samuelson has also questioned the Kennedy approach:

> Since the 1932 publication of J. R. Hicks' *Theory of Wages* there has
> been the vague notion that high wages somehow induce 'labor-saving'

inventions. Rothbarth, Kaldor, and Habakkuk have attempted to use this theory to interpret the history of American prosperity. . . . Since at minimum-cost equilibrium, all inputs are equally marginally dear and productive, the simplest interpretation of the high-wage theory of induced innovation is ill-founded.[22]

Another contrary example has been cited by Fernand Braudel:

> In textiles for instance, the two major processes are spinning and weaving. In the seventeenth century, one weaver required the services of seven or eight spinners. . . . Logically therefore it was in spinning, the operation requiring the greatest workforce, that technical innovation was needed. Nevertheless it was the loom which in 1730 saw the first labor-saving device, Kay's flying shuttle.[23]

The explanatory power of the bias in invention (or innovation) concept is limited.

ROLE OF LARGE-SCALE, PLANNED RESEARCH PROJECTS

In the process of accumulating scientific and technical knowledge individuals work independently and people work, frequently for pay (or financed by grants), in organized, planned projects. Possibilities include on the one hand the work of organizations such as the National Science Foundation (government financed) and the Ford Foundation (privately financed). These organizations pass judgment on individual or group projects and proposals and finance some and not others. On the other hand, either a governmental or a private organization may actually operate a research and experimentation organization such as the federal government with NASA (National Aeronautics and Space Administration) or the privately run Bell Laboratories of the American Telephone and Telegraph Company.

These would seem to be activities that involve induced research. A decision is made to try to advance knowledge in some certain areas and to fund projects and scientists for research in those areas. This is not necessarily the standard profit-motive motivated operation, but there may be an induced factor in the sense that the research subject is targeted.

When the NASA project to send someone to the moon was implemented in the 1960s, the scientists were reasonably sure that they already had the scientific knowledge to do it. So, the goal of NASA was not to generate the scientific knowledge to permit the flight, it was to utilize knowledge already in the cookbook and to implement flight. A lot of scientific research was involved in that implementation: work on appropriate food to take along, outfits for the astronauts to wear, psychological research, and so on. There was a lot of new knowledge developed as more or less incidental fallout from all this research, knowledge that could be used in other areas.

Thus there has been a significant difference in the assigned roles of cancer research and of NASA. One project involved an effort to go out and generate a designated discovery. The other involved effort to do something using knowledge already in hand. One project has not accomplished its assigned chore. The other has, and has provided useful fallout knowledge as well.

One can confidently say two things about the likely results of large-scale planned research projects. If they are intended to generate a specific bit of new knowledge they will be successful only if, shall we say, "its time has come" so far as that discovery is concerned; however, there may be a good deal of not-planned-for knowledge, whose time has come, generated in the course of the futile search for something else.

Money thrown at science can accelerate the pace of knowledge accumulation, but it cannot insure that any particular discovery will be made.

The institutionalization of research goes on apace, in part because certain types of research require large outlays if they are to be conducted at all, in part because research organizations once established, have an interest in continuing and expanding, regardless of their success in fulfilling their ostensible mission.

In general one may well say, where is the harm? The accumulation of knowledge presumably is desirable and it is respectable that scientists make a reasonable income while they are doing their research. But research is one of the more pleasant occupations and it is not entirely clear that it is appropriate for some of them to profit in a major way from their, generally subsidized, activities.

Some misgivings of a different sort have been expressed by John Jewkes:

> Under the influence of this doctrine the process of discovery and
> invention is becoming progressively institutionalized. The disposition
> of individuals to pursue their own ways with their own resources is
> weakened in many ways. . . . The lure of adequate equipment, conge-
> nial intellectual society and a secure livelihood provided by the institu-
> tion is strong. In turn, institutions will naturally place emphasis upon
> the formal training and academic qualifications of those they employ:
> they will therefore become increasingly staffed by men who have been
> subject to common moulding influences. There is a possibility of in-
> breeding from which the more eccentric strains of native originality
> may be excluded . . . .[24]

CONCLUSION

Some of those engaged in scientific and technological research are motivated by pure idle curiosity. Others have chosen such work as a profession, but it is a profession that has considerable appeal. The particular areas where the individual does research may be selected because of some felt need for solutions or useful products in the area where the research is being done. Successful work, the scientist hopes, will be rewarded, perhaps handsomely.

No matter how badly the new knowledge is needed it is still going to be true that it is findable only if the necessary knowledge base is already there. Given this knowledge base, the scientist motivated by idle curiosity is about as likely to be successful as the scientist strongly influenced by the profit motive.

In the case of neither invention nor innovation does there exist the possibility of measuring with any accuracy the likely amount of profits that may be realized. This is especially true in connection with pure science research. The mathematics designed to model this process and identify where the new developments will occur in response to such and such felt needs, or profit possibilities, or such and such changes in relative factor costs is mostly a pure waste of time unless the practitioner of the mathematics is blissful while going through the exercise.

NOTES

[1]Robert Aaron Gordon, *Business Leadership in the Large Corporation* (Washington: Brookings, 1945).

[2]*New York Times,* January 27, 1981, p. 26.

[3]Frank H. Knight, *Risk, Uncertainty, and Profit* (Boston: Houghton Mifflin, 1921).

[4]Adolf A. Berle, Jr. and Gardiner C. Means, *The Modern Corporation and Private Property* (New York: Macmillan, 1933); Thorstein Veblen, *Absentee Ownership* (Boston: Beacon Press, 1967 [1923]).

[5]Michael Maccoby, *The Gamesman* (New York: Bantam Books, 1978 [1976]).

[6]George W. Stocking and Myron W. Watkins, *Cartels in Action* (New York: Twentieth Century Fund, 1947); Thorstein Veblen, *Vested Interests and the Common Man* (New York: Kelley, 1963[1920]).

[7]Kenneth Arrow, "Economic Welfare and the Allocation of Resources for Invention," in *The Rate and Direction of Inventive Activity* (Princeton: National Bureau of Economic Research 1962), pp. 609-626.

[8]*New York Times,* Feb. 6, 1979, pp. C1, C2.

[9]Harry Elmer Barnes, *Economic History of the Western World* (New York: Harcourt, Brace, 1937), p. 301.

[10]Arrow, p. 618.

[11]Christopher Freeman, *Economics of Industrial Innovation* (Baltimore: Penguin, 1974), p. 233.

[12]Paul A. Samuelson, comment on Sherman Krupp, "Analytic Economics . . .," *American Economic Review* 53 (May 1963), p. 233.

[13]Joseph Schumpeter, in review of "Mitchell's *Business Cycles,*" *Quarterly Journal of Economics* 45 (November 1930), pp. 150-172; Joseph A. Schumpeter, "Analysis of Economic Change," *Review of Economics and Statistics* XVII (May 1935), pp. 2-10.

[14]Robert Solo, *Positive State* (Cincinnati: Southwestern Publishing, 1982), esp. ch. 10.

[15]For a substantial table dating differences between invention and innovation dates see: John Enos, "Invention and Innovation in the Petroleum Refining Industry," in *Rate and Direction of Inventive Activity* (Princeton: Princeton University Press [for the National Bureau of Economic Research], 1962), pp. 307-308.

[16]John Dewey, *Reconstruction in Philosophy* (New York: Holt, 1920), p. 41.

[17]J. R. Hicks, "An Inaugural Lecture," *Oxford Economic Papers* V (June 1953), pp. 117-135.

[18]Charles Kennedy, "Induced Bias in Innovation and the Theory of Distribution," *Economic Journal* LXXIV (September 1964), pp. 541-547.

[19]Alan S. Milward, *The Economic Development of Continental Europe, 1780-1870* (London: Allen & Unwin, 1973), pp. 172-173.

[20]Joseph Needham, *The Grand Titration* (Toronto: University of Toronto Press, 1969), pp. 33-34.

[21]Kenneth Arrow, in Raymond Vernon, ed., *Technology Factor in International Trade* (Princeton: Princeton University Press [for the National Bureau of Economic Research], 1970), p. 130.

[22]Paul A. Samuelson, "Theory of Induced Innovation," *Review of Economics and Statistics,* XLVII (Nov. 1965), pp. 343-356, esp. p. 355.

[23]Fernand Braudel, *The Perspective of the World, Civilization and Capitalism, 15th-18th Century,* Vol. 3 (New York: Harper & Row, 1984 [1979]), p. 566.

[24]John Jewkes, David Sawers, and Richard Stillerman, *The Sources of Invention* (2nd ed.; New York: Norton, 1969 [1958]), pp. 179, 180, 183, 97, 98.

Chapter VI

Philosophy of Science

It is useful to identify two different approaches to understanding the process of acquiring knowledge. One views what is happening as an ongoing process. The other sees what is happening as a problem-solving process.

In chapter 2, "Theory of Change: Technical Knowledge," the acquiring of knowledge, and especially of technical knowledge, was viewed as an ongoing cumulative process with its own internal dynamic. The primary effort was to explain the circumstances involved in the sequence by which one bit of knowledge leads to another. This is probably the more basic and important approach.

A second kind of discussion in the philosophy of science has examined the procedure for dealing with particular problems. Is the inductive or the deductive (logical) method to be applied? Philosophers have engaged in heated and arcane debate on these issues.

Down to the sixteenth century the prevailing view in the world of scholarship was that results are proven by deductive methods (by syllogistic logic). Assumptions of general principles are made and from those assumptions particular results are derived. If it is assumed that all dogs are animals (the major premise or thesis), and this specimen is a dog (minor premise or antithesis), then it follows that the specimen is an animal (conclusion or synthesis). Given the assumption involved in the major premise (a big if), and the correctness of the minor premise, the conclusion follows with 100 percent certainty. QED.

THE NATURE OF THE SCIENTIFIC METHOD

In contrast to pursuing this sort of methodology, Francis Bacon (1561-1626) argued for the importance of induction and what has come to be called the scientific method. One works from observed data and experience to reach conclusions as to general principles. Observation of the temperature over the year may lead to the conclusion that it is generally colder in January than in July.

The nature of the logic involved in the application of the scientific method to a specific problem is the following: (1) a problem is identified, (2) relevant data are gathered, (3) on the basis of the perspective given by these data, a hypothesis or theory is formulated as to how to deal with the problem, (4) the hypothesis is tested empirically, and (5) it is *tentatively* verified (validated or corroborated) or rejected. The tentative nature of the verification is to be noted. There is no harm in turning step (5) around and saying that the hypothesis (or law or theory) may have been falsified by the empirical test.

Unemployment may be viewed as a problem. Information about possible ways to deal with unemployment may be assembled. It may be hypothesized that among the possible policies, it is worth experimenting with unemployment insurance. Such a program is put in operation to see how it works. Society may be reasonably satisfied with the result and the program continued on a permanent basis. Or, with the passage of time the judgment may be that the program is not working too well. Some other program, such as a job guarantee, may be tried as an experiment.

Or, cancer may be viewed as a problem, much information may be assembled about the disease, various possible cures may be hypothesized, tested, and rejected, or validated, at least for the present.[1]

This conception of the nature of the scientific method corresponds, in the classification presented at the beginning of chapter 5, with "outside influences tending to induce new discoveries," influences which are different from the profit motive.

EMPIRICISM AND HUME

Isaac Newton (1642-1727) and others practiced variations of the scientific method in the seventeenth and eighteenth centuries. Thomas Hobbes, John Locke, George Berkeley, and David Hume were beginning to philosophize about the method. Other philosophers of the period (Leibniz, Descartes, and Spinoza) remained more in the deductive and metaphysical tradition.

David Hume (1711-1776) especially developed the aspect of the scientific or inductive method that has been called empiricism. He worked with the presumption that it is as possible to prove definite results with certainty by the inductive method as it is by the deductive method.

Hume wrote: "But when one particular species of event has always, in all instances, been conjoined with another, we make no longer any scruple of foretelling one upon the appearance of the other, and of employing that reasoning, which can alone assure us of any matter of existence. We then call the one object, *Cause,* the other, *Effect.* We suppose that there is some connection between them, some power in the one by which it infallibly produces the other, and operates with the greatest certainty and strongest necessity."[2] But where is such infallible certainty in this world? This troubled Hume.

Hume had the notion of probability: "Though we give the preference to that which has been found most usual, and believe that this effect will exist, we must not overlook the other effects, but must assign to each of them a particular weight and authority, in proportion as we have found it to be more or less frequent." Hume's understanding of probability did not include the belief that there is chance or the possibility of fortuitous events. "Though there be no such thing as *Chance* in the world; our ignorance of the real cause of any event has the same influence on the understanding, and begets a like species of belief or opinion."

There is little wonder that Hume, after trying to take these considerations into account, remained a sceptic, troubled by his inability to reconcile infallibility with probability.

POSITIVISM AND COMTE

Positivism is both in and not in the tradition of the scientific method and empiricism. It is an approach developed by Auguste Comte (1798-1857), the founder of sociology and the exponent of an explanation of history in terms of stages: a theological stage, a metaphysical stage, and a positive stage.[3] This is the law of three stages, and it presumably applies to society as a whole and to each of the major branches of human knowledge taken separately: mathematics, astronomy, physics, chemistry, biology, and social physics (sociology). Comte's positivism is concerned with positive facts and phenomena and excludes from consideration speculation and introspection about ultimate causes or origins. That is to say: metaphysics is without validity. What is involved is a search for invariable laws, Hume's infallibility. The process of gradually working out the features of these invariable laws is what Comte meant by progress. The expression "order and progress" is the slogan of positivism. The words appear on the Brazilian flag and indicate the influence of positivism in Latin America during the late nineteenth century.

According to Comte and positivism, society is susceptible of analysis in purely objective and mechanistic terms. Social values and normative standards are mere epiphenomena (epiphenomena being secondary phenomena accompanying other phenomena and caused by them). One of the invariable laws of Comte was: Society must develop in a positive direction. Comte visualized a scientific elite who would identify the invariable, fixed, and stable laws controlling the positive society, which resulted from the process. In fact the "order" implied in the expression "order and progress" had as an aspect the protection of the elite, the already dominant groups, from revolutionary influences. This is the reason Comte's positivism has been considered a conservative approach.

Positivism rejected metaphysics, but in the cleavage between the inductive and deductive methods, Comte did not take sides. Whichever method (inductive or deductive) was appropriate for dealing with the particular problem should be used. Along the way, in the search for the invariable laws, which inevitably would be forthcoming, Comte was flexible as to the degree of precision involved in the verification of hypotheses.[4] And yet invariable, fixed, and stable laws would seem to leave no room for flexibility, as to the degree of precision. Where are we?

PRAGMATISM AND INSTRUMENTALISM
(PEIRCE, JAMES, DEWEY)

A different approach, also oriented to induction and the scientific method, was developed in the United States during the late nineteenth and early twentieth centuries. Related but somewhat different arguments under this general umbrella have been variously called: pragmatism, pragmaticism, radical empiricism, and instrumentalism. This is, some have said, the only significant American contribution to philosophy. The chief figures in this development of pragmatism and instrumentalism have been Charles Sanders Peirce (1839-1914), William James (1842-1910), John Dewey (1859-1952), and Clarence Ayres (1891-1972).

First, a few comments about Peirce should be made.[5] Peirce's test for a clear idea, his pragmatic maxim, in one of numerous restatements, runs: "Consider what effects, that might conceivably have practical bearings, we conceive the object of our conception to have. Then, our conception of these effects is the whole of our conception of the object."[6] A reader may react to this definition of a clear idea with the thought that the definition itself is not all that clear.

Peirce is endorsing a procedure in which various scientists repeatedly make experiments in a given line of inquiry and this process is expected to give results which more and more closely approximate the truth until finally a consensus—the truth—will be arrived at. The possibility of reaching a definite conclusion does manifest itself in the presentation of Peirce: "On the other hand, all the followers of science are animated by a cheerful hope that the processes of investigation, if only pushed far enough, will give one certain solution to each question to which they apply it. . . . They may at first obtain different results, but, as each perfects his method and his processes, the results are found to move steadily together toward a destined center. . . . The opinion which is fated to be ultimately agreed to by all who investigate, is what we mean by the truth, and the object represented in this opinion is the real."[7]

Beyond this opinion, Peirce offers no proof that the process of scientific investigation is ultimately leading to final truth. Maybe it is, and maybe it is not, or maybe the process is uncertain and changeable.

A difference between Peirce and William James is James's use of the term pragmatism to include the situation where the ultimate conclusion as to truth is validated by a psychological feeling of the individual as to its reasonableness. For Peirce the meaning of a proposition lay in its logical and experimentally testable consequences. He depended on a sequence of experiments by many scientists rather than on individual intuition. And he thought the term pragmatism was being misused by James and decided to rename his concept pragmaticism. Peirce wrote: "This word is so ugly that it should be eternally safe from 'kidnappers'."

Nevertheless, one may view James as the second major figure in the development of pragmatism. James wrote in *The Will to Believe:* "Objective evidence and certitude are doubtless very fine ideals to play with, but where on this moonlit and dream-visited planet are they found? I am, therefore, myself a complete empiricist so far as my theory of human knowledge goes. I live, to be sure, by the practical faith that we must go on experiencing and thinking over our experience, for only thus can our opinions grow more true; but to hold any one of them—I absolutely do not care which—as if it never could be re-interpretable or corrigible, I believe to be a tremendously mistaken attitude."[8] Peirce seems to have been committed to the possibility of definitive truth where James was not.

The instrumentalism of John Dewey and Clarence Ayres embraces the pragmatism or radical empiricism of Peirce and James while leaning to the James view that truth is not definitive. There is also an additional aspect with Dewey and Ayres that involves values and the theory of valuation. Peirce and James spoke much about truth and what is real, but not much about value as such. Values and valuation will be discussed at more length in chapter 7.

Dewey had already used the term instrumental as early as 1903. Dewey wrote: ". . . the activity of thinking is instrumental, and . . . its worth is found, not in its own successive states as such, but in the result in which it comes to conclusion. . . . Judgment is essentially instrumental."[9] It is this use of the word instrumental that is the basis for calling Dewey's approach instrumentalism. Clarence Ayres adopted Dewey's terminology.

In all events, instrumentalism in the Dewey-Ayres tradition has to do with a subjective judgment as to whether things are working satisfactorily. Are the tools or ideas effective instruments in generating the results that are desired? And the crucial stage in this process is the observation of results, and the taking of corrective measures if the results are deemed not to be satisfactory. This is ongoing process. There is no presumption that one has at one's disposal all the relevant information on the basis of which positively certain results can be anticipated. But then, to repeat, in between in all this is the issue as to whether a particular policy measure taken now will work in what is considered a desired way.

In instrumentalism, this espousal of trial and error distinguishes it from an approach that overtly relies on statistically validated predictions. Properly stated, the instrumentalist test is not merely "does the procedure work satisfactorily?" but, more fully, "in the opinion of those involved, does the procedure work better than the available alternatives?" And whether it works better is a value judgment which is subject to change as a result of further experience or as a result of the further consideration of alternative possible procedures. In making this judgment, statistical tests of probability may be appropriate, but other and more subjective tests may also be relevant.

LOGICAL POSITIVISM AND THE VIENNA CIRCLE (THE 1920s)

Logical positivism, which developed among a circle of philosophers in Vienna during the 1920s, is an outgrowth of positivism, but not too direct an outgrowth.[10] Figures in the movement, or associated with it, included Moritz Schlick, Herbert Feigl, Hans Hahn, Rudolf Carnap, and Ludwig Wittgenstein. Carnap and Wittgenstein diverged in other directions in later years.

The verifiability principle was a basic tenet of the group. It said that propositions should not be accepted as meaningful unless they are verifiable. Since the basic propositions of transcendental metaphysics are not verifiable (for example: "The Absolute is beyond time"), metaphysics was considered meaningless.

A prime concern of the group was the development of the implications of induction and the scientific method. These efforts were continually frustrated by realization of the difficulties that had plagued Hume in his search for definitive results. Moritz Schlick wrote: "Thus neither through experience nor through reason is a proof to be had. That Hume's objections are convincing cannot be doubted. . . . The point of view we arrive at through considerations such as these is basically Hume's. I do not believe that it is possible to move essentially beyond him."[11]

These considerations do not take into account the position of Dewey and Ayres.

DEDUCTION, FALSIFICATION, AND POPPER

Karl Popper, who took strong exception to the views of the logical positivists of the Vienna Circle, was Viennese. Inductive logic, the methodology which he attributed to the logical positivists, was a particular anathema to Popper: "My own view is that the various difficulties of inductive logic here sketched are insurmountable. . . . Now in my view there is no such thing as induction."[12]

It is a rather simplistic conception of induction that Popper sets up as the victim of this summary dismissal: "it is usual to call an inference 'inductive' if it passes from *singular statements* . . . such as accounts of the results of observations or experiments, to *universal statements,* such as hypotheses or theories." He then assumes that those who use induction commit the mistake of believing that the universal statements are definitively proven: "Now it is far from obvious, from a logical point of view, that we are justified in inferring universal statements from singular ones, no matter how numerous; for any conclusion drawn in this way may always turn out to be false: no matter how many instances of white swans we may have observed, this does not justify the conclusion that *all* swans are white." Popper set up his strawman and knocked it down. "But I shall certainly admit a system as empirical or scientific only if it is capable of being *tested* by experience. These considerations suggest that not the *verifiability* but the *falsifiability* of a system is to be taken as a criterion of demarcation. In other words: I shall not require of a scientific system that it shall be capable of being singled out, once and for all, in a positive sense; but . . . *it must be possible for an empirical scientific system to be refuted by experience.*"

Popper then proceeded to advocate something he called deductivism (the hypothetico-deductive method), which, depending on the definition one adopts, is actually a rather sophisticated mixture of induction and deduction, flavored with a bit of new terminology: the distinction between verification and falsification.[13]

A noteworthy feature of this argument is the proposition that falsification is a clear-cut concept, one example of which destroys a theory which had been considered verified or operationally meaningful up to this point. This is a conclusion which is too strong. And Popper did relax this conclusion. But then where is one? It may be noted that Einstein, by finding one false element in the Newtonian system, did not destroy its usefulness as a working tool. An instance of falsification is not necessarily the end of the usefulness of a theory or a paradigm.

More important than the verification-falsification issue, so far as institutionalism is concerned, is the position that Popper takes on something he chose to call instrumentalism, which he equates with logical positivism. The issue is fairly important since Popper's conception of instrumentalism has been taken over in the philosophy of science literature in recent years. Popper's use of the term instrumentalism to categorize and castigate the work of Bishop Berkeley, Ernst Mach, Poincaré, and Duhem is gratuitous. The comment is subject to correction, but apparently none of those people ever used the term instrumentalism as the appropriate label for what they were talking about,[14] and the term logical positivism was readily available, as also was the term operationalism, which was used by P. W. Bridgman in the 1920s.

Popper describes what he means by instrumentalism: "By instrumentalism I mean the doctrine that a scientific theory such as Newton's, or Einstein's, or Schrodinger's, should be interpreted as an instrument, *and nothing but an instrument,* for the deduction of predictions of future events (especially measurements) and for other practical applications . . . .[15]

Popper seems to believe that for instrumentalism the basic concern is with prediction and the accuracy of prediction rather than with understanding, with the accuracy of understanding, and with truth, or with value judgments.

Popper is not talking about the instrumentalism of John Dewey and Clarence Ayres, nor about the pragmatism of Peirce and James. His writing does not show familiarity with the work of these men, nor with the fact that Dewey and James had been using the instrumentalism terminology as early as 1903.[16] So Popper has created a situation where writers of philosophy of science allege that instrumentalism and logical positivism are the same thing and that both are discredited (or credited, if one happens to be on the other side in the argument).

According to Peirce, pragmatism does not repudiate metaphysics, although he did believe that many of the ideas purveyed by practitioners of metaphysics lacked worth.[17] Also, according to Dewey, instrumentalism does not deny the possible usefulness of the deductive method.[18]

Actually, when Popper comes to describe his own views, as distinct from the logical positivism he rejects, in the preface to *Conjectures and Refutations* he is pretty close to describing instrumentalism in the sense of Dewey and Ayres.[19] Popper, whatever else he has done, has created a terminological muddle.

POSITIVE ECONOMICS AND FRIEDMAN

In 1953, Milton Friedman, an economist, declared that economists should concern themselves with what "is" instead of with what "ought to be." This was hardly a novel proposition. As Friedman pointed out, John Neville Keynes had said this in 1891 and had urged the importance of "recognizing a distinct positive science of political economy."[20]

In much of the discussion of the role of Friedman in these matters, it has been presumed that the advocacy of checking on what "is" and, more specifically, the advocacy of hypothesis testing by Friedman represented an endorsement of logical positivism, induction, and the use of the scientific method in economics. It is also widely thought that a commitment to logical positivism has been generally characteristic of the Chicago economists. Perhaps so, but one does not get a basis for this view from the essay on "The Methodology of Positive Economics," which begins Friedman's *Essays in Positive Economics*. No reference to logical positivism or to the Vienna Circle is made in the article.

Friedman explicitly said: [21] "Economics as a positive science is a body of tentatively accepted generalizations about economic phenomena . . . ." So, Friedman has accepted the tentative nature of the results generated by whatever method he is using to determine what "is." Also Friedman is not casting normative or value judgments into limbo, merely also endorsing inquiry into what "is." Since Friedman has thrived on making value judgments, it would be presumptuous of him to try to outlaw them. Thus far it is hard to take exception to what Friedman is doing.

Then he says: "The ultimate goal of a positive science is the development of a 'theory' or 'hypothesis' that yields valid and meaningful (i.e., not truistic) predictions about phenomena not yet observed." [22] Here the trouble starts. Accurate prediction would be fine, but is it the whole story? Friedman really is doing the thing of which Popper, with or without reason, accused the logical positivists whom he identified with instrumentalists.

More trouble comes with the use that Friedman makes of his methodology in the balance of his essay. It is hardly a model example of scientific rigor to be shown to graduate students. There is no use of hard empirical data as part of an inductive process designed to establish with reasonable, if tentative, credibility the validity of conclusions. The rest of the essay uses involved ratiocination to claim that assumptions do not matter and that the profit motive operates and the economy behaves as though it is purely competitive, whether it is or not.

A large proportion of the Friedman essay is devoted to defending the use of unrealistic assumptions. He says: "Truly important and significant hypotheses will be found to have 'assumptions' that are wildly inaccurate descriptive representations of reality, and, in general, the more significant the theory, the more unrealistic the assumptions (in this sense)." [23]

Since what is involved is the usefulness of testing hypotheses which will validate competitive price theory, it is appropriate to notice the nature of Friedman's argument. Aside from the farfetched analogies with the attraction of gravity, the habits of leaves, and billiard players, Friedman uses the following argument to support the profit maximization aspect of price theory:

> Confidence in the maximization-of-returns hypothesis is justified by
> evidence of a very different character. This evidence is in part similar
> to that adduced on behalf of the billiard-player hypothesis—unless the
> behavior of businessmen in some way or other approximated behavior
> consistent with the maximization of returns, it seems unlikely that
> they would remain in business for long. [24]

This argument scarcely includes hard evidence, and the discussion which follows does no better.

One may surmise that the real appeal of orthodox economics and of traditional price theory is that they create and endorse a world that is extremely convenient for the affluent. They validate laissez faire and the market solution and discredit effort by reformers to use the government to try to redistribute income or to improve the general welfare. And a large enough percentage of the United States population is now affluent so that their resistance to governmental measures designed to aid those who continue disadvantaged is effective, ably and strongly presented, and well financed.

A slightly different aspect of the Friedman argument is also interesting. The reader might be tempted to believe that Friedman is making sophisticated use of the falsification criterion of Karl Popper, especially when he says: "The evidence *for* a hypothesis always consists of its repeated failure to be contradicted. . . ."[25] But this cannot be a proper use of Popper's falsification proposition because that proposition calls for the hypothesis to be one that is capable of being falsified. To the extent that the maximization-of-returns hypothesis is capable of being falsified, it has been falsified a million times, every time anyone does anything for a reason other than profits. Also, it is not required that the falsifier produce a better hypothesis, at least not by Popper.

From the viewpoint of institutionalism, an unfortunate by-product of this convoluted scholarship is the manner in which Milton Friedman becomes identified as an instrumentalist. Lawrence Boland wrote Friedman and asked if he would accept the label of instrumentalist.[26] Friedman replied in the affirmative. Dewey must be turning over in his grave.

An institutionalist could perhaps leave the matter at that and be moderately bemused except for the fact that instrumentalism is frequently rather cavalierly dismissed in the philosophy of science literature on the ground that it represents nothing more than Popper's definition or Friedman's conception of a prediction process reveling in inaccurate assumptions. Guilt by association then discredits the instrumentalism of John Dewey.

THE ACTUAL METHODOLOGY OF SCIENCE

Is the preceding discussion of the scientific method and the philosophy of science particularly relevant to the way scientists actually behave?

So far as the experimental methods are concerned, the economist should not forget that there are test tubes, and machine shops and laboratories, and accelerators, and maybe decelerators involved in what physicists, chemists, biologists, and pharmaceutical research workers do.

Actual and effective procedures may bear little relation to the scientific method as discussed in philosophy of science literature. In fact the really major new insights are likely to be "one of a kind," that is the say: *sui generis*.

Even the not particularly knowledgeable outsider can imagine significant differences in the ongoing research procedures in different areas. Much ongoing research in chemistry consists in experimenting with thousands of different combinations of elements and compounds and then checking out the behavior of the new compound under different circumstances and speculating on its usefulness and on the implications for further experiments. Then there exists the possibility of additional combinations with yet different elements and compounds. Still, there is probably much chemical research that does not fit this stereotype, although much of the research in the pharmaceutical industry fits this chemistry stereotype fairly well.

Physics is close to following the cumulative knowledge process described in chapter 2, when physicists pursue the ultimately small particle from the molecule through the atom, protons, neutrons, electrons, and quarks to where?[27] There certainly occurs, at various stages in the ongoing research process in physics, the formulation of hypotheses (or even metaphysical speculations) about all sorts of things: black holes, the relation between space and time, the curvature of space, and so on. Also, the accumulation of knowledge goes on as a more or less continuous process as the physicists expand the capabilities of their accelerators, proceeding from one day to the next and one year to the next to do the additional things that the improved accelerator is capable of doing. The process is not dissimilar from the ancient progression from copper, through bronze and brass, and lead and zinc, to iron and steel. How many formal hypotheses or theories do you suppose anyone actually bothered to formulate in that process?

In geology and archeology, knowledge is being accumulated pretty much as ongoing process. There may be stages, punctuated by speculations such as "What do you suppose is under that hillock over there?" Or, "Let's check in this area rather than that for oil because . . . ." In geology there is a famous example of a mistaken argument and its correction cited by Stephen Jay Gould.[28] Lord Kelvin in 1866 ostensibly demolished the standard view in geology as to the age of the Earth, arguing that the Earth must be much younger than geologists were arguing because of the speed with which heat was being dissipated from the Earth. Gould's comment is: "Fortunately for a scientific geology Kelvin's argument rested on a false premise—the assumption that the earth's heat is a residue of its original molten state and not a constantly renewed quantity."

The trouble runs deeper than the observation that "there is still no systematic way of generating hypothesis." The article in the *Encyclopedia of Philosophy* on "Scientific Method" goes on to say: "The advance of science was not secured by reasonably intelligent persons following the methods of Bacon or Descartes; it was secured by very exceptional persons following their own methods. Why were Galileo and Newton better scientists than Bacon and Descartes?"[29] Perhaps there is no way to estimate precisely the relative proportions of "exceptionality" and luck in the make-up of the scientists who have made the major contributions. They have gone about their work in many different ways, frequently without hypotheses in any formal sense. And quite generally, once they are embarked on their work, the process looks much more like the cumulative and dynamic process described in chapter 2 on technology, which began this work, than like the stylized model of hypothesis testing.

As to verification and falsification in connection with significant scientific discoveries, one might well say: "indeed." A major discovery, such as Einstein's special theory of relativity may be confirmed, not by a large number of repeated experiments, but by two or three key observations made during one eclipse of the sun. Or a significant discovery may first be confirmed by one experiment, then falsified by a different experiment, and then reconfirmed by even later experiments. Who knows what will happen next? According to Steven Weinberg, this was the history of the Weinberg-Abdus Salam demonstration of the unification of the "weak force" and electromagnetism.[30]

"Philosophy of science" courses, as taught in philosophy departments, have very little to do with the actual methods of scientists, and, the philosophy of science courses taught in science departments are very largely anecdotal in nature and really do not effectively generalize the methods involved.

Do scientists believe they are practicing induction or deduction? If you ask one at random, the answer will be ambiguous. If the inquiry is whether a hypothesis is being tested, the scientist is likely to know that the answer is supposed to be "yes." But inquiry as to what the hypothesis actually is may well leave several doors open. A scientist is creating new compounds and checking their properties. What is the hypothesis being tested? There is hope that one will detect whether one of the new compounds has some useful properties. The hypothesis is that enough trial and error may lead to something useful. To put it mildly that is not much of a hypothesis.

Is testing supposed to decide on the validity of a hypothesis that the Universe is forever expanding, or expanding and contracting? Is the procedure inductive or deductive? Perhaps it depends on the nature of the tests. One could leaf through a collection of the aphorisms of some prophet or consult the "Revelations of St. John the Divine" and find the pronouncement, allegedly made from on high, that the Universe is standing on its head and use that as evidence and call that analytical process deductive. One might find some exotic technique that would let one get out with a yardstick and measure the distance to the edge of the Universe, and repeat that process every day for a million consecutive days, observe that the Universe seems to be getting bigger, and claim that this is a large enough sample to justify the tentative conclusion that the Universe is expanding and will expand forever, and call that method inductive, or perhaps hypothetico-inductive.

CONCLUSION

Knowledge is something more than accurate predictions arrived at by statistical correlations; it also involves understanding why and how.[31]

Beyond this, the accumulation of knowledge is a process with its own internal dynamic. It is not merely an agglomeration of isolated hypotheses which are either verifiable or falsifiable. It is a process rather than a series of isolated, disjointed events.

Hypothesis testing, problem solving, and other such activities, which involve refinements of deductive, inductive, and hypothetico-deductive logic, are a part of the pursuit of knowledge. A scientist may make careful use of the hypothetico-deductive method and discover something important, but such events have been rare. Most scientists have not mastered the algebra of George Boole or the symbolism of set theory in the tradition of Georg Cantor. And sentential calculus is a mystery not particularly worth solving.

They probably do not pay much attention to the methodology of science as that methodology is elaborated in the philosophy of science literature. For the most part they pursue their work as an ongoing process punctuated by sudden insights and occasional shifts of interest which may or may not be accurately described as involving, in a formal sense, the formulation and testing of new hypotheses.

NOTES

[1]A fuller treatment of the range of procedures for validating scientific knowledge may be found, for example, in Janet A. Kourany, ed., *Scientific Knowledge* (Belmont, Calif.: Wadsworth Publishing, 1987), pp. 112-226.

[2]David Hume, *An Enquiry Concerning Human Understanding* (1748), par. 59, 46, 47.

[3]Gertrud Lenzer, ed., *Auguste Comte and Positivism: The Essential Writings* (New York: Harper & Row, 1975); Auguste Comte, *Cours de Philosophie Positive* (1830-1842); Auguste Comte, *Systeme de Politique Positive* (1851-1854).

[4]Lenzer, ed., p. 146.

[5]Justus Buchler, ed., *Philosophical Writings of Peirce* (New York: Dover Publications, 1955 [1940]); Philip P. Wiener, ed., *Charles S. Peirce: Selected Writings (Values in a Universe of Chance)* (New York: Dover Publications, 1966 [1958]); Charles S. Peirce, *Collected Papers*, Charles Hartshorne, ed., (Cambridge, Mass.: Harvard University Press, 1931-1958).

[6]Buchler, ed., p. 31.

[7]Ibid., p. 38.

[8]William James, *Pragmatism and the Meaning of Truth* (Cambridge, Mass.: Harvard University Press, 1975 [1907]), p. 125; John J. McDermott, ed., *The Writings of William James* (New York: The Modern Library, 1967, 1968); William James, *The Will to Believe and Other Essays in Popular Philosophy* (New York: Longmans Green, 1896), pp. 20-24.

[9]John Dewey, *Studies in Logical Theory* (Chicago: University of Chicago Press, 1903), pp. 78, 128; John Dewey, *The Quest for Certainty* (New York: Minton, Balch, 1929); John Dewey, *Reconstruction in Philosophy* (New York: Holt, 1920); John Dewey, *Theory of Valuation* (Chicago: University of Chicago Press, 1939); John Dewey, *Human Nature and Conduct* (New York: Holt, 1922).

[10]See the article on "logical positivism" in the *Encyclopedia of Philosophy*, and also individual articles on the various members of the Circle.

[11]Moritz Schlick, *General Theory of Knowledge* (LaSalle, Ill.: Open Court, 1985 [1925]), pp. 395, 398-9.

[12]Karl R. Popper, *The Logic of Scientific Discovery (Logik der Forschung)* (New York: Harper Torchbooks, 1968 [1959, 1934]), pp. 27, 29, 32-33, 40-41. The first edition appeared in German in 1934. A substantially modified English translation appeared in 1959.

[13]Ibid., pp. 32-33.

[14]Ibid., pp. 36, 59, 61, 100, 373, 423, 425, 426.

[15]Karl R. Popper, *Realism and the Aim of Science* (Totowa, NJ: Rowman & Littlefield, 1983 [1956]), pp. 111-2.

[16]Dewey, *Studies in Logical Theory*, pp. 78, 128.

[17]Buchler, ed., p. 313.

[18]John Dewey, *Reconstruction in Philosophy*, p. 148.

[19]Karl R. Popper, *Conjecture and Refutations: The Growth of Scientific Knowledge* (New York; Harper and Row, 1965 [1963]), "Preface."

[20]Milton Friedman, *Essays in Positive Economics* (Chicago: University of Chicago Press, 1953), p. 3.

[21]Ibid., p. 39.

[22]Ibid., p. 7.

[23]Ibid., p. 14.

[24]Ibid., pp. 22-23.

[25]Ibid., p. 23.

[26]Lawrence A. Boland, *Foundations of Economic Method* (London: Allen & Unwin, 1982).

[27]Emilio Segrè, *From X-Rays to Quarks* (San Francisco: W. H. Freeman, 1980).

[28]Stephen Jay Gould, "False Premise, Good Science," *Natural History*, October, 1983, p. 20.

[29]A statement in the article on the "Scientific Method" in the *Encyclopedia of Philosophy*.

[30]Paul Davies, *God and the New Physics* (New York: Simon and Schuster, 1983), p. 156.

[31]Pierre Duhem, "Physical Theory and Experiment [1954]," in Kourany, ed., pp. 158-169, esp., p. 168.

Chapter VII

Theory of Valuation
(Value Theory)

The theory of valuation results from considering the process by which judgments about values are formed. Valuations are continually being made and modified by those making the valuations. This is a subjective, human-directed value theory with an instrumental aspect (using instrumental in the sense of John Dewey not Karl Popper). But it is not subjective in the sense that the individual's ideas about worthwhileness are taken as fundamental data. On the contrary, the most important part of the story involves looking behind the facade of people's expressed values in order to determine how these attitudes arose.[1]

It is better to call this a theory of valuation rather than a theory of value. The reason is that attention is centered on the process by which valuations, or value judgments, are made and changed. There is no presumption that there is an identifiable, quantifiable value inherent in whatever is under consideration. The job of the theory is not to identify values that remain intact and unchanging over time and distance, irrespective of the interests of the beholder.

THE CONCEPTS OF VALUE AND VALUATION

The theory of valuation is the study of the process by which value judgments or valuations are made by an individual (or, in some sense, perhaps also, by an institution or by technology) as to what is desirable, esteemed, or satisfying (ends-in-view in the sense of John Dewey) or as to what is instrumental or useful in effecting results conceived to be desirable, estimable, or satisfying (the means aspect of the ends-means-ends continuum). Those results thought to be desirable, estimable, or satisfying are subjective values. Those thought to be instrumental or useful in implementing such subjective values are instrumental values. These are not, however, mutually exclusive categories. Good workmanship is both instrumental and a source of personal, subjective satisfaction to the worker.[2] Note, also, the substantial equivalence of instruments and technology.

In this approach, values are attributed to both means and ends. Dewey says: "But it may be noted here that ends are appraised in the same evaluation in which things as means are weighed."[3] (This distinction, between values representing *desirability* and instrumental values embodying *usefulness* in accomplishing desired results, is different from the true values-false values distinction or the instrumental-ceremonial distinction. These two distinctions have been made in the institutionalist literature with a pejorative implication. There is no pejorative implication in the distinction between desirability and effectiveness.)

The identification of a value because it is desirable, esteemed, or satisfying corresponds with the identification of one of John Dewey's ends-in-view. The identification of an instrumental value corresponds with the means aspect of Dewey's means-end continuum—the ongoing, perhaps never ending, ends-means-ends-means process.[4] That is to say: The realization of an end-in-view may suggest further ends-in-view requiring new means for their attainment. The realization of full employment, a possible end-in-view, may leave unattained the implementation of another possible end-in-view such as a pleasant life for all.

This is not a utilitarian (pleasure-pain) or hedonistic value theory. For one thing, pleasure and pain cannot be measured in a way that permits use of the so-called hedonistic calculus to quantify the best possible mix of pleasure and pain. There are other problems. Short-term euphoria may provide only a temporary test of desirability and a long-run ticket to misery. And the individual may very quickly regret some euphoria-generating activities, but nevertheless be trapped by a habit that is difficult to shake. Dewey has made this distinction between the immediate urge and the more thoughtful opinion on desirability:

> [P]ast experience has shown that hasty action upon uncriticized desire leads to defeat and possibly to catastrophe. The "desirable" as distinct from the "desired" does not then designate something at large or a priori. It points to the difference between the operation and consequences of unexamined impulses and those of desires and interests that are the product of conditions and consequences.[5]

The urge to take dope or smoke a cigarette does not necessarily establish the desirability of doing such things, even from the viewpoint of the individual involved. Tax reduction may mean fun in the short run and deficits in the long run.

Unfortunately there exists no objective procedure for identifying and ruling short-run mistakes to be out of order except the self-correcting value judgment process, unless society wishes to abrogate responsibility.

There is a value-in-use versus value-in-exchange distinction in classical and Marxist economics. The concept of value used in this work is close to value-in-use. But the discussion of value-in-use in the classical and Marxist literature takes usefulness as assumed. Institutionalism tries to understand the origins of criteria for usefulness or desirability. Thus the frame of reference of institutionalism is sufficiently different so that it is probably not helpful to identify the institutionalist concept of value with the value-in-use concept of classical economics.

Certainly the institutionalist concept of value does not give credibility to the classical economics concept of value-in-exchange. Because of distortions in the marketing process and assorted other reasons, discussed at length in chapters 9 and 10, there can be no legitimate presumption that price (or value in exchange) identifies any result that can usefully be identified as value in a theoretical sense. Market price may be a useful approximation of value for certain purposes. And, for better or worse, market prices are pretty important. But if society finds reason for being unhappy with the valuations imputed by market prices, society will take actions that override the judgments of the market.

The labor theory of value—that labor time measures relative value—may for some purposes provide a useful approximation of value. This would be true if the labor time involved was the "socially necessary unit of labor time" of the Marxists, if such a quantity were consistently identifiable. But, as will be indicated in chapter 12, basically, the socially necessary unit of labor time turns out to be just as ambiguous as price.

There is no satisfactory way to identify and quantify the amount of value inhering in objects. And economists and philosophers could save a lot of time by ceasing trying. Nor is there a higher power up in the sky who is willing to provide a value yardstick. There may be a higher power up there, but it seems to have other interests than assuring perfection in the operation of the free market system. (It may be added that, also, there is not out there, or in the Kremlin, a clairvoyant, well meaning autocrat capable of managing a beneficent society with perfection.) For better or worse we are feeling our way in an uncertain but interesting process.

Society as a whole may have a consensus about certain values (institutionalized behavior norms), and institutions are the custodians of those judgments. And it may be repeated that institutions are likely to be a little slow in changing these norms in response to the exigencies of new circumstances.

One may classify the cast of characters in the theory of valuation as follows: the subject who makes the value judgment or the evaluation is either an individual or an institution. The objects to which values are imputed are goods and services. The goods and services are subdivided into the ends-in-view—the objects of consumption—and the means, which are technology and resources. One bears in mind meanwhile that there is an overlap between ends-in-view and means, and even between subjects and objects. One can see the overlap between ends-in-view and means in the case of the individual who takes pride in one's own work.

The foregoing represents an assertion as to what the important relationships in the theory of valuation actually are. Observation of the way people behave, and consideration of the alternatives, may convince one that this is a reasonable statement of the relation among the actors in value theory—or may not. But one's view in this matter is itself subject to the self-correcting value judgment process which is being discussed.

IDENTIFICATION OF THE SUBJECT WHOSE
VALUATIONS ARE RELEVANT

Who is this individual who makes judgments about values? The answer would seem rather simple: It is any biological being capable of having an opinion about the desirability or estimability or usefulness of something. Thus, all kinds of creatures are capable of making value judgments: smart people and morons, women and men, people of different races, monkeys, dogs, horses, the old as well as the young, and maybe the birds and the bees.[6]

The social and institutional structure of human society influences which people have the greater effect in determining the social consensus, that is, the institutionalized behavioral norms (the valuations of institutions) that society imposes on individuals. Who, or what species, is most influential in this process varies as time passes and the process of self-correcting value judgments works itself out.

It is the individual who matters—to the individual if the individual thinks so and if that individual, at the moment, happens to have been thrown into a position of "power" by the self-correcting value judgment process. But being in this position does not mean that the values of such people are unique, or permanent, or instinctive, or definitive, or clairvoyant. Quite the contrary: values are changeable results of changing circumstances.

We choose to be concerned about the individual's stake in things because we are individuals. The concern of some individuals is pretty much concentrated on themselves. The concern of others might extend to yet other individuals, or at least to selected other individuals.

In a democracy, the rules at a given time determine who can vote and who cannot: 18-year olds or 21-year olds? And the 18-year olds might have a voice in determining whether the voting age would be raised from 18 to 21, but not in determining whether it should be lowered from 21 to 18. There is an asymmetry here. This is to say, institutionalized behavior norms which are in being, influence how institutionalized behavior norms get changed. As Clarence Ayres has said: ". . . the system itself grows by a process that can be understood only as a cultural phenomenon."[7]

THE LOCUS OF VALUE AND OF VALUATION

In identifying who is doing what in this valuation process, we must be clear as to who is "subject" and who or what is "object" in the process. On the one hand there is the object to which value is being assigned; on the other hand there is the subject making the assignment. In the institutional literature, when technology is referred to as a locus of value, it is in the sense that technology is an "object" to which value is being assigned. Technology is valued because it is instrumental in implementing desired results, thereby affecting our life process in which we have a considerable interest.

Although beings or individuals are the subjects making the judgments about values, they are also changing their attitudes as part of the ongoing process. Institutions, or society viewed as a whole, are also entities functioning as subjects and expressing value judgments and imposing those value judgments on individuals.

SENSE IN WHICH INSTITUTIONALISM IS NORMATIVE

In modern economics, and especially in the first or second chapter of recent elementary textbooks, normative economics (economics concerned with value judgments and with "what ought to be") is contrasted with positive economics (economics concerned with what "is"). The value judgment is then made that positive economics is the proper realm for economics. This assigns to economists the role of mechanical technicians and makes it seem that economics is not a social science. If mention is made of institutionalism at all at this juncture, it is to say that institutionalism is to be rejected because it is normative. The picture is then given of the institutionalist as a pseudo-economist running around making gratuitous or even irresponsible value judgments about everything. The claim is that at the very least the economist, when making a value judgment, should be careful to say that one is not making it as an economist. A remarkable job has been done in giving the word "do-gooder" a pejorative content.

This caricature of the place of value theory in institutionalism is not very helpful for promoting understanding in the social sciences. Properly stated, the position of institutionalism with regard to norms, values, and valuations is as follows:

(1) Institutionalism as institutionalism has no commitment to any particular value judgment.

(2) It does assume that explanation as to where normative or value judgments come from is not only appropriate to economics but an obligation of economics as a social science.

(3) Normative judgments matter.

(4) Value judgments (like "scientific" conclusions) are tentative and subject to reappraisal.

THE SELF-CORRECTING VALUE JUDGMENT PROCESS

The Basic Argument

The self-correcting value judgment process involves continuously evaluating and re-evaluating value judgments against the consequences of efforts to implement those value judgments. The value judgments as to the desirable, the estimable, or the instrumental, which the individual or the institution holds, are determined and modified in this process of appraisal and reappraisal; and both types of value judgments (instrumental and ends-in-view) may be thus modified in the process.

Value judgments (valuations) as to both means (instruments) and ends (ends-in-view) are made and modified by both individuals and institutions in an ongoing process. This process involves evaluating the technology or instrument against the results obtained when one uses a particular technology in an effort to implement a value. It involves re-evaluating the value or end-in-view in terms of whether one really wants it or not after one has had an opportunity to see the implications of the implemented value. It involves individuals as actors in this process. It involves institutions and their role in the process as they influence individuals and try to defend their institutionalized behavior norms or institutionalized values. It involves the interaction among individuals and institutions as they influence and are influenced by each other. It involves the interaction among technology (with its own inherent dynamism), resources, individuals, and institutions, as they react and interact.

In a sense the quality and changing nature of dynamically accumulating technology dominates the whole process and the physical look of the world. This is the ends-means-ends continuum, which has no beginning and no end. The value process is thus not teleological—pointed to some preordained end or ends. There is no paradise to be had at the end of the road or after some revolution which is just around the corner. Rather, this is a process which is ever ongoing. In the course of this process, individuals are continually reappraising. They are changing their opinions as to which technologies work best, and they are discovering new technologies as a by-product of the internal dynamic of the technology accumulation process. They are discarding some technologies and assimilating others. They are looking at the products of those efforts. The innovation and use of the technologies which are considered to be better and more desirable force changes in the structure of institutions and their behavior norms. People, caught up in this process, are continually changing their opinions as to desirable, estimable, and useful. The process is conditioned by available neutral stuff and resources. And life is more interesting as a result.

Wolfgang Friedmann has provided an example of the working of this process:

> A convenient illustration of this approach might be the question of
> prohibition of alcohol, which deeply influenced American legal,
> economic and social life for more than a decade after the First World
> War. Absolute prohibition [involving intoxicating liquors] could be
> stated as a value goal. Means of its execution consist in the appropriate
> Constitutional amendments, statutory prohibitions, administrative
> regulations, and the policing of the legal prohibitions (as well as the
> technology used in attempted enforcement—the speed of the Coast
> Guard ships, the investigatory techniques of the law enforcement
> officers, etc.) An enquiry into the means of execution may show that
> the purported enforcement of prohibition leads—as in fact it did—to
> a vast increase in the consumption of illegal and often lethal alcohol,
> bootlegging, gang warfare, murder, and a general increase in criminal-
> ity. The results of such enquiries may lead to an abandonment or the
> modification of the original value postulate. Abandonment of the ethical
> postulate, in the light of practical experience, is expressed in the repeal
> of the Constitutional amendment in the U.S. Constitution.[8]

The test of an end-in-view or of a technique for obtaining it is our collective opinion as to the results. The theory, then, runs to the effect that tentative valuations are tested in a process involving self-correcting (or self-adjusting) value judgments. One does things differently next time if a previous method did not work out satisfactorily, or if the ends-in-view do not look too attractive when attained. "The proof of the pudding is in the eating." A child who touches a hot skillet makes a self-correcting value judgment in a hurry. An aggressive dog, which is squirted with Halt by a mailcarrier, may leave that mailcarrier alone in the future. That is the instrumental side. On the ends-in-view side one may decide, after trying it, that cigarette smoking is not such a good idea.

As John Dewey expressed it: "An individual within the limits of his personal experience revises his desires and purposes as he becomes aware of the consequences they have produced in the past."[9]

Or, if the institution rather than the individual is viewed as the custodian of value, as Wolfgang Friedmann pointed out, society may experiment with prohibition to discourage the consumption of alcohol, decide the process does not work very well, and give up on the effort.

No definite judgment is made now regarding what is best for all time. No master plan for a perfect society can be drawn up with the thought that this is the ideal social order for which we shall all work and that, once we have arrived at this promised land, all will be for the best in this best of all possible worlds—permanently. This is simply not the name of the game, and life would be a bore if it were.

According to this approach, there are no identifiable, intrinsic values, given from on high or convincingly demonstrated by philosophers. There are no values to which individuals or institutions will adhere regardless of the state of technology, the stage of biological evolution, the availability of resources, or the prevailing social scene. A vision of "sudden blinding good or monstrous evil," or the value "thou shalt not kill," might well leave the spitting cobra unimpressed.

Nevertheless, society has accumulated a good deal of wisdom as to what it takes to constitute a reasonably pleasant, livable society and it would scarcely be good judgment to toss this knowledge, and the institutions we have developed, completely aside. Starting with a clean slate is neither desirable nor feasible nor anything but an invitation to chaos and another round of dark ages characterized by the strong making life miserable for the weak.

The End Does Not Justify the Means

Means and ends are interrelated. Both are part of ongoing process. We have to live with the means as well as with the ends. Our prevailing judgments as to what is ethical apply to the means as well as to the ends, and this is the position of institutionalism, or at least of Dewey and Ayres.

The Self-Correcting Value Judgment Process as Scientific Method

This self-correcting or instrumental value judgment (valuation) process follows much the same logical process as does the scientific method. The initial value judgment is a hypothesis. One puts it into practice and later makes a judgment about the results. Similarly, when the question is whether a technique or instrument, viewed as a value, can get the job done, the appropriateness of the technique is a hypothesis. One applies the technique and decides whether one is satisfied with the result. If not, one tries another technique or writes off the value that one was trying to implement with the technique.[10]

According to William James: "All this amounts to saying that . . . ethical science is just like physical science, and instead of being deducible all at once from abstract principles, must simply bide its time, and be ready to revise its conclusions from day to day . . . ."[11]

FURTHER EXAMPLES OF PROCESS

The use of hard drugs is an example of the self-correcting value judgment process in relation to ends-in-view. One may provide a somewhat stylized description of the way this process has worked, at least with some people. During the 1960s, children, who typically rebel a bit against parental constraints anyway, found themselves in a situation that gave them considerably more leverage than usual. The generation of parents following World War II was consciously permissive in their ideas about raising children. So, the parents were conditioned not to be as authoritarian as the previous generation of parents. The automobile, a technology readily available to the children, has compounded the ability of children to experiment indiscriminately. Then came the Vietnam War and subsequently Watergate, which produced pretty credible bases for being disrespectful of authority.

In this setting a major new behavior pattern was the use of drugs by young people. As the process gained momentum, the slightly older young people challenged the younger to experiment with drugs. And, free-private-enterprise-type entrepreneurs discovered the drug traffic as a profitable line of business. Some of the young people were capable of experimenting a little with drugs and stopping. But large numbers, once they had started with the experimenting, could not stop. And the drug culture dominated their lives from then on, and permissive parents could do little to help when they, too late, came to realize the seriousness of the situation.

Many looked around at the world of the 1970s, with its permissiveness, disorder, terrorism, and crime, and reacted strongly. And, in reaction, an influential, role-setting, dominating young generation of the 1980s emerged as socially and economically conservative. They were business and profit oriented and prone to impose moral standards on others.

In the ongoing process, a swinging pendulum does not come back to where it was before. There is no equilibrium. So, in the society of the 1980s, some of the ingredients in the permissiveness of the immediate post World War II period have been retained and some have not been. Considerable drug use remains but there is also widespread condemnation of drug use. Condemnation of abortion is strong, but there is much promiscuity and much use of the abortion procedure. On many such matters, in the 1980s, it is difficult to identify a social consensus or generally accepted institutionalized behavior norms in United States society.

The shift back and forth between soap and detergents is a very different example of the self-correcting value judgment process at work. When detergents were developed several decades ago the instrumental value judgment was made that in many respects they were superior to soap. Their use proliferated. Then the difficulties with disposing of the detergents were discovered. They contaminated soils and rivers and destroyed life in the rivers. So, the instrumental value judgment as to their usefulness was reappraised and they have been used much less.

DDT, dichloro-diphenyl-trichloro-ethane, appeared during World War II as a miracle chemical for dealing with mosquitoes and insects and bugs that were destructive to crops. So, a highly favorable instrumental value judgment was made. Then, later, harmful side effects were observed and the chemical has since been widely condemned.

Students (and faculty) are often unhappy with registration procedures at their university. The computer appeared to offer a miraculous solution to the registration headache. But the computer did not turn out to be a miracle cure for registration hassles. This does not mean that it would be best to give up the computer in registration procedures in large schools, or in processing airline reservations. Instead, the computer is reprogrammed and procedures are modified. In ongoing process one does not return to the former norm, at least in all probability.

In laboratory experiments on animals a distinction may be made between rats and mice on the one hand and dogs and cats on the other. Some university laboratories have been charged with cruel and inhuman treatment of dogs and cats. But the complaining groups might not object to such treatment if it was meted out to rats and mice. Opinion as to where such lines are best drawn may change as a result of rethinking of valuations.

People, alerted by the press or even by President Reagan, may be very generous in support of some individual to whom fate has been unkind. Hundreds of thousands of dollars may be donated to finance one child's organ transplant. Meanwhile the administration in Washington and society as a whole may be quite indifferent that the proportion of the population living in poverty is rising.

In medical malpractice suits, some people get hundreds of thousands or millions of dollars. Others are the victims of similar afflictions and get nothing or next to nothing. Society may reconsider these situations and change the ground rules, again influenced by evolving perceptions as to what is fair.

SOME ISSUES
Definitive Values, Eternal Verities, and Truth

Lack of certainty as to the definitiveness of truth or the existence of identifiable eternal verities and absolute values is characteristic of institutionalism and instrumentalism.

Marc Tool writes: "What sets off the following formulation of instrumental value theory from the social-value theory of other belief systems is that it is derived exclusively from the experience continuum of people and that it articulates what often has historically been meant by progress, reform, or betterment. . . . The following value theory is different in kind; it is a product of inquiry; it may be modified or replaced by subsequent inquiry. . . . The formulation here is thus provisional and exploratory." [12]

Clarence Ayres states: "The discovery that values are culture-borne—that men prize and abhor what they have been taught to prize and abhor—is one of the great intellectual achievements of modern times." [13]

In spite of this Ayres does seem to say in certain places that various values do represent eternal verities: freedom, equality, decency, honesty, loving and kindness, gentleness and non-violence, helpfulness, the absence of crime, health, the continuation of the life process, keeping the machines running, science and technology, the technological process. [14]

Speaking of freedom, equality, security, abundance, and excellence, which would seem not to be technological values in an obvious sense, Ayres says: "These are values all mankind has sought. . . . But it is also true that the effective working relationships which constitute the life process of mankind spell out values which thus derive not from our sentiments but from our necessities, and this likewise is just as true of the values that prevail in intimate personal relationships as of those which pertain to whole societies. The truth is that honesty, decency, and veracity are not only the best policy but the only policy in terms of which human beings can work together to live better than the animals."

Marc Tool also endorses the existence of an eternal verity in his social-value principle, which he refers to as a value referent: "We now affirm that that direction is forward which provides for *the continuity of human life and the non-invidious re-creation of community through the instrumental use of knowledge.*" [15]

There is a difficulty which both Ayres and Tool recognize in other contexts. Ayres says with regard to the meaning of the absence of crime:

> Noses, we now realize, detect odors but do not select them. The selection is done by society, by social habit and tradition; that is by the mores. There is no odor, however foul it may seem to certain people, which is not enjoyed by other people with different traditions; and the same thing is true of behavior generally. There is no act which is universally condemned. "Crime" is universally condemned. But "crime" is an abstraction, not an act. What is crime in one set of circumstances or to one set of people may be highly meritorious in other circumstances or to other people. [16]

One, personally, may endorse Ayres's values—freedom, equality, security, abundance, and excellence; and one may endorse Tool's instrumental value principle. To endorse these values and to believe that they actually do or that they ought to represent the values of society does not, however, establish that these are definitive valuations.

William James wrote: "[T]here is no such thing possible as an ethical philosophy dogmatically made up in advance. . . . [T]here can be no final truth in ethics any more than in physics. . . . [N]othing can be good or right except so far as some consciousness feels it to be good or thinks it to be right, ... If one ideal judgment be objectively better than another, that betterness must be made flesh by being lodged concretely in some one's actual perception."[17]

Possible Sources of Definitive Values and Eternal Verities

If there were, or if there are, definitive values or eternal verities, what are the possible processes by which they might be identified? Three chief possibilities suggest themselves: (1) revelation by a supreme being, (2) natural law, and (3) rational thought.

The first, and perhaps historically the most important, procedure by which definitive values and eternal verities might be revealed to people has been revelation by some supreme being via the priesthood. One might say this is the function of the priesthood in any religion, almost by definition: to enlighten the people as to what the Lord, Jehovah, Allah, or some other conception of the supreme being, envisions as valuable or meritorious. When people were emerging from savagery this was probably the only feasible way to civilize (and we might agree that some measure of civilizing was a pretty good idea) the beasts, especially if the message as to what is desirable behavior was accompanied by the prospect of Hell and damnation for the non-conformists. Divine revelation by respected priests was a most useful civilizing device as humanity evolved into society.

Then as society evolved and people got a bit skeptical about the priests, the possibility presented itself that order in nature, or natural law, could be observed and these observations could provide the basis for identifying eternal verities and definitive values. This happened at the time of The Enlightenment during the seventeenth and eighteenth centuries. Philosophers then were especially imaginative in conceiving that in early times people lived together in a state of nature involving cooperative, communistic bliss before people agreed to a social contract and began to squabble and fight. Of course, the possibility that some mistaken interpretations have been made does not refute the possibility that eternal verities may be revealed to the observant as a by-product of the workings of nature and of natural law.

The third possible source of knowledge as to definitive values and eternal verities is rational thought. If one chooses to see a considerable overlap between this possibility and the conception of the philosopher observing and thinking about the workings of nature, there is no quarrel. Also, there may be some overlap between a supreme being revealing truth to a priest and nature revealing truth to a philosopher.

When Clarence Ayres says that freedom, equality, security, abundance, and excellence represent eternal verities as values, then the arguments he uses to support this claim are an example of the use of rational thought to identify such truths.

John Rawls's argument for his two principles of justice is an example of a similar rational process. First Principle: "Each person is to have an equal right to the most extensive total system of equal basic liberties compatible with a similar system of liberty for all." Second Principle: "Social and economic inequalities are to be arranged so that they are both: (a) to the greatest benefit of the least advantaged, consistent with the just savings principle, and (b) attached to offices and positions open to all under conditions of fair equality of opportunity."[18]

Another example as to a thoughtful process for arriving at an eternal verity is Immanuel Kant's categorical imperative. A categorical imperative is (according to *Webster's Unabridged*, 3rd ed.) "a moral obligation or command that is unconditionally and universally binding." The famous categorical imperative of Immanuel Kant is that people should "act as if the maxim from which you act were to become through your will a universal law." This proposition has the implication that "thus people must recognize that they ought to pay their taxes, because, although it would be in their interest not to, it would not be in their interest to have a system in which no one did." This proposition might have been worth a little attention on the part of Proposition 13 fanatics in California back in the 1970s. One may endorse, as of the here and now, Kant's proposition and yet be of the opinion that it is not a categorical imperative in the sense of being an eternal verity or a definitive value. How would one *prove* that it is such?

The natural law and the rational thought approaches to identifying eternal verities may overlap. Cicero is cited as having said: "There is in fact a true law—namely right reason—which is in accordance with nature, applies to all men, and is unchangeable and eternal." And John Cogley has said about this proposition: "fundamentally, the idea of natural law . . . is based on a belief that there exists a moral order which every normal person can discover by using his reason and of which he must take account if he is to attune himself to his necessary ends as a human being."[19]

The proposition that some laws are basic and fundamental and are discoverable by human reason has been held by the Greek Stoics, by the Roman Cicero, by Thomas Aquinas, Hugo Grotius, Rousseau, Tom Paine, John Locke, and many others. Rousseau, of course, is a prime source for the doctrine that natural law is a basis for democratic and egalitarian principles, such as those expressed in the United States Declaration of Independence. John Locke's catalog is slightly different than that in the Declaration of Independence. His catalog includes freedom of worship, right to a voice in one's own government, and the right of private property. Tom Paine makes natural rights theory a justification for revolution.

One can doubt that any one of these procedures conclusively identifies a definitive value and at the same time be grateful for the roles these approaches have played historically. Resort to the authority of a "supreme being" was probably very useful in civilizing our ancestors. Recourse to the natural law argument during the seventeenth and eighteenth centuries was probably most useful in refuting the "divine right of kings" claim. And the statement in the American Declaration of Independence: "We hold these Truths to be self-evident, that all Men are created equal, that they are endowed by their Creator with certain unalienable Rights, that among these are Life, Liberty, and the Pursuit of Happiness— . . ." made a major contribution in the long struggle for a better world. Yet, the propositions stated there are probably not literally self-evident truths and they are not demonstrably eternal verities.

Implication for Morality and for the Importance of the Individual

Some individuals, when confronted with the prospect that there are no definitive values dictating appropriate behavior, may be concerned that morality in society has been lost. There need be concern only if people fear a situation where society and the individuals in it are rethinking their values all the time. If they face up to the implications of challenge, those implications become interesting, stimulating, and challenging. The value theory of institutional economics offers the exciting prospect of progress because at each stage in the process we can be working to improve matters according to our conception of improvement. We can work to improve ourselves and we ourselves are making the meaningful judgments regarding how to do it. This is no picture of a utopia after revolution, which might seem pretty empty once we had it: it is a picture of ongoing struggle, improvement, and progress. We do have an ongoing, worthwhile, challenging, ever changing future.

The implication for morality of all this is not what one might expect at first thought. The implication is not that there is a decline in ethical standards because there are no eternal verities to guide us. Actually, the implication for the quality of individual ethics is quite the contrary and quite wholesome. The individual is on her or his own and society is on its own. They can make something of themselves that they can be proud of, if they will. But people as a group have to do it for themselves. They have to do it again and again every day. And people can only do it for themselves as a cooperative venture—not in a dog-eat-dog contest. This way of thinking is conducive to the creation of improved ethics and improved relations among people. (Adam Smith and the Western obsession with the virtues of competition contributed to putting economics on the wrong track.)

A quotation from Ayres is appropriate: "This naturalistic, instrumental, technological theory of value is not 'mere' theory. As I have already said and will continue to repeat, it is not a theory of how value judgments ought to be made. It is an account of how we do, now and always, actually evaluate the things we value." [20]

Yet, it is also a theory which permits us, even enjoins us, to have an opinion as to how things ought to be, even if there is nothing eternally definitive about this quality of oughtness. This is normative, not positive, economics. We do make value judgments, and economists (as economists) should take an interest in understanding where values come from as well as how economics can contribute to their implementation.

Also, it is within the realm of reason that this institutional value theory, in truth, is in the United States frontier tradition endorsing freedom and change. If the truth be told, static price theory is not in that tradition.

William James wrote: "[E]thics have as genuine and real a foothold in a universe where the highest consciousness is human, as in a universe where there is a God as well."[21]

Cross-Cultural Values and Cultural Relativism

The theory of valuation as set out here is (if the approach is correct) common to all cultures. That is to say, it involves a principle that can be applied to all cultures. Certainly, different cultures at a given time may value particular goods or circumstances differently. But that is not the crux of the matter. There is here a common principle. The value theory methodology is general even though what is held valuable may vary from culture to culture. What is common to all cultures is the process of self-correcting value judgments.

One may presume with some assurance that historically when one culture has imposed its religion on another culture it has self-righteously believed that it was imposing a correct set of values upon a civilization living in error. This is true whether it was the victor in some ancient war enforcing a religion on the vanquished; or, the Arabs forcing Islam on the people of the Near East and North Africa; or, the various European countries, following the discovery of America, forcing Christianity on the Indians of the New World.

Toward the latter part of the nineteenth century, incipient anthropologists began to poke around among primitive cultures all over the world and to react against the idea that western European culture had all the correct values and the rest of the world had things all wrong. Franz Boas and his student, Ruth Benedict, and her student, Margaret Mead, were among the anthropologists trying to make sense out of cultural differences in values and behavior patterns. Out of the study of cross-cultural values came the proposition of cultural relativism. Melville Herskovits has defined cultural relativism: "[C]ultural relativism is a philosophy that recognizes the values set up by every society to guide its own life and that understands their worth to those who live by them, though they may differ from one's own. Instead of underscoring differences from absolute norms that, however objectively arrived at, are nonetheless the product of a given time or place, the relativistic point of view brings into relief the validity of every set of norms for the people who have them, and the values these represent."[22]

It is worth mentioning the, perhaps obvious, point that, although valuations may differ from culture to culture, there is nothing about this argument that requires that they must differ. A pipe wrench may well be considered, in many or all cultures, to be better than a monkey wrench for screwing and unscrewing pipe. Certain instruments and ends-in-view may well be similarly regarded in many cultures.

As to whether all values of all cultures are sacrosanct, in the sense that outsiders cannot legitimately question them, something more needs to be said. As world society becomes more and more integrated the possibility arises that the social unit which imposes values on people may well be world society as a whole. World society in the future could well "decide" (by processes not yet clearly identifiable) that there is a degree of polluting the atmosphere that no individual nation will be allowed to engage in. It will not matter how highly that nation esteems its right to engage in the polluting activity. Or, possibly, the world community will organize itself well enough to permit it to impose peace on the bellicose "sovereign" nations.

Herskovits does argue that cultural relativism is to be sharply distinguished from the relativity of individual behavior.[23] He argues that a society simply cannot allow each individual freely to get away with any behavior the individual whim leads one to fancy. At some point, Herskovits's argument will be applied to the individual nation in a world of nations.

Valuations at Cross-Purposes

This chapter has been based on the presumption that the making of valuations by individuals is the heart of the process. Such an approach might seem to imply that such valuations are coherent. Unfortunately, subjective valuations are not necessarily coherent. (Some may think this makes the process more interesting.) There remains, for better or worse, the complicating circumstance that one may be at cross-purposes with one's self. As an example, at one and the same time, the individual may experience a craving for a cigarette and a realization that it is in one's own interest not to smoke. Similar inconsistencies may exist at the level of the institution, perhaps when a nation both desires peace and relishes war.

Here there is no claim that the self-correcting value judgment process maintains coherence in the judgments at all stages as the process goes on. Ongoing inconsistency remains with us like death and taxes. The inconsistency is a fact of life that we will have to live with, adjusting to the inconsistency as best we may by the self-correcting value judgment process.

ESSENCE OF VALUATION PROCESS

The valuation process has two aspects: an ends-in-view aspect and an instrumental aspect.

Judgments as to desirable ends-in-view are made by individuals (and, in a somewhat different sense, by institutions). Comparisons are made with other possible goals and there is some sort of ordering of priorities. But it is an imperfect ordering because of mixed-up considerations.

Efforts may then be made to implement the valuations. Tentative judgments are made as to the relative merits of different instruments. Individuals use instruments to try to influence society to endorse their ideas. Society uses instruments to try to implement such of the ideas as it has been induced to endorse. At both levels, the individual and the institutional, judgments will be made as to how well the instruments have worked.

Ends and means will be continued or modified depending on these judgments.

Some of these judgments may be checked by quantifiable techniques. In the case of other judgments the checks will be subjective in varying degrees. Whose opinion as to which judgments will prevail will be controlled by the then prevailing institutional arrangements of society in a setting where those arrangements themselves are subject to change in the ongoing process.

What is going on is ongoing process not circular reasoning.

NOTES

[1]The literature in the field of value and valuation theory has been extensive. A small sample of this literature includes: John Dewey, *Theory of Valuation* (Chicago: University of Chicago Press, 1939); C. E. Ayres, *Toward a Reasonable Society* (Austin: University of Texas Press, 1961); W. H. Werkmeister, *Historical Spectrum of Value Theories,* 2 vols. (Lincoln, Nebr.: Johnsen Publishing, 1973); C. I. Lewis, *An Analysis of Value and Valuation* (LaSalle, Ill.: Open Court Publishing, 1946); Ralph Barton Perry, *General Theory of Value* (New York: Longmans, Green, 1926): also there is a professional journal specializing in this area: *Journal of Value Inquiry.* Economics has a long history of concern for value theory: value in use, value in exchange, labor theory of value, price theory as value theory (Adam Smith, David Ricardo, Karl Marx). Per contra, see: Karl P. Popper, *The Logic of Scientific Discovery* (New York: Harper Torchbooks, 1968[1959, 1934]), p. 423.

[2]For discussion of some of the terminological problems see Dewey, pp. 5-6, 29.

[3]Dewey, p. 24.

[4]John Dewey, "The Field of 'Value'," in Ray Lepley, ed., *Value: A Cooperative Inquiry* (New York: Columbia University Press, 1949), pp. 64-78.

[5]Dewey, *Theory of Valuation,* p. 32.

[6]Peter Singer, "Ten Years of Animal Liberation,"*The New York Review* XXXI (January 17, 1985), pp. 46-52; the January 1987 issue of *The Monist* is entirely devoted to the subject of "Animal Rights."

[7]Ayres, p. 119.

[8]Wolfgang Friedmann, *Legal Theory* (New York: Columbia, 1967 [1944]), pp. 31-2.

[9]Dewey, *Theory of Valuation,* p. 58.

[10]The argument is developed by John Dewey in his *Theory of Valuation,* in fac the argument pervades the book.

[11]William James, "The Moral Philosopher and the Moral Life [1891]," in *The Writings of William James,* John J. McDermott, ed., (New York: The Modern Library, 1968), p. 625.

[12]Marc R. Tool, *The Discretionary Economy* (Santa Monica, California Goodyear, 1979), p. 292.

[13]Ayres, p. 289.

[14]Ayres, pp. 113, 170, 265; C. E. Ayres, *Theory of Economic Progress* (New York: Schocken Books, 1962 [1944]), pp. xxiv, 230, 231; C. E. Ayres, *The Industrial Economy* (Boston: Houghton Mifflin, 1952), p. 19.

[15]Tool, p. 293.

[16]Ayres, *Theory of Economic Progress,* p. 70.

[17]William James, "The Moral Philosopher and the Moral Life," pp. 610, 611, 616.

[18]John Rawls, *A Theory of Justice* (Cambridge, MA: Harvard University Press, 1971), p. 302.

[19]John Cogley, *Natural Law and Modern Society* (Cleveland: World Publishing Co., 1961), pp. 15, 19-20.

[20]Ayres, *Toward a Reasonable Society,* p. 34.

[21]William James, "The Moral Philosopher and the Moral Life," p. 619.

[22]Melville Herskovits, *Cultural Relativism* (New York: Random House, 1972), pp. 31-32.

[23]Ibid., p. 10.

Chapter VIII

Currently Held
Value Judgments

The value theory of institutionalism holds that the value judgments of individuals and society (or institutions) are not eternal verities but are subject to change in the self-correcting value judgment process. Of course, at any given time there will be values that are subscribed to by individuals and by groupings. It is of considerable importance to identify these values, understand how they arose and what their implications are. This is part of understanding the society in which one is living.

What follows is an effort to catalog, schematize, and one might even say over-simplify, the value pattern existing at present on Planet Earth (or perhaps, more specifically, in so-called Western society). The effort is worthwhile even though there will be major disagreement with the classification, disagreement on where to draw the more meaningful lines, disagreement even on the question as to whether such and such a value is generally held. Also, value patterns are in a considerable state of flux and one may identify values that once were generally held but are now increasingly rejected. And we may not have become aware of important attitudes that are coming into being as a result of the instrumental value judgment (valuation) process. In the Reagan-Thatcher era, self-centered selfish-ness is the order of the day in Western society. Perhaps it is more accurate to say that present day conservative attitudes endorse generosity on a person–to–person basis but not action by society as a whole to eliminate poverty and hardship. This attitude might, somewhat unfairly, be summarized as: We want the garbage picked up, but let us fire the garbage collectors in order to balance the budget.

The basic valuations discussed in what follows are the desirability of (1) a decent minimum, (2) getting along pleasantly, (3) constructive self-expression, and (4) security.

101

THE DECENT MINIMUM

The first item in the list is the desirability of a decent, minimum, material level of living for all, accompanied by the possibility that the individual may pursue, not too obstreperously, an improved level of living.

The implementation of the decent minimum involves several things. For those able to work and who live in a developed country the crux of the matter may well be the implementing of a job guarantee (discussed in chapter 15).

Most people in the United States are now living in comfortable affluence. The same can be true in the not too distant future for the world's population in general. The standard of living is high for many and it is rising for most. But the usefulness (marginal utility) of each $100 increase in income is decreasing and considerations other than material level of living are becoming more important, especially in rich countries.

Basic welfare can cease to be a problem. But this is not necessarily what will happen. Some self-correcting value judgments need to be made, and it is not entirely clear that society, especially a society characterized by what we might call the Reagan mentality, will choose to make the necessary changes in attitudes. To the extent that holding down taxes and keeping down the size of government remain an obsession with those already affluent, this attitude may frustrate the possibility for obtaining general material welfare. People have reason to be suspicious of big government, irresponsible bureaucracy, and unfettered spending. But the solution to this problem is not gutting government but for a responsible citizenry to cooperate to improve government.

GETTING ALONG PLEASANTLY

In an affluent society, all of those who are ready, willing, and able to work have jobs paying well enough to support a decent life. A lot of people have more than that. Such a society is not, however, automatically a pleasant society. After one has stuffed oneself and napped, what does one do? Especially if it is a moonlit night, the cats get out and yowl and fight.

Among people, as well as cats, there are problems. There are the indecent telephone calls, surliness, truculence, public and private gruffness and rudeness, inconsiderate behavior, bullying and elbowing and violence, the mugging of the elderly, and the exploiting of the young (frequently by the young or the slightly older). And there are drugs and dope. We litter, make noise, blow cigarette smoke around, drink and lose our judgment and ability to coordinate, drive with zest and screeching tires, think it is funny to frighten or humiliate others, or mistreat animals.

Someone chewing with the mouth open, popping bubble gum (especially after the person realizes it irritates others), cigar and cigarette smoke, remarks about the mother-in-law, failure to do something about the ring around the bathtub after one has taken a bath, elbowing in pedestrian traffic when things are a bit crowded, perennially borrowing the roommate's clothes, belching (which may or may not be interpreted as an expression of approval after a fine meal)—all these practices may thoroughly irritate some people. To other people, under other circumstances, they may not be an irritation at all, they may be institutionalized behavior norms. In one setting one may enjoy bargaining with the second-hand car salesperson. Under other circumstances one may feel bitter about being taken in by a high-pressure salesperson. There is much here that under slightly different circumstances would be trivially unimportant. But at a certain time and place the behavior may destroy friendships or even lives. We and our dogs expect behavior to conform to custom.

Things happen, and some of the participants are seething, others are being intentionally irritating, and others have a knack, it seems, for being utterly oblivious.

The Aggressive Social Animal and Civilization

Homo sapiens is both agressive and social, belligerent and generous, needful of fellowship and camaraderie but demanding and vindictive.[1]

To quote Elliot Aronson: "Man is an aggressive animal. With the exception of certain rodents, no other vertebrate so consistently and wantonly kills members of his own species. . . . Psychologists . . . are in disagreement over whether aggressiveness is an innate, instinctive phenomenon or whether such behavior has to be learned."[2]

Freud has written: ". . . the inclination to aggression is an original self-subsisting instinctual disposition in man. . . . But man's natural aggressive instinct, the hostility of each against all and of all against each, opposed this program of civilization."[3]

Is the aggressiveness in the genes or created by the conditions of one's rearing? Maslow says: "Aggression, we have learned, is both *genetically* and *culturally* determined."[4]

In some circumstances aggressiveness may be understandable and defensible, in other circumstances society may not approve. It may be "defensive" or "malignant" according to the expressions of Erich Fromm: "We must distinguish in man *two entirely different kinds of aggression*. The first, which he shares with all animals, is a phylogenetically programmed impulse to attack (or to flee) when vital interests are threatened. This *defensive*, 'benign' aggression is in the service of the survival of the individual and the species, is biologically adaptive, and ceases when the threat has ceased to exist. The other type, 'malignant' aggression, i.e., destructiveness and cruelty, is specific to the human species and virtually absent in most mammals; it is not phylogenetically programmed and not biologically adaptive; it has no purpose, and its satisfaction is lustful. . . . However, man differs from the animal by the fact that he is a killer; he is the only primate that kills and tortures members of his own species without any reason, either biological or economic, and who feels satisfaction in doing so."[5]

Something needed to be done about this aggressive behavior if people were to live together in a halfway viable manner, in a halfway pleasant and civilized way, so that many people much of the time would not be living in genuine fear. Veblen, speaking of the inception of civilization in the Baltic states wrote: ". . . the common understanding that made group life practicable appears to have been in effect the rule of live and let live."[6]

Perhaps thinking in these terms, Leonard D. Eron has had some thoughts about the women's liberation movement: "Here is where the women's liberation movement has it all wrong. Rather than insisting that little girls should be treated like little boys and given exactly the same opportunities for participation in athletic events, Little League activities, and the like, as well as in all other aspects of life, it should be the other way around. Boys should be socialized the way girls have been traditionally socialized, and they should be encouraged to develop socially positive qualities such as tenderness, sensitivity to feelings, nurturance, cooperativeness, and aesthetic appreciation."[7]

The 1978 president of the American Psychological Association did not speak kindly of one of the features of Western tradition: "The individualistic version of selfhood that has characterized our Western tradition since the Renaissance, which we Americans have managed even to exaggerate, seems an increasingly poor fit to our requirements for survival in unavoidable interdependency."[8]

The problem is compounded by the tendency of other people to cater to the aggressive. "Out of nervous desire to avoid hassles, . . . we tolerate daily outrage. Being passively shoved around spills no blood, but rights undefended fade away."[9]

All this has significance for the world of the 1980s, characterized by widespread reliance on terrorism to advance noble or not so noble causes: bombing abortion clinics, airplane hijacking, contesting on either side in the Middle East or Central America. A given government may not be worth much and the Establishment in a given society may be pretty self-serving to the detriment of the rest of the population. But, surely the effort to improve matters should not be allowed to endanger the veneer of civilization that we have. The affluent, however, who have much to gain by the furtherance of civilized behaviors, may be well advised to realize that substantial concessions to the underprivileged is often good judgment.

Much of the meaning of civilization is in the control of aggressiveness and meanness so that people can live among their kin in a viable relationship. The essence of civilized behavior has to be that one will do voluntarily, the things which it is obviously desirable that the average person should do in the process of making the community livable.

The preceding comments have emphasized the problem of aggressiveness rather than the felt need to socialize. The desire to socialize and the desire for love and affection and a bit of ego gratification have tempered the tendency to aggressiveness and contributed to the attaining of the degree of civilization that we have. That should be obvious without extensive effort to elaborate. Awareness that people can be generous does not abrogate the desirability of reducing aggressiveness and interpersonal violence.

Behavior Modification

So, one comes to what is a most difficult and controversial issue: behavior modification or induced character change.

Various behavior modification possibilities may be identified: (1) Changing technology causes changes in institutions (values, attitudes, and behavior) as society adjusts to the use of the new technology. This is behavior modification, affecting both institutions and people, of a sort that is inherent in the institutionalist explanation of the technology-institutions relation. (2) An institutionalized motive, such as the profit motive, may result in character modification in other aspects of behavior; for example, the implementation of the profit motive may result in less generosity toward one's fellows. (3) The demonstration (or emulation) effect—tendency to copy—may operate. People may behave better, or worse, because they see other people behaving better, or worse. (4) Cajoling, arguing, and Madison Avenue advertising may influence the attitudes of people. (5) Force and power and violence and the threat of violence (à la the Nazis and terrorists of more recent vintage) may modify the character of people affected.

(6) There are two types of professional scientists with roles in this area: the biologists and the psychologists. (a) The biologists, such as Hermann Muller, Francis Harry Compton Crick, and James D. Watson, have ideas about modifying the nature of people. The accumulating knowledge of DNA and the biology of the human cell has opened a sort of Pandora's box of possibilities for controlled modification of the biological characteristics of people and of all other forms of life. There was a brief discussion of these matters in chapter 3.

(b) Then there is the role and interest of the behavioral psychologists in behavior modification. Involved is the behaviorism school in psychology from John B. Watson shortly after the turn of the century to B. F. Skinner at the present time.[10] Why not finagle to make human behavior correspond more nearly to the heart's desire— of the dominant social group? In fact behaviorism proper in psychology goes a good deal farther than this and, as in the *Random House Dictionary,* may be defined as: "The theory or doctrine that regards objective and accessible facts of behavior or activity of man and animals as the only proper subject of psychological study." Introspective data or references to consciousness, or mind, or subjective values are excluded from consideration. Behaviorists conceive that "motivation" is a concept that cannot be gotten hold of. So the domain of psychology, according to them, is the explanation of human behavior entirely in terms of overt physiological activity, behavior caused by the working of the nervous system in response to identifiable stimuli. The value of introspection is denied. Thinking is merely subvocal speech. Emotions, except perhaps for rage, fear, and love, are conditioned by habit and can be learned and unlearned.

So, the behaviorists run rats through mazes to condition their behavior and are intrigued by the possibility of doing the same thing with people.

B. F. Skinner has been an active proponent of such activity. In *Walden Two* he has said that "When we've once acquired a behavioral technology, we can't leave the control of behavior to the unskilled. . . . The fact is, we not only *can* control human behavior, we *must* . . . . By a careful cultural design, we control not the final behavior, but the *inclination* to behave—the motives, the desires, the wishes, ... Eventually we shall have no use for Planners at all. The Managers will suffice."[11] And he seems to be saying that the bulk of the population will be happy to live under a planned society provided the planners use only positive reinforcement methods and not negative reinforcement. That is to say: the enforcement tool should be the carrot and not the stick.

What is one to think of such activity?

In a modest way, people are doing this to each other all the time. Wives are trying to make their husbands shape up. Parents are trying to mold the character of their children and their dogs. Certainly a good deal of this sort of thing can be done, is being done, and should be done.

A somewhat different question is whether one major social group might appropriately try to condition another social group. Here again, it seems, a lot of this is going on. In fact, in some sense, this is what formal education is all about. Perhaps one should say that society as a whole does and should oversee the education that its children get. There is a reasonable presumption that over millions of years the human race has learned something which youth can absorb to advantage through the educational process so that each generation does not have to learn everything all over again from the ground up. To say, however, that education is desirable and that the process has to have some socially determined order is not to say that everything done in the educational process is sound, well-meaning, and disinterested. Plenty of individuals and groups are grinding plenty of private axes, and dealing with this situation involves the process of ongoing, self-correcting value judgments.

There are further varying conditions and problems. Should psychologists, such as B. F. Skinner, be allowed to use people as guinea pigs in behavior modification experiments? The answer is, for better or worse, that they are doing it all the time. If some criminals may thereby be induced to mend their ways, the results may be deemed desirable. At the same time, society has an obligation to itself to supervise pretty observantly the manner in which such things are done.

To try again: Should certain groups (such as either professional psychologists or the hatchet men of the political party in power) be allowed to try to control the behavior of large groups of the ordinary population and of the school-age youth? What were the implications of Hitler's doing this to the German people?

Maybe it makes a difference whether the character or behavior modification is attempted by the use of drugs and brain surgery, mass hysteria, or group intimidation of other groups, or whether the modification is attempted by logical, reasonable persuasion (either education-type or Madison-Avenue-type—advertising is a studied effort at behavior modification on a grand scale). Whether the use of drugs and brain surgery to effect behavior modification should be entirely ruled out is an issue to argue about. But surely we can say that, in the present state of our civilization and attitudes, the accepted and acceptable view is that the use of high-handed behavior modification procedures should be highly circumscribed.

With a slightly different slant at behavior modification, it may be observed again that people are practicing behavior modification on themselves all the time by the use of medicinal drugs, aspirin, whiskey, marijuana, cigarettes, cigars, heroin, and coffee—generally without quite understanding what they are doing. Yet, surely there is a difference between the voluntary private use of heroin and the public spectacle often made by the heroin addict. Also, perhaps, the voluntary taking of drugs by more or less conscious and intelligent individuals may be viewed as morally different from the administration by psychiatrists or secret police of LSD to unknowing subjects. All these acts have certain consequences, however, and in no case can the actors expect to be entirely excused from answering for the consequences, if society chooses to hold them accountable. This is not a world in which society need allow everyone or anyone total freedom to experiment without regard to what the results may be. Anyone believing that one has the right to "do one's thing" may well find out the hard way that there is no such right.

Perhaps, at least for now, given our presently conceived values, we should reject Skinner's proposal to authorize behavioral psychologists to control individual behavior on the basis of their unmonitored judgment as to what is appropriate. But the issues are not simple, and a lot of self-correcting value judgments are going to be operating in this area in the years to come.

It may be helpful, for perspective, in this controversial subject to identify a few behavior modification situations where the reader may be willing to subscribe to the idea that the planned behavior modification is a good idea.

Hunger is biological. But one's preference as to what one prefers to eat and what one will refuse to eat are very largely culturally determined. Some societies reject pork or ham for various reasons. Some reject red meat on Friday. Some people like raw oysters. Some do not. In the poorer countries of the world many of the children who survive to adulthood have impaired mental capacity because they did not get enought protein when they were very young. Temporary famine may have been involved. Also, the diet of the culture may not have contained adequate supplies of protein, even though an adequate supply might have been obtainable at not unreasonable cost if the appropriate knowledge and channels of supply had been available. But even when the difficulties of limited knowledge and inadequate channels of supply have been surmounted it frequently turns out that the people will not eat or provide to their children the appropriate food. Cultural inhibitions operate. How to get the people to change the attitudes that are involved is a problem in behavior modification. [12]

In poor countries, economic development requires a change in people's attitudes. Effective use of the production and distribution methods that will raise the material standard of living will involve change in patterns of work and consumption and related values. David McClelland has argued that what is needed is the inculcation into the youth of an underdeveloped country of a need for achievement (n-Ach). He has done a major amount of writing on why this is and how the appropriate behavior modifications might be effected. [13]

Muzafer Sherif in the 1940s and 1950s worked on developing satisfactory and pleasant and cooperative relations among all races. He believed that placing members of different races together in situations where they had common superordinate goals was an effective means. His experiments put blacks and whites at summer camps on the same teams in athletic contests. The superordinate goal of the blacks and whites on the same team was winning. And, in the process of trying to win, friendly, workable relations evolved.[14] This particular method may appear rather banal in the 1980s. It was not in the 1940s and 1950s.

Perhaps about all one can or should say, by way of conclusion, on this touchy subject is that peoplekind, as it goes along, will be modifying its views as to what is appropriate in the area of behavior modification. Such are the workings of the self-correcting value judgment process. This is an area where it will be good judgment to move slowly and to double-check the consensus as society evolves. It would be especially dubious to attempt to develop a definitive national policy of behavior modification involving the establishment of unsupervised official agencies authorized to implement that policy.

The Dual Role of Advertising

Is the purpose of advertising to modify behavior, or is it merely to make people better aware of the nature of the options available to them? In reality, few claim that the role of advertising is merely to provide balanced information without influencing attitudes. So, purposeful behavior modification is a significant part of the story.

If this is true, economists are not entitled to avoid thinking about the influences that lie behind the demand curve or the consumer indifference curve. Advertising represents a significant aspect of production cost. And, if advertising influences the location of the demand and the supply curves in price theory, how can price theory justify the assumption of the independence of demand from supply, the assumption that permits one to draw independent demand and supply curves in the first place?

Things Are Not So Bad

It is comforting and legitimate to speculate that the world may not be in such bad shape as much of the foregoing (plus the morning newspapers) imply. Most people are not neurotic wrecks. Dewey once wrote: "Never before in history has mankind been so much of two minds, so divided into two camps, as it is today."[15] But he was talking about the 1930s, not more recent times. When William Wordsworth denigrated life in London he was talking about 1802, not the 1980s. World War II, a horrible nightmare, when ruthless dictatorships almost conquered the world, is a thing of the past. Vietnam was a minor aberration by comparison with that struggle. Maybe the troubles of the 1980s are really even less serious. We have the technology to provide a decent living for all, if we will. We have the technology and the management skills necessary to dispose of the garbage, if we will. (We might just put it into six or eight really big piles in the six or eight states with the highest per capita incomes; let it season for a while; and sell it to Du Pont.)[16]

The truth of the matter is that never in the history of the human race have so many people and such a large proportion of the population "had it so good" as in the United States in the 1980s. It is a bit hard to understand why this affluent population should feel so sorry for itself and be so obsessed with limiting programs to help the poor, cutting back on supportive public programs, strengthening the military, crime prevention (which they are unwilling to pay taxes to support), stiff jail sentences (while being unwilling to finance the penitentiaries), and having an absolute obsession with tax cutting, and a pseudo-obsession with balancing the budget. The Russians are probably as afraid of us as we are of them. Maybe the moral is that we need a more effective United Nations rather than a larger military budget.

CONSTRUCTIVE SELF-EXPRESSION

The third value is the desirability of constructive, self-fulfilling self-expression; that is, the freedom permitting individuals to express themselves in ways that they themselves approve. Involved is one's own attitude on the matter, not somebody else's, and not society's (except to the extent that one's own attitudes are what they are as a result of social conditioning). People need to have a feeling of accomplishment if they are to respect themselves, a feeling of doing something constructive, worthwhile, even important. Otherwise they are likely to go sour. An opulent society, even one that also provides a pleasant place in which to live, may not be quite enough.

The Instinct of Workmanship

What is involved in constructive self-expression? Thorstein Veblen wrote a book entitled *The Instinct of Workmanship and the State of the Industrial Arts.*[17] The implication of Veblen's use of the term instinct was discussed in chapter 3. Here the concern is with the concept of workmanship as an expression of constructive self-expression.

For Veblen, workmanship "is a proclivity for taking pains." In behavior, the instinct of workmanship "is effective in such consistent, ubiquitous and resilient fashion that students of human culture will have to count with it as one of the integral hereditary traits of mankind."

This conception of human nature has some psychological respectability. It is close to the phenomenon A. H. Maslow calls self-actualization, which Erich Fromm says is a deeply-rooted impulse in people.[18] The behavior involved is viewed from the perspective of the individual concerned. The professional boxer may well have pride in workmanship as may the pickpocket. Of course social and peer pressure influence the individual's attitude as to the type of workmanship that the individual prizes.

Service

Another attitude involved in constructive expression and self-actualization is service to others. Strangely enough, the self-indulgence that characterized the more blatant mores of the 1960s was accompanied by a very considerable amount of self-denying service to others on the part of many people, young and old. The Peace Corps was an example of willingness on the part of volunteers to try to help others at very considerable self-sacrifice.

Self-Expression and Skill

Vents for the need to have a feeling of accomplishment are the arts, crafts, hobbies, and sciences—and bridge. Work in writing, painting, music, or drama can go a long way toward making life worthwhile for those with the appropriate talents, or maybe just a little interest in participating. Crafts, such as woodworking, boat-building, gardening, creating an attractive yard, work with textiles, with clay, and with ingenuity, can play a role. Sailing and nature study (if we can somehow manage to preserve a little nature) can be of consuming interest. And then there is golf. There are also cooking and sewing. A lot of people like to eat and dress well and these activities require skill. For those who relish conflict and display of physical prowess there are football, soccer, basketball, rugby, ice hockey, and many more sports involving varying degrees of violence and skill. International war and military preparedness should not be necessary as a vent for instincts of this sort.

It is easy to say these things and that the solution for boredom is for the individual to show a little responsibility and to cultivate a skill. It is not so easy to implement this prescription. Shiftless and lazy people seldom change their ways because somebody reads them a sermon. Nevertheless boredom and frustration are, mainly, states of affairs for which the bored and frustrated individual is alone responsible.

Even Marx said as much, at least according to Eric Fromm:

> Only in being productively active can man make sense of his life. For
> Spinoza, Goethe, Hegel, as well as for Marx, man is alive only inasmuch
> as he is productive, inasmuch as he grasps the world outside of himself
> in the act of expressing his own specific human powers, and of grasping
> the world with these powers. Inasmuch as man is not productive,
> inasmuch as he is receptive and passive, he is nothing, he is dead. [19]

What happens to orthodox price theory if some work is fun? Price theory depends upon the assumption that all work is unpleasant, burdensome, and undesirable and is therefore a cost of production. People, according to economics, will not work unless they are materially rewarded. So, believers in supply and demand may not be entirely happy with the concept that work may be regarded as a self-fulfilling activity, which one would, at least up to a point, presumably be willing to do for nothing.

Alienation and Anomie

Miserable conditions and danger on the job can make one's job undesirable. Still, even garbage collecting can be handled in a way that makes the activity rather pleasant outside work, involving a good deal of camaraderie. It helps if the householder ties the garbage in a plastic bag and puts it in front of the house. Also, there is the white collar work of the computer programmer. Work with computers is much in vogue. It is well paid, and prestigious, and the universities are offering majors in the area, and the courses are crowded with students. Nonetheless, the programmers may find out five or ten years down the road that programming computers to solve problems for other people is about as alienating a type of work as there is around.[20] In fact, Abraham Korman cites evidence that some of the most alienated (perhaps one might say: overtly disaffected) people in modern United States society are young executives, professional people, and "responsible" managerial people.[21] There may be a tendency for blue collar workers to be less alienated than white collar workers. What is going on?

A study by the National Institute of Occupational Safety and Health found stressful work to involve: inspectors who do inspection tests in blue-collar assembly line operations, health technicians, clinical laboratory technicians, miners and mine workers (not necessarily working underground), industrial laborers, warehouse personnel, office managers, public relations workers, licensed practical nurses, waiters (but not waitresses).[22] The least stressful jobs were found to be: librarians, professional technicians, stock handlers, sewers and stitchers (in factories), store checkout workers, college or university professors, office machine operators, vehicle washers, surveyors, bank tellers. These classifications do not correlate with the level of pay or status of the job. Why?

Intelligent, well-educated young professionals may be disaffected because they are not getting ahead as fast as their expectations call for, but at the same time their work may not be particularly stressful in any meaningful sense. They are well fed and prosperous. And do they ever hate taxes, as any politician speaking out for higher taxes quickly finds out. These people are not only alienated, they are vocal about it. They, along with their spouses, are heard by politicians.

Perhaps, in spite of Marx and the Marxists, alienation is more a psychological problem than an economic problem.

SECURITY

The fourth goal, security, is a hodgepodge of job security (which may be provided by the job guarantee), care during illness, care during old age and childhood, and security against the terror of war. Some of these matters are discussed elsewhere in the book. To others, justice is not attempted here. Regarding the importance of the desire for security, John Dewey has written in his *Quest for Certainty* that security in some absolute and final sense is probably unattainable.[23] What would be involved anyway: eternal life in a state of drugged bliss? But much more protection for the population in general against the woes of the world, many of them created by inconsiderate or power-hungry people, is, one can make the value judgment, possible and desirable. Efforts along this line should not be frustrated by an uncaring anti-tax attitude.

ALTERNATIVE LISTS
Maslow's Basic Human Needs

A. H. Maslow, a psychologist, has described a hierarchy of basic human motives, which is similar in several respects to the above catalog of currently-held values.[24] There are (1) the physiological needs such as food, clothing, and shelter. But, since "a satisfied need" will no longer motivate behavior, if we already enjoy adequate food, clothing, and shelter, our behavior thereafter is going to be motivated by other considerations.

If the basic physiological needs are satisfied, but those are the only needs that are satisfied, the prime human concern will be for (2) safety—security against danger, threat, and deprivation. The organism may well be almost wholly dominated by these considerations if it lacks what it conceives to be security. It will hunger for order, routine, and normality if it believes existence is unreliable, unsafe, or unpredictable. (Children with quarrelsome parents are thought to wish for an organized, peaceful family and world.) But, just as was the case when the physiological needs are met, the person who enjoys security will then become almost entirely unconcerned about security needs.

Satisfied in the need for safety, the person may experience a need for (3) love and affection. If that need is satisfied, the prime concern may then be (4) ego-gratification. The person may seek esteem and recognition. If this need is met and the individual, in consequence, feels self-confident, strong, and capable, loved, well-fed, and secure, the highest level of basic need and motive may be expressed as (5) self-actualization. The emergence of self-actualization as the overriding motive rests on the prior satisfaction of the other needs.

Such is Maslow's hierarchy of human motives or needs and the nature of the relationship among them; and the highest need in the hierarchy is for "self-actualization," a concept which is, by no means, equivalent to the profit motive of economics.

Of the values alleged above to be currently held, Maslow's physiological needs roughly parallel the minimum, decent standard of living. But it is not clear whether the "getting along pleasantly" consideration has any clear parallel in his scheme. The concept of constructive self-expression, in ways that permit people to be proud of their own behavior, has a parallel in Maslow's self-actualization and also in Thorstein Veblen's instinct of workmanship. Security has a clear parallel in Maslow's security need.

Maslow's needs for love and for ego-gratification were not listed, perhaps because they cannot represent valuations that society is likely to feel it has an obligation to help implement. Perhaps they are and always will be privileges rather than rights—so far as society is concerned. Society is not likely to be any more successful than some parents in telling their children "Love (and marry) so and so."

The satisfaction concept as used by Maslow is interesting, but perhaps simplistic. It is an all or nothing proposition. One is very concerned about a given need under certain circumstances. Under other circumstances, after the need has been satisfied, one is alleged not to be concerned about it. This concept is in sharp contrast to the diminishing marginal utility concept prevalent in economics. It would make considerable difference to price theory and revolutionize the graphs used in economics texts if attitudes about desirability changed abruptly rather than by small increments.

The Ayres List

The Ayres listing of values in *Toward a Reasonable Society* is: freedom, equality, security, abundance, excellence, plus certain additional "moral" values.[25] Ayres seems to be listing these as definitive values. But they may also be viewed as values subject to change and thought of in much the same way as the above list of "currently-held" value judgments.

RIGHTS AND DUTIES

Do people have a right to the enjoyment of the valuations represented by the currently-held value judgments? The answer has to be: not necessarily. The nature of the institutionalized behavior norms involved with the rights is such that there are powerful pressures urging compliance with and implementation of the valuations involved. This is not quite the same thing as a legally enforceable right or an effectively implemented right.

For implementation to be effectively or enforceably meaningful, two conditions must be met. (1) It must be physically possible for the right to be implemented. And (2) there needs to be an entity or an individual, capable of doing so, with the duty to implement the right.

What is involved may be illustrated using the value judgment as to the decent minimum standard of living as an example. For people to have a right to the decent minimum it would need to be physically possible for the system to produce the quantity of goods that would be involved. And there would need to be a government agency, or some entity or individual, capable of providing the goods, which or who has a duty to make good on the obligation to provide for the right. Rights without correlative duties are likely to be meaningless.

A verse by Stephen Crane runs:

> A man said to the Universe:
> "Sir, I exist!"
> "However," replied the Universe,
> "The fact has not created in me
> A sense of obligation."[26]

The implications of these relations suggest a further thought with regard to the claim, oft repeated by people, to the effect that they as individuals have some sort of a natural right to "do their thing" or live their lives as they see fit according to their whims and fancies. Sometimes the issue is posed as a right to "do one's thing" in private, in other times it is posed as a right to do it in public as well. Behavior that others may consider obscene, or offensive, or immoral is involved. (The reader should not have any trouble imagining examples.)

The answer is pretty clear. In an absolute sense no such right exists. Society can make the value judgment that you cannot do *that* and make the judgment stick. Whether society will do so or not is another matter. What we actually have is a system where self-correcting value judgments, and implementing laws and court judgments, are being made and reconsidered about specific examples of behavior that may or may not be protected or interdicted under the First Amendment to the Constitution of the United States or thousands of other laws and moral precepts observed in the various societies that exist in The Universe.

You do not even have a right to die when you want to.[27]

THEORY OF CHANGE OR THEORY OF PROGRESS?

Is the explanation of ongoing process that is involved in institutionalism merely a theory that tries to explain change or is it also a theory explaining progress in the sense of improvement? Perhaps it was the Industrial Revolution, with its tremendous potential for expanding production, that made it meaningful for the first time for people to think in terms of progress and improvement as distinct from mere existence. Some people conceived of the possibility of an ideal society, a Utopia, in the ascertainable future. For others, continuing improvement or progress was conceived as possible in a process that did not prejudge the nature of the end result.[28]

Institutionalists, generally, have believed in the concepts of progress and improvement. They believe increasing technical knowledge makes possible the furtherance of the life process in a desirable manner. But they have generally not visualized Utopias and Promised Lands as meaningful.[29]

Strangely, in present times, despite the high and rising standards of living, people appear discontented with the state of affairs and pessimistic about the future. Is, in some sense, our effort at progress a self-defeating process, like Sisyphus futilely trying to roll the stone up the hill? Is all the change failing to improve the quality of life? Do more technology, the change in institutional attitudes, the evolving patterns of resource use, combined with our evolving biological structure, net out to no long-run gain in satisfaction? Do some get more or less satisfaction and others get more or less frustration, just as it has always been?

A tentative conclusion about the reality of progress may seem simplistic, but it is offered nevertheless. Here we are in our current state. It is obvious that conditions could be better. So, let us worry about how to make them better. We may or may not succeed. But, for our own self-respect, it is worth trying. Progress, in a sense that most people would call progress, is not inevitable. But it is conceivable. The possibility of an existence that people in general consider more satisfactory is worth some effort. We do not need to answer the question as to how happy, relative to us, dinosaurs were in Mesozoic times.

Progress is not movement toward a conceived utopia nor is it perpetual ongoing improvement. It is change in a manner that the people involved at the time consider to be improvement.

SYNTHESIS OF EVOLUTIONARY OR INSTITUTIONAL THEORY

Society exists in an ongoing scheme of things; and it behooves us to appraise and reappraise our goals and values as we go along.

The accumulation of technical knowledge is a dynamic process. This means that the drive, or the motivation, that makes the process go is inherent in the manner in which the assimilation of one bit of knowledge leads to another. In a meaningful sense, this is an automatic, ongoing process, not requiring outside motivation, although it is a process that may be speeded or slowed by factors from outside the process, such as the felt need for a technique that will accomplish such and such a result. This possibility is conditioned by the fact that felt need cannot call forth a bit of knowledge whose time has not yet come.

Society holds values in the manner of a consensus and changes them. It is important to try to understand the influences guiding these changes. And it is reasonable to notice that we as individuals are at the center of concern in this process, at least from our own point of view.

Although values are ever changing, it is instructive to identify the values prevailing during a given period. The value pattern that exists at the present time is assumed to involve: (1) bringing everyone up to a decent minimum standard of living and, beyond the decent minimum, (2) emphasizing the necessity for making society pleasantly livable, (3) permitting the constructive expression of the personality of individuals, and (4) implementing security.

Individuals with varying degrees of understanding of the process, at any given time, will have ideas about appropriate behavior (on abortion, the death penalty, profit making, the use of drugs, deregulation). With varying degrees of adroitness they can use the means made available by the existing institutional order, technology, and resources in an effort to change that order. For better or worse, the norm at any given time is what society says it is, not what the individual believes it ought to be. Then, to complicate matters, world society is not one coherent whole; it is many institutions, many societies, and many nations practicing behavior norms that may well contradict the behavior norms of other institutions, societies, and nations.

The prevailing institutionalized behavior norms at any given time are an expression of the concepts about value of the people involved. And, society's ideas as to valuation are changing in the same process (they really are the same thing) as the institutionalized behavior norms. In terms of the fourfold complex of enacted laws, religious fiat, reason, and institutionalized behavior norms, enacted laws merely play a role as one of the possible processes by which behavior norms are identified and changed. If religious fiat (or some higher wisdom as to valuations) actually exists, that would be a continuing "given," a permanent factor in this process. Perhaps no useful purpose is served by trying to resolve whether some such factor exists.

NOTES

[1]Wilbert E. Moore, "Social Structure and Behavior," in Gardner Lindzey and Elliot Aronson, eds., *The Handbook of Social Psychology* (2nd ed.; Reading, Mass.: Addison Wesley, 1969), IV, p. 283; Edward Zigler and Irvin L. Child, "Socialization," Lindzey and Aronson, III, pp. 521-33; Elliott Aronson, *The Social Animal* (San Francisco: W. H. Freeman, 1972); Sigmund Freud, *Civilization and its Discontents* (New York: Norton, 1962 [1930]), p. 69; Erich Fromm, *Anatomy of Human Destructiveness* (New York: Holt, Rinehart, and Winston, 1973); Stanley Milgram, *Obedience to Authority* (New York: Harper & Row, 1973); Abraham H. Maslow, *Motivation and Personality* (New York: Harper & Row, 1954).

[2]Aronson, pp. 142, 144.

[3]Freud, p. 69.

[4]Maslow, p. xix.

[5]Fromm, p. 4.

[6]Thorstein Veblen, *Imperial Germany and the Industrial Revolution* (New York: Kelley, 1964 [1915]), p. 166.

[7]Leonard D. Eron, "Prescription for Reduction of Aggression," *American Psychologist* 35 (March 1980), p. 251.

[8]M. Brewster Smith, "Perspectives on Selfhood," *American Psychologist* 33 (December 1978), p. 1062.

[9]Thomas Moriarty, "A Nation of Willing Victims," *Psychology Today* (April 1975), p. 43.

[10]J. B. Watson, *Behaviorism* (New York: Norton, 1925); B. F. Skinner, *Beyond Freedom and Dignity* (New York: Knopf, 1971).

[11]B. F. Skinner, *Walden Two* (New York: Macmillan, 1948), pp. 166, 249-276.

[12]Wendell Gordon, *Economics from an Institutional Viewpoint* (Austin, Texas: University Stores, Inc., 1974), ch. 19. "Institutionalized Consumption Patterns in Underdeveloped Countries."

[13]David C. McClelland and David G. Winter, *Motivating Economic Achievement* (New York: The Free Press, 1969).

[14]Muzafer Sherif, "Experiments in Group Conflict," *Scientific American* 195 (November 1956), pp. 54-58.

[15]John Dewey, *Intelligence in the Modern World: John Dewey's Philosophy* (New York: Modern Library, 1939), p. 1003.

[16]L. C. Cole, "What to Do with Waste?," *The New York Times Magazine*, April 2, 1972, p. 30 et seq.

[17]Thorstein Veblen, *The Instinct of Workmanship and the State of the Industrial Arts* (New York: Augustus M. Kelley, 1964[1914]), pp. 2-3, 13, 27-28, 33.

[18]A. H. Maslow, "A Theory of Human Motivation," *Psychological Review* L (July 1943), pp. 370-96, and esp. p. 382; Maslow, *Motivation and Personality*, chs. 6, 11; Fromm, p. 36. A psychologist who questions this approach is Leonard Berkowitz, "Social Motivation," in Lindzey and Aronson, eds., III, p. 87.

[19]Erich Fromm, *Marx's Concept of Man* (New York: Frederick Ungar, 1961), p. 29.

[20]Jon M. Shepard, *Automation and Alienation: A Study of Office and Factory Workers* (Cambridge, Mass.: MIT Press, 1971).

[21]Abraham K. Korman, *Organizational Behavior* (Englewood Cliffs: Prentice Hall, 1977), pp. 206-207. Chapter 9 deals with alienation.

[22]Reported in *Austin American-Statesman*, March 30, 1977.

[23]John Dewey, *The Quest for Certainty: A Study of the Relation of Knowledge and Action* (New York: Minton, Balch, 1929).

[24]Maslow, "A Theory of Human Motivation."

[25]C. E. Ayres, *Toward a Reasonable Society*, (Austin: University of Texas Press, 1961), pp. 165-273.

[26]Stephen Crane, *The Collected Poems of Stephen Crane*, Wilson Follett ed. (New York: Knopf, 1930 [1895]), p. 101.

[27]There is much more sophisticated discussion of rights and duties in many places, for example: John R. Commons, *Legal Foundations of Capitalism* (Madison: University of Wisconsin Press, 1968 [1923]), pp. 83-100.

[28]Charles Van Doren, *The Idea of Progress* (New York: Praeger, 1967).

[29]C. E. Ayres, *The Theory of Economic Progress* (2nd ed.; New York: Schocken Books, 1962 [1944]), p. 122.

Part II

Implications for Alternative Approaches

Chapter IX

Maximization and General Equilibrium

What are the implications of the evolutionary or institutional approach for other approaches or paradigms prevailing in economics, such as general equilibrium theory, price theory, national income theory, and Marxism?

THE NATURE OF GENERAL EQUILIBRIUM ANALYSIS

General equilibrium analysis in economics attempts to take into account all the relevant influences in one pattern.[1] It does this, perforce, in a highly simplified setting. Taking everything into account, in actual practice, would be, to put it mildly, a large order. It is alleged in the model that there are no relevant conditions that are being left out of account, that is to say: there is no ceteris paribus assumption. It is true that the simplifying assumptions may be made that there are only two factors of production, only two products, and only two countries (a so-called $2 \times 2 \times 2$ assumption). It is supposed that other factors, commodities, or countries may be ignored. Two of each is all there are. The full implications of this need to sink in. This is an unreal world, but is it a useful approximation? Then, assuming pure competition, the analysis proceeds to find the production and distribution patterns that will generate either an equilibrium or a welfare maximum.

The model is tempting and simple. It reflects some credit on the economists involved that they assume that the maximization of human welfare is the prime goal of society. General equilibrium analysis does represent an effort along this line.

BACKGROUND

Historical Background

Economics has long been concerned with value, with the meaning of wealth, and with questions of desirability. For the mercantilists of the period 1500-1776, gold was wealth and "people value wealth." For John Locke, about 1690, there was pleasure and pain both here and in the hereafter. Locke also had an embryonic labor theory of value: the values of things may be examined by comparing the amounts of labor time that go into their production.

The concept of utilitarianism (the greatest good for the greatest number) evolved from Thomas Hobbes through Locke, Jeremy Bentham, John Stuart Mill, and Herbert Spencer from the 1650s to the mid-nineteenth century. More or less involved was the solution of a maximization problem in which pleasure was offset against pain for the whole population in an effort to maximize the end result. Locke included pleasure in the hereafter as part of his netting operation; others, Bentham, for example, did not try to take into account possible compensation in the hereafter.

For Adam Smith in 1776, goods in general, rather than gold in particular, were wealth and of value. He also distinguished between value in use and value in exchange, the former being the desirability of goods to oneself as distinct from the latter, what could be gotten for them in the market. In the tradition of this distinction, economists have worried much about value in exchange (price) and not much about value in use. Value in use, the individual's concept of desirability, is generally assumed as "given" information.

Adam Smith argued that a desirable result could be accomplished where pure competition prevailed and each individual pursued only personal gain: "Every individual necessarily labors to render the annual revenue of the society as great as he can . . . . He intends only his own gain, and he is in this case . . . led by an invisible hand to promote an end which was no part of his intention."[2] For Adam Smith, the desirable result was apparently an article of faith, a provident invisible hand being assumed. That pure competition effectively generates a meaningful welfare maximum for society as a whole was not really proven.

David Ricardo, in 1817, presented a labor theory of value in the tradition of John Locke and Smith, but with considerably more logical rigor. Karl Marx reworked the classical Locke-Smith-Ricardo labor theory of value and the conception of value in exchange in a manner calculated to show that capitalists exploited labor.

During the latter decades of the nineteenth century, in large measure to obviate Marx's devastating use of the labor theory of value to denounce the capitalist system, the neoclassical economists, Stanley Jevons, Alfred Marshall, and many others, dropped the labor theory of value. They substituted orthodox price theory and evolved the demand and supply curves that have symbolized economics in the twentieth century.

Vilfredo Pareto, around 1900, developed indifference curve analysis to describe how people assign relative values to different things and relate their desires to what is attainable. The resultant, for Pareto, was not necessarily a value maximum.

It might only be a situation that would be as favorable as possible for one party without making anyone else worse off. Pareto's work ushered in general equilibrium analysis which became the heart of modern, orthodox value theory in economics.

Abram Bergson and Paul Samuelson, from 1938 to 1956, attempted to reformulate the Pareto approach by using modified concepts:[3] utility possibility frontiers, revealed preferences, and social welfare functions, which had the implication that a welfare maximum can be identified.

Kenneth Arrow and others have, more recently, tried to identify the conditions necessary for identifying a "general welfare" general equilibrium, but Arrow and others abstain from the effort to prove that such an equilibrium also corresponds with a welfare maximum. It is also not entirely clear whether Arrow believes that the conditions necessary for equilibrium are a reasonably accurate description of the real world.[4]

General equilibrium analysis in the manner of Bergson and Samuelson and Arrow is the value theory of modern, orthodox, neoclassical economics. Others, such as Milton Friedman and the University of Chicago people subscribe, despite the jousting and name-calling that has gone on between Chicago and Cambridge, Massachusetts.

But this is a strange value theory, one from which the protagonists have striven mightily to separate the valuation content from the value theory. Whatever these leaders may actually believe, the economics profession in general is obsessed with a felt need to show that competition *maximizes* the general welfare. In his 1981 presidential address to the American Economic Association, William Baumol said: "[I]n the received analysis perfect competition serves as the one standard of welfare-maximizing structure and behavior."[5]

In a similar vein, Mark Blaug has written: "Anyone who has been attentive to the recent resurgence of the neoclassical research program in regional analysis, urban economics, applied welfare economics, cost-benefit analysis, the economics of education, labor economics, the economics of time, the economics of search and information, the economics of crime, the economics of fertility, the economics of marriage, the economics of private property rights—the list is really endless—can hardly doubt that there is life yet in the concepts of maximization, equilibrium, substitution and all the other tricks of the trade of mainstream economics."[6]

Definitions: Optimum and Maximum

In the jargon of general equilibrium (or welfare) economics, an optimum is the best situation that can be worked out in a process that involves making people as well off as possible without making anyone worse off. The optimizing procedure, so defined, is unable to handle the situation where a loss to one person may make possible a greater gain to someone else. And it may well be argued that a dollar loss to a wealthy person is of less importance than is a dollar gain to a poor person.

A maximum occurs at the greatest total, aggregate amount of welfare, a state of bliss that might be reached only by making some people worse off and other people better off. In general, welfare economists, old style, would have said that it is impossible to take the step from optimum to maximum because it is impossible to quantify and compare the loss of the loser to the gain of the gainer. In particular, it is difficult to compare the pleasure of the fortunate with the pain and despair of the less fortunate.

The realization of this impossibility uses good psychology, and it would have been best if economists had left things at that. But it is more fun and more impressive if the game involves maximizing, and maximizing is also the game the politicians and the public want the economists to play. So, a lot of economists are spending a lot of time trying to solve maximization problems, which are now frequently called optimization problems or control theory problems. And a rigorous distinction between optimization and maximization is not consistently observed.

Conditions for Optimum Resource Allocation

Welfare economics, new style, in its effort to do the best it can by society, specifies three conditions for an optimal (welfare maximizing) resource allocation. (1) In order to have "optimal allocation of commodities among consumers . . . the marginal rate of substitution between any two commodities must be the same for any two consumers." (2) In order to have "optimal allocation of inputs among producers . . . the marginal rate of technical substitution between any two inputs must be the same for any pair of producers." (3) In order to have "both the optimal allocation of inputs among industries and the optimal allocation of commodities among consumers . . . the marginal rate of substitution between any two commodities must be the same as the marginal rate of transformation between these commodities for any producer."[7] If these conditions are met, all is for the best in this best of all possible worlds. The theory also laboriously probes the possible existence (even the necessary existence) of a general equilibrium that can encompass these characteristics for all commodities. This occurs: if we have pure competition, we disregard the income distribution problem, growth is nonexistent, everybody's tastes are alike and unchanging, and there is full employment—a whole mare's nest of nonexistent conditions.

(Many readers, with good reason, may wish to skip the next few pages and the accompanying graphics. The argument is understandable from the prose discussion, but presenting the relations using the standard graphics may be of help to some, especially those already familiar with the standard general equilibrium argument.)

At all events, figure 9-1 is a general equilibrium graph representing the conditions for optimum resource allocation.[8] The two products produced in this two-product world are x and y. Physical quantities, V_x and V_y, are measured on the two axes. The curve c–c is the production possibility curve, and represents the varying ratios of x and y that the economy is capable of producing at full employment. If it produces only product y, it can produce approximately 7 million; if only x then approximately 6 million. If it produces 4 million of y, it is capable of producing 5 million of x. Any one of the indifference curves, I–I, I'–I', I"–I", represents along its length mixes of x and y that are considered equally desirable by the people of the society. As an example, looking along the curve I–I, they would consider the mix of 4y and 5x to be equally desirable with a mix of 9x and .8y. (For simplicity the word million will generally be omitted.)

FIGURE 9-1
General Equilibrium

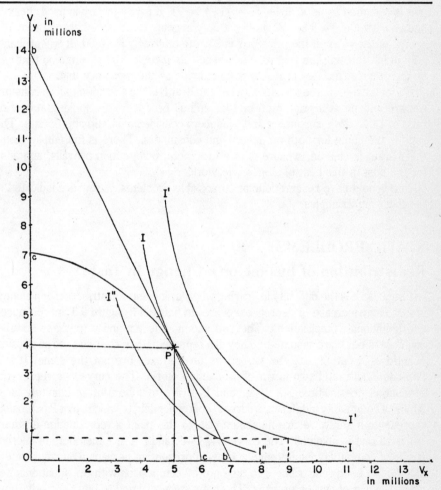

The welfare of society is maximized at the product mix where the production possibility curve, c–c, is tangent to the furthest outlying community indifference curve, I–I, that it can reach. This relation occurs at point P. The so-called price- or budget-line, b–b, through P is drawn so as to be tangent to both c–c and I–I. The slope of this line represents the exchange ratio, or the price ratio in the market, between x and y. An exchange ratio of 7x = 14y, or 1x = 2y is considered appropriate by both producers and consumers. That price ratio will clear the market, assuming pure competition and all that.

At a price ratio of 1x to 2y the value of the gross national product, which is the same as the national income, is 14 million if the monetary unit, or numeraire, is assumed to be y. (It includes 4 million of y plus 5 million of x, valued in y according to the ratio 14:7; that is: $5 \times 14/7 = 10$, and $4 + 10 = 14$, which is also the y intercept of the budget or price line). It is 7 million if the monetary unit is assumed to be x: $(5 + [4 \times 7/14]) = 7$. If paper money is used, heaven knows what GNP will be. Whatever it is, y is going to be priced at the ratio: 14y = 7x, or 2y = 1x; if the price of x is \$1, the price of y is \$0.50. It will probably help in interpreting the real relations here to stick with the assumption that one or the other of the two products is functioning as the monetary unit.

For optimal resource allocation, what exists at P is the condition that all consumers are looking at a price ratio of 14:7 and all producers are looking at a price ratio of 14:7. Both consumers and producers consider this ratio appropriate. The ratio is the same for both producers and consumers. There is full employment, the market is cleared, welfare is at a maximum, competition prevails, and all is for the best in this best of all possible worlds.

One should have reservations as to possible problems. A few are indicated in the following examples.

STATIC PROBLEMS

Redistribution of Income or a Change in Taste

First, there is the difficulty in proving whether income redistribution or a change in taste may increase or decrease welfare. In figure 9-2, figure 9-1 is reproduced with additional complications. The two commodities, x and y (perhaps luxuries and necessities), are assumed.[9] They are represented on the two axes as physical quantities of output; so, the yardsticks on the axes are not the same. It is a two-commodity and two-factor-of-production world. The curve c–c represents production possibilities. I–I, I'–I', and I"–I" are members of an infinitely large family of community indifference curves, corresponding to which point P ostensibly represents a static welfare maximum. Up to this point a reproduction of figure 9-1 is all that is involved. The curves i–i, i'–i', and i"–i" are members of another family of community indifference curves, representing perhaps a situation where income has been redistributed to the poor by comparison with the situation when the I–I family of curves prevails. The poor are presumed to buy relatively more y, or necessities, than do the wealthy. Or perhaps there has merely been a change in tastes as a result of changing fashions. At any rate, point P' becomes the new welfare maximum. Has welfare, in general, improved or worsened? One cannot say. We have lost our criterion: tangency with the furthest reachable outlying community indifference curve. No such curve is identifiable, since the two families of community indifference curves are crisscrossing.

FIGURE 9-2
Maximization: The Income Distribution and Change in Taste Cases

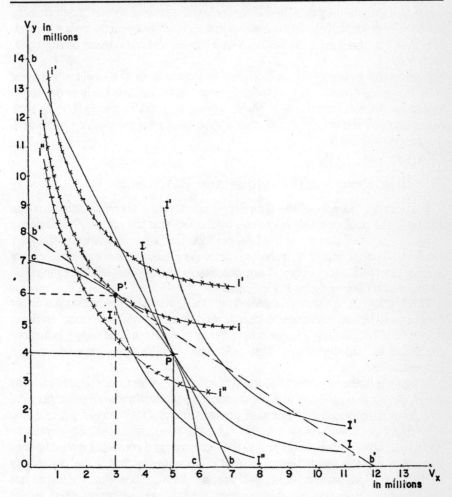

At this point one might merely say that the welfare maximum is indeterminate, and the case for pure competition as a welfare maximizer is unproven. But it is interesting to spell out more fully the nature of the difficulty.

If one alleges, as is appropriate in the setting of general equilibrium analysis, that the slopes of the tangents at P and P′ represent relative prices and that either of the two commodities may equally well serve as the yardstick, then, if y is taken as the yardstick, the move from P to P′ has lowered GNP from 14 million to 8 million. But if one takes x as the yardstick, the move P to P′ has raised GNP from 7 million to 12 million. One gets contradictory signals as to the direction of change of GNP, not just a difference in magnitude, depending on which commodity is used as money, and one has no criterion for identifying which commodity makes the more appropriate yardstick.

This example confirms the earlier indication that, so far as general equilibrium analysis and pure competition have anything to say by way of identifying a general welfare maximum, they lose their leverage and the result becomes indeterminate when the possibility of either income redistribution or change in tastes is admitted. In economics, this conclusion has been well known, and consistently disregarded, since Pareto.

What is the nature of the self-denying ordinance or institutionalized behavior norm that leads economists to disregard these considerations? Perhaps one tends to disregard these influences, if one's interest is to justify the system of pure competition by the article of faith that a system of pure competition maximizes the general welfare.[10]

The Best-Practice Technique and Efficiency

Next, as an example of the difficulty in identifying a maximum, there is the matter of the confusion that is created by the fact that the meaning of efficiency in production, the identity of the best-practice technique, is not unambiguously determined on the supply or technology side. A rose is a rose is a rose, efficiency is efficiency is efficiency; but it is not necessarily so. Demand influences must be taken into account as figure 9-3 indicates.[11]

In the graphics of a general equilibrium, the appropriate production possibility curve has to be unique. It has to be independent of demand side considerations, in order for a maximum to be identified. Otherwise demand and supply influences are mixed up and the concept that production efficiency is a pure engineering concept is lost.

In figure 9-3, the algebraic production functions represent two possible patterns for producing two products in a two-factor, two-product frame of reference; the two patterns generate the indicated production possibility curves AA and BB. (The figure *is* drawn to scale.) In this case, the production possibility curves do cross each other. There is nothing in the standard pure competition assumptions that rules out this quite likely possibility. This means that if the community indifference curve pattern I–I and I′–I′ prevails, then the best-practice techniques (as between these two possible production patterns) are represented by the production functions: $V_x = 1.01 \, L^{.75} K^{.25}$ and $V_y = 1.01 \, L^{.25} K^{.75}$. If the community indifference curve pattern i–i and i′–i′ prevails (perhaps representing alternative tastes), the best-practice techniques are represented by the production functions: $V_x = 1.01 \, L^{.25} K^{.75}$ and $V_y = 1.01 \, L^{.75} K^{.25}$.

The identification of the best-practice technique, that is, which set of production functions is more productive, must await taking demand patterns into account.

Failure to appreciate the ambiguity in the concept of efficiency is general among practicing economists. Witness the following extract from an article in *The New York Times*: "'The argument is that in a textbook world, nobody can allocate resources better than the free market,' said Joel L. Prakken, an economist at Lawrence A. Meyer & Associates in St. Louis, a forecasting firm. 'So any form of Government intervention is less efficient.'"[12]

FIGURE 9-3
Best-Practice Technique

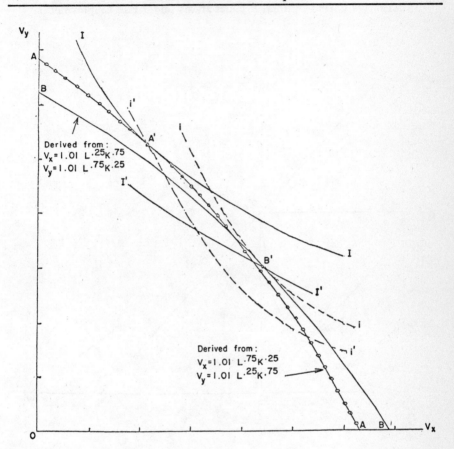

Use of Alternative Factors as Yardsticks

(The following argument, regrettably, assumes on the part of the reader some knowledge about the representation of production functions in Edgeworth boxes. Some readers who have endured the graphics to this point may wish to skip this section.)

Another example of a static contradiction, shown in figure 9-4, arises in the quest for a welfare maximum. It occurs in the Edgeworth box, $O_xOO'_yO'$, where the contract line is derived from the production functions already used in figure 9-4: $V_x = 1.01 \, L^{.75}K^{.25}$ and $V_y = 1.01 \, L^{.25}K^{.75}$. In this case one is comparing the GNP at Q with the GNP at Q′ to ascertain whether there is a contradiction in the identity of the welfare maximum depending on the numeraire used. In this example, a factor of production, capital (K) or labor (L), alternatively, is used as the numeraire for measuring GNP.[13] The slopes of the straight lines tangent to the isoquants at Q and Q′ represent the wage/rate-of-return-to-capital (w/r) ratios

FIGURE 9-4
The Edgeworth Box and Gross National Product
(Alternative Pareto-Optimal Product Mixes under Full Employment)

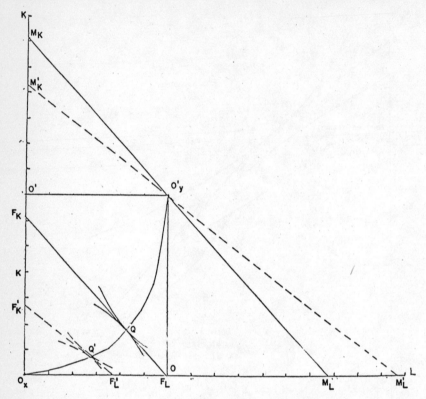

at those points (on the full employment and other assumptions generally used in this paradigm). $M_K M_L$ has the same slope and therefore represents the same w/r ratio as prevails at Q. This means $O_x M_K$ corresponds to GNP using K as the numeraire when production is at Q. Similarly if production is at Q', by similar reasoning, $O_x M'_K$ represents GNP. So GNP is less at Q' than at Q if capital (K) is the yardstick. (Incidentally, $F_K F_L$ is correctly drawn steeper than $F'_K F'_L$.)

The procedure for establishing that $O_x M_K$ or, alternatively, $O_x M'_K$ represents GNP is similar to that used in the "redistribution of income" case. To use $O_x M_K$ as an example: the distance $O_x O'$ represents the share of GNP provided by capital in the production of both goods, and the distance $O' M_K$ represents the share of GNP represented by the amount of labor ($O_x O$) used in the production of both goods, with that amount of labor being valued in capital at the ratio represented by the slope of $F_K F_L$, which is the same slope as that of $M_K M_L$. The additional restriction on $M_K M_L$ was that it had to pass through O'_y, thus representing full employment of both capital and labor.

The principal act of faith that the reader is being asked to observe is that the slopes of $F_K F_L$ and $F'_K F'_L$, when these lines are drawn tangent to the tangent isoquants at Q and Q' on the contract line, really represent the relative prices of capital and labor at Q and Q'.[14]

The direction of change in GNP is apparently reversed if labor is used as the numeraire. $O_x M_L$ is GNP corresponding to Q and the greater amount $O_x M'_L$ is GNP corresponding to Q'.

It is worth noting and emphasizing that in the income redistribution case, figure 9-2, and the Edgeworth box contract line case, figure 9-4, not only does one get somewhat different orders of magnitude in the answers depending on the choice of yardstick (under circumstances where there are no clear grounds for preferring one yardstick to another), but the *sign* (or the direction of change of GNP) is, in general, reversed.

Marxist Socially Necessary Unit of Labor Time

This argument has implications for the Marxist concept of socially-necessary-unit-of-labor-time. Make the inputs two qualities of labor instead of capital and labor, and the concept of the socially-necessary-unit-of-labor-time (which involves aggregating different qualities of labor) loses its precision. Whether the size of the product is increasing or decreasing (whether exploitation, according to Marxism, is increasing or decreasing) depends on which quality of labor one uses as a numeraire. Again, there is no clear criterion for identifying the better yardstick. So, one loses the ability to identify exploitation in the manner associated with Karl Marx.[15]

Implications for Consumer and Producer Surplus Concepts

In policy recommendations a standard criterion as to the desirability of a policy is whether the sum of consumer and producer surplus generated by one policy is greater than that generated by another. A statement by William Branson and Alvin Klevorick is illustrative. "The object of each government is taken to be the standard criterion of social welfare—the sum of domestic consumer and producer surpluses."[16] The use of these concepts has been frequent in energy and resource studies since the 1973 energy crises and in connection with evaluating efforts to stabilize prices in raw commodity control schemes.

It has been well understood for many years that the use of consumer and producer surplus areas under and over ordinary Marshallian demand and supply curves, the cross-hatched areas in figure 9-5, is theoretically questionable because of the inherent implication that the marginal utility of money is constant, when it clearly is not, either to the individual or to society as a whole. The poor probably get more satisfaction from a one dollar increase in income than do the wealthy.[17]

In recent years it has been argued that this difficulty can be avoided by the use of compensated demand and supply curves. Such curves allegedly represent demand and supply on an assumption of unchanged utility or unchanged welfare.

132
Gordon & Adams

FIGURE 9-5
Industry Demand and Supply: Consumer and Producer Surplus

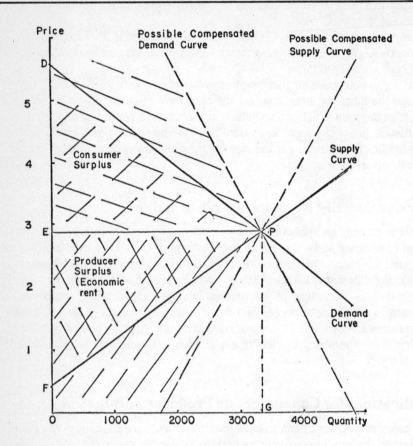

The consumer and producer surplus areas are then the areas under and over the compensated curves.

The ability to draw such compensated curves requires the ability to identify unambiguously an amount of welfare or utility corresponding to a given mix of commodities, and to equate that amount of welfare to some amount of welfare corresponding to a different mix of commodities being consumed by different people. Difficulties involved in doing this have already been noted, difficulties on both the demand and supply sides.

The critical argument developed above should not be interpreted as denying the rough and ready usefulness, in a ceteris paribus (not a general equilibrium) setting, of comparisons of areas under demand and over supply curves, provided one can identify demand and supply curves at all. But it does mean that the effort to validate such comparisons on the ground that they are theoretically precise is unwarranted. It is worth quoting Kenneth Arrow in a related context: "What I want to emphasize here and repeat later in varying contexts is that this price adjustment mechanism is *not* independent of the choice of numeraire. More specifically, the movements of relative prices can be different with different numeraires."[18]

Nevertheless, use of this approach as a basis for making policy recommendations continues apace.[19]

DYNAMIC PROBLEMS

If static equilibrium, on conventionally reasonable assumptions, cannot generate a unique welfare maximum there should be a strong presumption that growth models cannot generate a meaningful unique, maximum solution either. Nevertheless, there have been efforts, going back at least to Frank Ramsey in the 1920s, to conceptualize a maximum to infinity. Also there have been less ambitious efforts. Such efforts are considered next.

Unambiguous Increase in Production Capability

There is the question as to whether an unambiguous increase in production capability in a setting of unchanged community indifference curves (and assuming full employment) produces an identifiable, consistent percentage growth rate by different, equally valid, yardsticks. In figure 9-6, to make the case fairly strong, it is assumed that the community indifference curves are linear homogeneous (U $= X^{.6}Y^{.4}$), a fairly common assumption in "the received analysis." New technology is somewhat favorable to Y production and moves the production possibility curve from qq' to rr'. The welfare maximum, taken in terms of tangencies between the production possibility curves and the furthest outlying community indifference curves they can reach, moves P to P'. This corresponds to moving the community indifference curve out by 50 percent relative to the origin. If one believes community curves can only be ordered, that tells us nothing in terms of providing a number for the percentage increase in welfare. If one believes these relations can be cardinalized, a 50 percent increase in welfare may be said to be involved.

But it is "welfare in terms of what" as a common denominator? If commodity X is then used as the numeraire, gross national product (in real terms) rises by about 27 percent from OB to OD. If commodity Y is so used, it rises by approximately 92 percent from OA to OC. It makes considerable difference which commodity is used as numeraire. And yet governments of underdeveloped countries fall or survive on the difference between a 3 percent and a 4 percent growth rate.

Without departing too much from the way economists typically draw graphs, it is even possible to make GNP rise in terms of one numeraire and fall in terms of the other. Figure 9-7 illustrates the possibility.

FIGURE 9-6
Increase in Production Capability: General Case

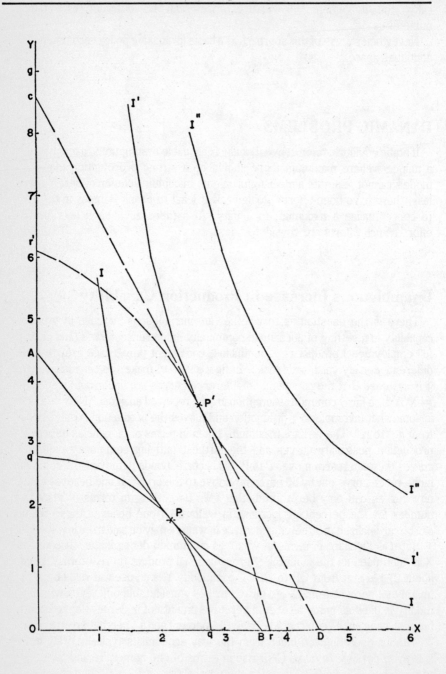

FIGURE 9-7
Increase in Production Capability: Special Case

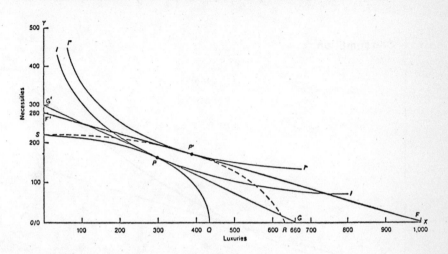

Maximizing a Rate

"Maximizing a growth rate" is a concept without a really useful role in defining and determining future welfare. In figure 9-8, the growth rate of per capita consumption begins more slowly in track A than track B, perhaps because there is a higher rate of saving in relation to income in case A. Eventually, in the tenth year, the earlier saving pays off with a higher growth rate in per capita consumption along track A thereafter. Which track implies a higher growth rate? Figures don't lie but liers do figure. A possible way to deal with this problem is to identify some particular year as the terminal year of concern or to say that we have some certain goal, such as a certain amount of capital stock (or as much capital stock as possible, or "in what proportions it would be nice to possess capital stocks at the end of the planning period," or some such) in some particular future year.[20] If this is done, it is then possible to pass judgment on the relative merits of two development strategies. But the price paid in order to be able to pass this judgment is high—we have prejudged that we are more concerned with the welfare of our children than with the welfare of our grandchildren (or vice versa).

FIGURE 9-8
Maximization of the Rate of Growth

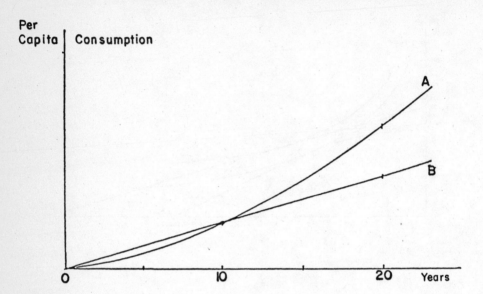

EVALUATION
Economic Significance of Maximization

The economics literature simply abounds with overly ambitious efforts to solve welfare maximization problems. Examples include the maximization of bliss to infinity by Frank Ramsey and Edmund Phelps's golden rule of accumulation.[21]

Among many difficulties with this sort of analysis is one pointed out by Kenneth Boulding. In a world where some people get their satisfaction out of the misery of others, the indifference curve pattern becomes a bird's nest of crisscrossing curves.[22] Johnnie gets his fun from tooting his horn. Mary likes quiet while she reads. Johnnie also enjoys irritating Mary. How is welfare to be maximized or a consensus obtained in that family?

The preceding exercises have been intended to indicate that the concept of a unique welfare maximum, expressible by a common yardstick, is not and in general cannot be theoretically meaningful.[23]

Frank Hahn has also denied meaning for the concept: "A bad nomenclature (Pareto-optimal) in the literature, together with much carelessness in textbooks, often misleads people into thinking that there is some theorem which claims that a competitive equilibrium is socially optimal. There is no such claim."[24]

Ludwig von Mises wrote: "If maximizing profits means that a man in all market transactions aims at increasing to the utmost the advantage derived, it is a pleonastic and periphrastic circumlocution. . . . Some economists believe that it is the task of economics to establish how in the whole of society the greatest satisfaction of all people or of the greatest number could be attained. They do not realize that there is no method which would allow us to measure the state of satisfaction attained by various individuals."[25] The implication of the statement is reasonably clear even if one temporarily stumbles over "pleonastic" and "periphrastic."

Changing conditions, changing knowledge, changing techniques, changing relative prices, changing relative use of factor inputs in given processes, in alternative processes, and in the production of different commodities, changing tastes, variations in tastes among people, decreasing (or increasing) utility, changing income distributions, and, above all, changing values mean that any attempt at a definitive conception of an overall, unique welfare maximum is a mirage. This is true both in terms of alternative conditions at a given time (the static situation) and in terms of changing conditions over time.

There is no way that a common yardstick of value can be identified, the amount of these different ingredients be quantified in terms of a common unit of measure, and the whole thing added up to give a unique number for gross national welfare or value. This sort of addition (in an effort to get a unique total) cannot theoretically be done, because the ingredients are not homogeneous (apples and onions), and they appear in continually changing proportions in the complete complex of welfare. Also, our judgments on *relative* values or desirabilities are or may be changing. That this arithmetical addition, in an effort to identify a unique total (and check whether it is a maximum), cannot be performed is a point that needs to be emphasized in economics because a large percentage of the profession is spending an awful lot of time playing with econometric models based on a presumption that some such aggregation is meaningful. The difficulty is basic. It is not a case where, if we could just improve our data gathering methods and the specification of our models, we could identify a desirable maximum of welfare. The point is that the concept of a welfare maximum is not meaningful. And this is true whether or not Nobel prizes are given for allegedly accomplishing this feat.

It should be added that these considerations do not deny the possibility that there may be situations where the solution of maximization problems is useful, particularly in decision making at the microeconomics level, in the short run, in the setting of certeris paribus assumptions. And none of the foregoing denies the importance of prices and profits. The individual buyer trying to pay less and the seller trying to get a higher price and higher profits are behaving in an intelligent and thoughtful manner. What has aborted in economics is the effort to aggregate these individual behavior patterns in an argument that leads to the conclusion that such behavior (in the setting of pure competition assumptions) tends automatically to generate a welfare maximum.

Also, one needs to shake the idea that the concept "marginal cost equals marginal revenue," at the microeconomics level, implies anything theoretically precise with regard to maximization of welfare at the general equilibrium level. MC = MR may imply some useful perspective as to the rational behavior of firms. But one needs to be chary in drawing any more general inferences from this much abused concept.

Then there is the case of the Pareto optimum, a position to which it is desirable to move because such movement may make somebody better off without making anybody else worse off. In reality, you cannot avoid setting one person's gain against another's loss. In fact, people are prone to make commotions over imagined losses, whether they are real or not.

True, it is good tactics for the businessperson or politician to operate in a fashion that will hurt as few people as possible. But this does not mean that practitioners of general equilibrium economics can solve this problem for the businesspeople or politicians. This is the politician's preserve not the economist's.

Of course, all this is well known to most welfare economists, so well known that they are likely to express some irritation when the matter is called to their attention. Yet, in general, they have refused to implement the appropriate conclusion: junking welfare economics and its effort to identify a welfare maximum and dropping this type of analysis as a basis for judgments on policy.

The Maximization Problem, Institutionalism, and Currently Held Values

If we realize we cannot identify a maximum (or an optimum), where do we go from there? Is all hope lost for economics? Or, is it possible that the problem of identifying and establishing reasonable social goals is simplified? Perhaps the latter is the case. We do not need Hamiltonians and Pontryagin maximizing methods or control theory in order to say a good deal that is useful about economic policy. We need a little common sense, a desire to assure that all people have a decent minimum, and beyond this that they get along pleasantly, have and make reasonable use of the opportunity for self expression, and enjoy security against hardship. These are the crucial distinctions that emerge when the value theory of institutional economics is contrasted with the value theory of neoclassical, general equilibrium economics.

CONCLUSION

The starting point of economics is, or ought to be, an understanding of how people behave. Psychological and other studies of human behavior do not support the commonly held position in economics that human goals are simple and, in general, involve some unique, aggregable, and maximizable concept of gain (individual or collective). Human motives are more complex than that. They are diverse, not susceptible to aggregation, and not maximizable, at least in any measurable way.

The significance of this for economics is that in many industry-level, firm-level, and individual-level situations it is useful to estimate the procedure that will maximize gain (perhaps monetary profit) in a given time period on some assumption or other as to what prices and other parameters will be). This procedure can provide a first approximation of a meaningful picture and be a useful indication of a reasonable production or pricing policy. Where economics has gone astray is in alleging that there is a useful way in which behavior at the microeconomic level can be aggregated into maximum general welfare.

Of course, all of us are mixtures of many characteristics, in varying degrees, and the composition of the mixture is likely to change at different periods in our lives. Much depends on the accident of the personality of the person one marries, the personalities of one's immediate associates at work, and the personalities of one's neighbors, and on the accident of health. Our composition depends on the institutional environment in which we live and on the way our personal biological makeup reacts to that environment. And it depends a lot on luck.

In their analysis, many economists have tried to keep the economics frame of reference apart from the frames of reference of other social sciences (some professional snobbishness being involved) and to separate the nature of the problems dealt with by the economists from other aspects of problems that the decision maker must take into account—and those efforts have done no service to economics or to decision making on the broader scene.

This is as far as the institutional theory goes. It is no criticism of the concept of self-correcting value judgments nor of the value theory of institutional economics that it fails to go farther and offer pseudo-solutions to what in fact are unanswerable questions. A theory is not required to provide answers to questions that do not have answers nor to find eternal verities where none exists.

NOTES

[1]Examples of the general equilibrium literature include: Vilfredo Pareto, *Cours d'Economie Politique* (Lausanne: F. Rouge, 1896); Kenneth J. Arrow and F. H. Hahn, *General Competitive Analysis* (San Francisco: Holden-Day, 1971); Gerard Debreu, *Theory of Value* (New Haven: Yale University Press, 1972); James Quirk and Rubin Saposnick, *Introduction to General Equilibrium Theory and Welfare Economics* (New York: McGraw-Hill, 1968).

[2]Adam Smith, *An Inquiry into the Nature and Causes of the Wealth of Nations* (Chicago: Encyclopaedia Britannica, 1952 [1776]), p. 194.

[3]Abram Bergson [Burk], "A Reformulation of Certain Aspects of Welfare Economics," *Quarterly Journal of Economics* 52 (February 1938), pp. 310-34; Paul A. Samuelson, "Social Indifference Curves," *Quarterly Journal of Economics* LXX (February 1956), pp. 1-22; Milton Friedman, *Essays in Positive Economics* (Chicago: University of Chicago Press, 1953).

[4]Arrow and Hahn.

[5]William J. Baumol, "Contestable Markets: An Uprising in the Theory of Industry Structure," *American Economic Review* 72 (March 1982), pp. 1-15, esp. p. 2.

[6]Mark Blaug, *The Cambridge Revolution, Success or Failure?* (London: Institute of Economic Affairs, 1974), p. 85.

[7]Edwin Mansfield, *Microeconomics* (New York: W. W. Norton, 1970), pp. 414-7.

[8]Quirk and Saposnik, p. 140.

[9]Hal R. Varian, *Microeconomic Analysis* (New York: W. W. Norton, 1978), p. 217, fig. 7.8(c).

[10]An example, in a standard textbook, of failure to take into account these relations can be found in Richard E. Caves and Ronald W. Jones, *World Trade and Payments* (2nd ed.; Boston: Little, Brown, 1977 [1973]), p. 447. For the argument involved in that case see: Wendell Gordon, "Welfare Maxima in Economics," *Journal of Economic Issues* XVII (March 1983), p. 6.

[11]Varian, p. 217, fig. 7.8(d).

[12]*The New York Times*, June 2, 1985, p. 19.

[13]Harry G. Johnson, *The Theory of Income Distribution* (London: Gray-Mills, 1973), p. 57.

[14]Ibid.

[15]Karl Marx, *Capital* (New York: Modern Library, 1906 [1867]), p. 52. Marx credits a "process that goes on behind the backs of the producers, and consequently appears to be fixed by custom" with solving the problem. See also: E. R. Berndt and L. R. Christenson, "Testing for the Existence of a Constant Aggregate Index of Labor Inputs," *American Economic Review* LXIV (June 1974), pp. 391-404.

[16]William H. Branson and Alvin K. Klevorick, "Strategic Behavior and Trade Policy," in Paul R. Krugman, ed., *Strategic Trade Policy and the New International Economics* (Cambridge, Mass.: MIT Press, 1986), p. 246; Alfred Marshall, *Principles of Economics* (6th ed.; London: Macmillan, 1910), pp. 124-133.

[17]Arnold C. Harberger, "Monopoly and Resource Allocation," *American Economic Review* 44 (May 1954), pp. 77-87; H. H. Liebhafsky, *The Nature of Price Theory* (rev. ed.; Homewood Ill.: Dorsey, 1968), pp. 202-212.

[18]Kenneth J. Arrow, in Daniel Bell and Irving Kristol, eds., *The Crisis in Economic Theory* (New York: Basic Books, 1981), p. 142.

[19]Charles L. Ballard, Don Fullerton, John B. Shoven, and John Whalley, *A General Equilibrium Model for Tax Policy Evaluation* (Chicago: University of Chicago Press [for the National Bureau of Economic Research], 1985); Herbert Scarf and John B. Shoven, eds., *Applied General Equilibrium Analysis* (New York: Cambridge University Press, 1984).

[20]This is done for example by: Robert Dorfman, Paul A. Samuelson, and Robert M. Solow, *Linear Programming and Economic Analysis* (New York: McGraw-Hill, 1958), p. 330.

[21]Frank Ramsey, "A Mathematical Theory of Saving," *Economic Journal* XXXVIII (December 1928), pp. 543-559; Edmund Phelps, "The Golden Rule of Accumulation: A Fable for Growth Men," *American Economic Review* 51 (September 1961), pp. 638-643. It is not entirely clear whether Phelps has his tongue in his cheek or not.

[22]Kenneth Boulding, *Economics as a Science* (New York: McGraw-Hill, 1970).

[23]This is no pathbreaking discovery. Many say the same: Max Weber, *Selections in Translation*, W. G. Runciman ed. (Cambridge, Eng.: Cambridge University Press, 1978), pp. 83-88; Robin Marris, ed., *The Corporate Society* (New York: John Wiley, 1974), esp. the articles by E. J. Mishan and Thomas Schelling; Mark

Blaug, *The Cambridge Revolution, Success or Failure?* (London: Institute of Economic Affairs, 1974).

[24]Frank Hahn, in Daniel Bell and Irving Kristol, eds., *The Crisis in Economic Theory* (New York: Basic Books, 1981), p. 126.

[25]Ludwig von Mises, *Human Action* (New Haven: Yale University Press, 1949), p. 243.

Chapter X

Implications for Microeconomics

Price theory (*micro*economics) and national income theory (*macro*economics) are the chief ostensibly practical paradigms available to orthodox economics. These theories are based on assumptions such as the profit motive, the desire for gain and utility, and the stability of relationships among economic variables. This latter constancy assumption is involved when mathematical models are being constructed. In price theory, the constancy of price elasticities is a rather standard working tool. In national income theory, the constancy of the marginal propensities to consume, save, and import is an equivalent working tool.

This chapter is concerned with price theory. Price theory generally involves an assumption that business enterprises are trying to maximize profits and individuals are trying to maximize their incomes or their utilities. Much of the analysis is conducted in a world of pure competition, especially so in recent years, although oligopoly, monopoly, and market rigidities may be considered.

To begin, it is best to look at microeconomics as though it were really microeconomics. The firm or the industry is visualized as acting in a context where conditions in the world outside the firm or industry are assumed to be unchanging or almost unchanging. That is to say, the rest of the world is taken care of by the *ceteris paribus* assumption. Free private enterprise, with no government regulation (laissez-faire), and pure competition are assumed.

Price theory, in these terms, is what is taught to economics students in the elementary course, then again in a junior level theory course, and then perhaps again in a graduate microeconomic theory course. You get it as many times as a student in Texas is required to repeat Texas history. In the end, some students believe it and some don't. So it is also in the Texas history courses where the Mexican-American student, even in the end, may not be entirely convinced that all the villains were in Santa Anna's army.

Price theory (pure competition version) runs to the effect that, at the industry level, the quantity of production and the price are determined at the intersection of demand and supply curves possessing certain characteristics. At the level of the firm, the quantity of production is set where marginal cost equals marginal revenue, and the meaning of those concepts is stylized.[1]

PURE COMPETITION ASSUMPTIONS

The assumptions of pure competition are as follows: The participants in the economic process (producers, consumers, resource owners) are (1) all-knowing "economic" men and women, with perfect knowledge of the relevant economic and technological data, (2) rationally pursuing the maximization of gain, and (3) existing in such large numbers that no one of them can perceptibly influence price or quantity of production. (4) Each economic actor can move freely, and immediately and costlessly, to other, more remunerative activities (the mobility assumption). Also, (5) all the items produced in an industry are exactly alike. This "identical product" assumption rules out competition-in-terms-of-quality. (6) There is always full employment.[2]

Full employment is an automatic result when the other assumptions hold, rather than an assumption. But the full employment condition so permeates microeconomics that it *is* worth listing, especially since it debars taking unemployment into account. So, economics thus dispenses with a serious social problem by assuming away unemployment. (In chapter 9, the exercises done with the Edgeworth boxes required a full employment assumption.)

THE MARKET SYSTEM
Representation of Market Prices

Neoclassical price theory seeks to show how demand and supply (for example for bales of cotton) interact to determine price at the point where demand equals supply—the famous "law" of supply and demand. Demand curves slope down because people will presumably buy more at lower prices; supply curves slope up. In figure 10-1, for instance, DD is a downward sloping demand curve and SS is an upward sloping supply curve. A fall in demand involves a movement of the whole demand curve to the left, perhaps to D'D', and a lower price, because the intersection with the unmoved supply curve will perforce be at a lower price: at P'' instead of P, since the supply curve is falling to the left. Similarly, a rise in supply to S'S' will lead to a price at P' if DD is the demand curve. A fall in the demand for cotton might be caused by a fashion change, a rise in supply by good weather.

Price theory claims that demand and supply interact this way and the market *works*. The chief tools of analysis are such solid and convincing-looking demand and supply curves. If the analysis is to be at all useful, it must be possible to identify the location of these curves with some precision.

FIGURE 10-1
Demand and Supply

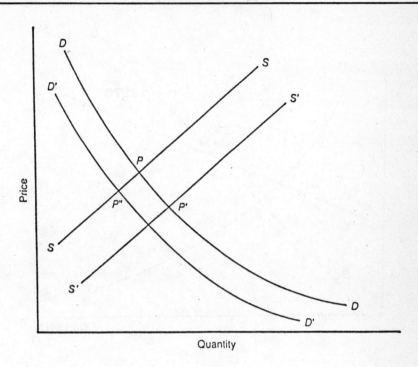

The Identification Problem

The information that economists possess is about quantities actually bought and sold during particular periods of time and market prices. Such information may be plotted in a scatter diagram (figure 10-2), where each dot represents average prices and sales during a given year, for example, 1969, 1970, or 1971.

It is possible to run a line (by using regression analysis) through the pattern of dots in a way that seems to strike a reasonable average among the dots. Such a line is RL in figure 10-2; it represents how much has been bought and sold at various prices. Is RL a demand curve or a supply curve? Pretty clearly it is neither. In econometrics, a great deal of ingenuity goes into rationalizing the slopes of demand and supply curves, starting from this sort of raw data and using additional information on related circumstances to justify pinning down the curves. It is a tricky game. But, when the demand and supply curves so derived are used for extended analysis, one does well to remember the extremely shaky basis on which they were constructed.

FIGURE 10-2
Quantities Bought and Sold: Scatter Diagram

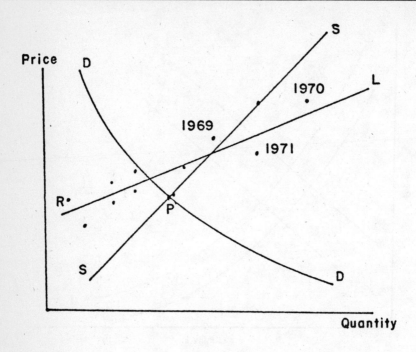

This ambiguity is called the identification problem. There are gimmicks (artifices, subterfuges, and proxy variables) for separating demand forces from supply forces. One may do a multiple regression using as additional independent information such variables as the weather, which allegedly affects only supply, or a change in style, that allegedly affects only demand. This procedure will separate demand influences from supply influences after a fashion. But it is difficult to find influences that are unique to demand or unique to supply. One still does not really know whether the demand (or supply) curve, so derived, as located, represents matters with any precision.

The identification problem is substantial and real. The concepts of demand and supply are not theoretically independent. Changes in the weather may well affect both demand and supply, and so may fashions. A change in demand may well affect supply—perhaps via national income changes. Demand and supply are not really independent as is assumed when one draws the separate curves. Or an increase in demand may lead to a nonreversible increase in production capacity, implying a different supply curve. But once the increase in supply is installed it is there; the movement of the supply curve is irreversible (in the sense that the new machinery is in place pretty definitively) even though the demand curve moves back to its former position. The mobility assumption is suspect.

The Elasticity Concept

A demand elasticity is a pure, but not particularly precise (or perhaps it is pseudoprecise), number that ostensibly describes, in a neat capsule, what will be the percentage change during a given period of time in the quantity demanded by buyers if there is a certain percentage price change:

$$\frac{\text{The elasticity of demand}}{\text{with respect to price}} = \frac{\%\ \text{change in quantity demanded}}{\%\ \text{change in price}}$$

Presumably the elasticity for salt is close to zero. People will buy about the same amount of salt regardless of price. And the elasticity for a durable consumer item such as a television set ought to be considerably larger than one. Price may be a major influence as to whether one buys a television; not so in the case of salt. Similar elasticities may be computed to describe the supply side. Producers would like to know what these elasticities actually are, since setting the right prices and quantities helps them maximize profits.

Graphs of demand curves representing the standard range of elasticity possibilities from zero to infinity are freely presented in the undergraduate texts. The demand curve in figure 10-2 probably has a constant elasticity of one along its length. A vertical demand curve has an elasticity of zero; a horizontal line is infinitely elastic. When the demand curve is a diagonal straight line falling to the right, it has an elasticity varying from much greater than one to much less than one.

Graphs of the standard supply curve elasticities are seen more seldom than the demand curve graphs. The possibilities are illustrated in figure 10-3. In the

FIGURE 10-3
Supply Elasticities

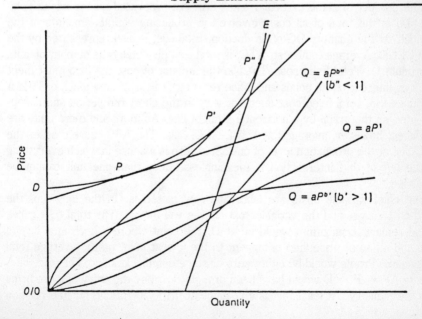

case of a simple parabola based on the origin, it turns out that the exponent on the independent variable is the elasticity. Thus, b′ and b″ are elasticities. A straight-line supply curve out of the origin has an elasticity of one. A curve rising to the right, such as DE, is elastic in the range where the tangents (for example at P) cut the vertical axis, inelastic in the range where such tangents cut the horizontal axis (for example, the line tangent at P″), and has unit elasticity at the point P′ where the tangent is also a ray out of the origin.

Demand and supply price elasticities are among the most basic concepts in economics. It is essential to be able to compute them if many price theory relations are to be mathematized in formulas of any reasonable degree of accuracy and simplicity. Consequently, it is revealing of the state of the economic science that the values of the elasticities cannot be computed from empirical data in a theoretically satisfactory manner by the methods presently at the disposal of the profession.

Cost Curves and the Marginality Concept

Total, fixed, variable, and marginal cost curves are other basic price theory concepts. The cost curves, when put together with information about the demand for a company's product, reveal the most profitable level of production for the firm. The demand curve for a firm's product under perfect competition is flat, or perfectly elastic. In figure 10-4, profit is greatest at point B, where nonconstant marginal cost equals constant marginal revenue. At this point the profits are the ABEC area, delimited by the vertical distance BE between B and the average total cost curve ATC.

In figure 10-4, price or cost (P = OA) and quantity of production (Q = OG) for the product of some particular small firm are presented on the axes. Total cost TC is the total of all costs involved in producing various amounts of the product. At the quantity OG of production, total cost is also represented by the area CEGO. Average total cost, ATC, is total cost divided by the number of units of product Q. Total fixed cost, TFC, is the amount of cost the firm must meet (such as interest on its bonds and office rent) regardless of how much or little it produces. So, total fixed cost does not vary in the short-run period and is represented on the graph by a horizontal straight line. As more and more units are produced, however, average fixed cost, AFC, falls. The AFC curve crosses the TFC line at the production level of one. So, there is a sense in which everything to the left of that intersection is meaningless. Less than one unit cannot be produced.

The chief variable costs are labor and raw materials. In the long-run, the fixed-cost curves and the variable cost curves will merge. The total cost curve would remain. Equilibrium would be at D, the point where a horizontal line (a new and different price line) is tangent to the lowest point on the average total cost curve. Profits would be either zero or some nominal amount. The price line, MR = AR = P = D would have been brought down by the entry of more firms into the industry. At least that is a possible scenario. (Working out the relation

FIGURE 10-4
Short-Run Equilibrium of the Firm Under Competition

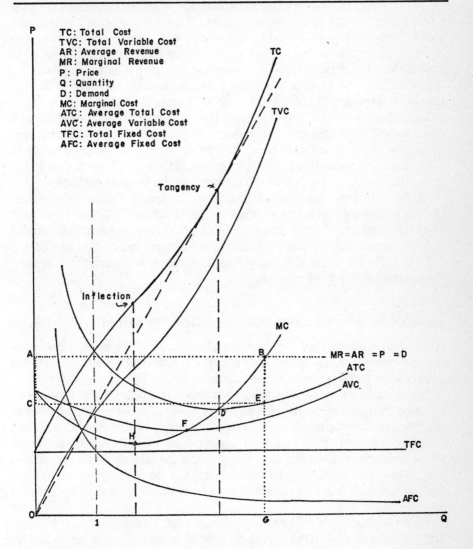

between the short run and the long run is a tricky and unsatisfactory part of the price theory.)

The marginal cost (MC) curve represents the change in total cost (and also in total variable cost, the two magnitudes being the same) as quantity of production is increased. The logic of these interrelations requires that the marginal cost curve intersects from below both the AVC and ATC curves at their lowest points. The AFC curve is always the same height as the vertical distance between the ATC and the AVC curves.

In the application of the marginality concept what is looked at is the impact of a slight change of a variable. What will be the impact on total cost of a slight change in the quantity of production? Production is said to stabilize at the level where marginal cost equals marginal revenue. If more is produced, the increased cost exceeds the increased revenue. Below this level, the firm will produce more as long as the revenue from increasing production exceeds the additional cost. This thinking brings one back to the conclusion that, in the short run, equilibrium is at point B. In the long run it is at point D after the entry of new firms into the industry has brought the MR = AR = P = D curve down.

Much of the curvature pattern in figure 10-4 derives from the shape of the total cost curve. It is argued that, at low levels of production, total costs rise ever more slowly up to an inflection point. Beyond that they rise ever more rapidly as the difficulty of expanding production mounts. The level of production at the inflection point corresponds with the minimum on the marginal cost line.

All this is to some degree black magic since calculating the curves at a point in time is impossible. Of course, the internally consistent relations must hold, given the definitions of variables and the belief (which may not be entirely correct) as to the shape of the total cost curve and the assigning of some costs to fixed cost.

How well the understanding of these relations will serve the average businessperson is a good question.

Monopoly, Monopolistic Competition, or Oligopoly

A slightly more (but not particularly) realistic model of the industry might still assume laissez-faire (the government does not interfere with business) but cease to adhere to all the precepts of pure competition.

Such models are those of monopolistic competition, oligopoly, and monopoly. They continue to assume that all the parties involved in the productive process are trying to maximize their gains. But they drop one or another of the assumptions of pure competition, most frequently the assumption that no one of the parties can influence price. Less frequently, they modify the assumption that productive resources can move freely and instantaneously from one employment to another. Joan Robinson, Edward Chamberlin, and John Kenneth Galbraith have toiled in this vineyard.

Figure 10-5 is a standard monopoly pricing model. The marginal cost, MC, and the average total cost, ATC, curves have the same meaning as in figure 10-4. In the monopoly case it is argued that the firm is looking at a downward-sloping demand curve because the firm is assumed to be big enough so that its production pattern is a factor in total industry supply.

Since, under monopoly, the demand curve for a firm's product probably does fall (lower prices calling forth greater demand), the marginal revenue curve, MR, is below the demand curve and is falling more steeply. It shows by how much revenue will be increased by one more sale. And, since average price is falling, the increase in revenue resulting from selling one more unit is less than the average revenue, where AR = D.

FIGURE 10-5
Monopoly Pricing

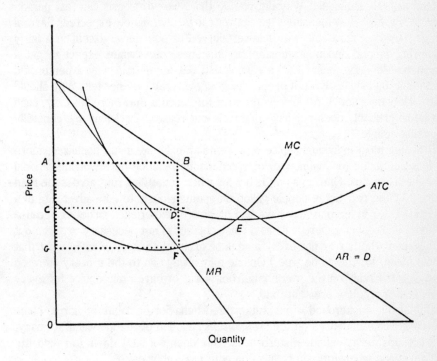

The profit-maximizing executive will produce output of GF, at which marginal cost equals marginal revenue. At that level of production the price the monopolist can effectively charge is OA, which is greater than average total cost of OC. So B is the point that indicates both price and quantity of production. The price of OA and the average cost of OC permit the monopolist to collect a so-called monopoly profit corresponding to the area ABDC.

This story indicates why public utilities, which are likely to be monopolies, are regulated by an appropriate level of government to protect consumers from the monopoly prices the public utilities will otherwise charge. This model does, therefore, have a practical usefulness as a clue to underlying relations, even though in particular cases the information is probably not available to permit putting real life curves into the model. In the jargon, the model has a genuine heuristic value: it transmits an important correct message.

Influences on Individual Choice

Price theory generally assumes that the profit motive, or the desire to maximize gain, is the one and only influence on choice. There was considerable discussion of the profit motive in chapter 5. In this chapter some additional discussion of the problem of choice may be helpful.

One asks an individual: Why did you do that? On what basis can that person give an answer? How meaningful an answer can be legitimately expected? Several things may be said, some with fair certainty. For one thing, except in a fairly clear-cut, simple, and nontraumatic circumstance, one cannot expect to get a complete, definitive answer. We cannot find out for certain why a person did something by asking. Even if people really know, they may not tell. Why should they? They may not be completely proud of the reason. But, more basically, each individual probably does not have one clear-cut reason. Decisions are generally "not that simple."

Probably most individual choice represents an habitual, institutionalized, more or less automatic (or instinctive) or spontaneous reaction not involving rational thought processes. One jams on the brakes when something runs across the road in front of the car. Some people gallop off spontaneously to take advantage of a bargain. Later in life one may have bad dreams or experience anxieties because of some unpleasant experiences as a small child (it is not necessary to argue out with Freud whether or not everything is sexually motivated, or even what that would mean, for this to be true.) Or one may always go to the grocery store on Tuesday or Friday on the way home from work, or have orange juice for every breakfast or a coffee break at 9:30.

Out of this background of institutionalized behavior or habits or norms come the controlling influences on the *spontaneous* reaction of the individual to many, and perhaps most, outside disturbances. One does not slow down to rationalize the whys and wherefores in connection with most choices.

Suppose there is a novel situation or difficulty. How does one react? Consider typical cases.

Spontaneous or fortuitous choice may occur in college football recruiting, and probably frequently does:

> Talk about the one that got away. If college football coaches were fishermen, the story of Harvey Williams—and how Texas A&M apparently had him on the hook only to lose him at the last possible second—would be legendary.
>
> Two days before national signing date last February, Williams called a news conference and said he had narrowed his choices to A&M and LSU. He told his coach he really couldn't decide—even 20 minutes before his second news conference two days later.
>
> Until Williams walked down the school hallway to meet the press and announce his selection, he didn't know which to choose.
>
> "I walked down the hall past a lot of people and policemen and TV cameramen," Williams said. "Then I passed some girls who started singing the Aggie fight song."
>
> "That kind of threw me to LSU . . . ."
>
> It seems an awfully pivotal decision to be based on one song. Is the Aggie fight song that bad?[3]

The accident of timing in decision making can lead to results that seem not to jibe with rationality. Take as an example buying a house, a pretty important decision.

The, until then, happily married couple is trying to decide whether to buy a three bedroom house with a sunken bathtub for $110,000 or a house with a patio and a swimming pool for $120,000. At five minutes of the hour they choose the sunken bathtub, on the hour the swimming pool. One minute their inclinations are in one direction and the next moment in the other direction. Each choice has its advantages and disadvantages. And the spouses are differently influenced by various of these advantages and disadvantages. So, the discussion as to what to do waxes complicated. Also, in the end, one or the other of the spouses, or both, may be inclined to lean over backwards to accommodate what is conceived to be the desires of the other, or each may lean the other way, or one may be more obliging than the other. At any rate, the tentative decision is first to buy one of the houses, then to buy the other, and so on back and forth. But the seller of one of the houses has set a two o'clock deadline on a certain day, maybe because of a payment that must be made to the bank. It may be pure accident which of the tentative decisions is endorsed by the buyers at the moment the decision has to be made. "The die is cast" at a certain moment in the typical purchase or sale. One was thoughtful and reasonably rational at five minutes of the hour and also on the hour. But the choice was different, despite the fact that the underlying ingredients conditioning the choice were unchanged.

This is a behavior pattern that most people can check for themselves as they reconsider their own behavior.

More generally, a decision has to be made. It has to be made in the sense that the thing will or will not be done. But the person is undecided. And the influence that tips the balance, even on important decisions, is frequently trivial, even irrelevant, or irrationally spontaneous. Some impulse jumps a synapse in the brain. And away one goes, with implications for oneself and others.

Of course, the preceding comments are not the whole story on choice. What they do represent is an important alternative to the sort of rationality generally assumed in price theory and synthesized in the profit motive.

HOMEOSTASIS AND BEHAVIOR REINFORCEMENT
The Equilibrium Concept

Price theory is oriented to the proposition that there is some kind of equilibriating force at work which, after things get out of order (when demand exceeds supply or vice versa), tends to bring the economy or the industry or the firm back to equilibrium and full employment. This is the condition of homeostasis—the tendency toward equilibrium. This concept is at the heart of the work of Alfred Marshall, of most price theory texts, and of the view of the knowledgeable public as to how the law of supply and demand works. (Keynes's *General Theory* also uses the equilibrium concept, but with the feature that there can be equilibrium in a setting involving something less than full employment.)

The tendency to equilibrium in economics has an analogy with centripetal force in physics. But then, in physics, there is also the concept of centrifugal force, involving the possibility that something being spun around in a circle may fly away at a tangent.

The economist's tendency-to-equilibrium concept also has an analogy with natural order or natural balance in nature, in the universe, or in human behavior. One hears a good deal about natural balance in nature, such as influences that kill off surplus populations in one species or another or influences that may reverse a falling population trend. But one also hears about the extinction of species and may not be entirely sure that survival in equilibrium with nature is a natural law.

In psychology, homeostasis may appear as a relatively stable state of equilibrium or a tendency toward such a state between the different but interdependent elements of an organism or group. But to the psychologists there are other possibilities. Organisms may behave in ways detrimental to bodily maintenance. Organisms may have no means of detecting some aspect of the environment of which they need to be aware if they are to maintain equilibrium. And organisms sometimes strive for goals which have no adaptive significance.

So, homeostasis, taken as the process for maintaining the physiological and psychological equilibrium of an organism by means of various regulatory mechanisms, is not the whole story in explaining behavior.

It may have been J. E. Meade who used a mountain-climbing example to indicate a difficulty with marginal analysis in price theory. Price theory alleges that the quantity of production appropriately establishes itself at the level where marginal cost equals marginal revenue. The decision maker has reached this point by proceeding by marginal increments. One does not need to know the "big picture," but only that the next step, and the next, are leading in the right direction, and one will eventually arrive at the most desirable level of production. In the Meade example, however, the problem is to climb the highest mountain in the range (the analogy being with maximizing profits). So one wears blinders and proceeds uphill, one step at a time. Each step leads always up—and is, therefore, always rational at the margin. Once a peak is reached, the climber takes off the blinders and is surprised to see that there is a higher mountain in the range. Only by chance would the climber have reached the highest point in the range (or the entrepreneur followed the most profitable policy).

Nevertheless, the competitive assumptions are basic in creating the setting that makes a natural tendency toward equilibrium an operationally meaningful concept in economics. Whether such a tendency is in fact generally operational is one of the most important questions with which economists ought to be concerned but in fact have neglected.

Discussion of a so-called cobweb theorem used to be fairly standard in elementary economics texts or the junior level price theory texts. The cobweb theory described a process by which an industry might arrive at a demand and supply equilibrium or fail to do so. The argument went that it was accidental whether the adjustment process followed a route that led to equilibrium or away from it. Which process prevailed depended on the relative slopes of the demand and supply lines and on the mechanics as to how the adjustment process got started. Are such models now largely disregarded in economics because it has been demonstrated that the tendency away from equilibrium is demonstrably unlikely? Or, has the typical economist been conditioned to believe that proper economics involves an assumption of a tendency to equilibrium?

The Tendency Away From Equilibrium (Behavior Reinforcement)

Many economic problems are better understood in a context where a movement toward equilibrium is not a natural tendency. There are various expressions for behavior leading away from equilibrium: social traps, bandwagon effects, cumulative causation, disaster myopia, cognitive dissonance, or, in economics, the cobweb theorem.[4]

In John Platt's terminology, people may be trapped into a behavior pattern that leads to long-run results that are both contrary to the social interest and contrary to their own interest. The tendency-toward-equilibrium analysis fails to get hold of the nature of such an ongoing process. One of many examples given by Platt is the working of Gresham's Law, "bad money drives out good," when a country is trying to operate under a system of bimetallism.

The decline of passenger service on the railroads, which led to results that were probably undesirable from almost all points of view, resulted from a process somewhat like this. People were using the automobiles and the airplanes more after World War II; so, the railroads cut back on the quantity and the quality of their service; and, as a result, people used the railroads even less, and so on. This is the sort of self-fortifying or self-reinforcing process that leads to a result quite different in kind from that visualized in equilibrium analysis.

A similar example involves inflation. Once an inflationary process has gotten underway, the labor unions want higher pay to offset the effects of inflation, the executives want more generous expense accounts and higher profits to offset inflation, the teachers want higher salaries, and so on. These higher wage costs then serve as justification on the part of businesses for further increases in prices. Spiraling inflation, self-reinforcing inflation, is underway, with the monetary system accommodating the process with increases in lending and expansion in the money supply. The attraction of rising interest rates makes bankers happy to cooperate in this process. The expansion in the money supply thus is in considerable degree a result of the process rather than a cause of the process. The quantity theory of money is working, but not in the way envisaged by Chicago. Milton Friedman may have cause and effect oversimplified. Individuals are under strong pressure not to fall behind in this race. It is not a situation where a few statesmanlike business or labor leaders can stem the tide by moderating their own demands. The price is too high. They go bankrupt or their real wages fall. They just get left behind.

A famous example of damaging interaction is free grazing on New England commons. One had better get there first with one's sheep before the other fellow's sheep nibble up all the grass. If everyone does the same thing, the commons is going to be a barren, vegetation-free area. The problem is not dealt with if a few people of good will abstain from grazing their cattle on the commons.

Another situation, the missing-hero case, is epitomized by a mattress fallen in one lane of a two-lane highway from Hyannis to Boston on a busy Sunday evening when all the weekenders are heading home. Each incoming driver, arriving at the mattress, waits patiently for a break in the outgoing traffic flow in order to get by the mattress. The result is a line of cars several miles long waiting to edge by the mattress. No hero, once arrived at the mattress, finds it judicious to go to the trouble of getting out of the car and removing the mattress. The only reward for that service is to be honked at and lose position in the traffic parade.

So-called one-person traps involve cigarette smoking, alcohol, and drug addiction. One becomes "hooked" on the habit and "cannot" quit even though the individual is well aware of the desirability of quitting.

Escalating expenditures by the United States and the U.S.S.R. on arms are an example of an international relations trap. Each country wants "to negotiate from a position of strength," and expenditures have to escalate on both sides.

Then there is the use of DDT. The results of its use are most profitable for the first few farmers who use it. DDT has a lethal effect on insects and initially reduces the incidence of malaria. But it takes stronger and stronger doses as the years pass to be effective and the effect upon wildlife and on life in the rivers that receive discharge containing DDT becomes devastating.

Or there is the case of the cumulative effects involved in the phenomenal growth of Mexico City. It is socially undesirable for 15,000,000 or 20,000,000 or more people to become concentrated in the Valley of Mexico. The ecology and atmosphere cannot stand it. But it is *the* place to go. And no one person is going to stay away because the city is larger than is ecologically desirable.

Pursuit of ends that make sense for the individual very often lead to generally undesirable results for society. Some decisions even make the individual better off in the present but worse off in the future. What behavior is *rational?*

EMPIRICAL MICROECONOMICS

During the 1930s, economists began to use data to compute demand curves, supply curves, and their elasticities. The thought was that the estimates would be of practical usefulness to business. They were to be more than theoretical constructs designed to help economists understand the system.

Since the 1930s empirical microeconomics has become one of the major fields of activity of economists. This is a rather strange phenomenon. This analysis does not help the owner of a little bookstore trying to decide how many copies of *Free to Choose* to order for the Christmas rush. And it is not much help to the owner of a shoe store trying to plan ordering, and it is even less help to the buyer for a department store trying to anticipate fashion trends. No one has ever observed the manager of a grocery store trying to compute the elasticity of demand for bananas.

Businesspeople do have method in their buying and selling practices. Frequently what is involved is a standard markup. How sensitive the people in a given industry are to the desirability of changing these rules of thumb in response to changing conditions is important, but is a consideration that price theory is not particularly well adapted to taking into account.

Whether any or all of the decision-making methods, and many more such as linear programming, input-output, and shadow pricing, made available by economists to business executives and planners with decisions to make, are much help seems debatable. In fact, businesspeople rarely use these economic methods to help with their decision making.

THE MORALITY OF PRICE THEORY

The market system, according to orthodox price theory, makes unadulterated selfishness into a virtue. How does one rationalize this attitude with the belief that charity and cooperation are virtues? Perhaps one does it by recognizing that a mixture of a self-serving incentive system and cooperative generosity is the system we actually have, and—all things considered—it is not all that bad a system.

If these are the facts of life, then the elaboration and proliferation of price theory models, which assume that the market solution and the profit motive are the whole story, is, to put it mildly, overdone. The eulogizing of the free market solution, unadulterated by recognition that it is appropriate for society to ride herd on eager entrepreneurs is, to put it strongly, an expression of a behavior pattern that society will in fact not tolerate.

Prices are meaningful and important; price theory is not particularly.

THE NATURE OF THE USEFULNESS OF PRICE THEORY

Almost any problem can be analyzed by price theory if one chooses to do so (and choosing to do so has become common in economics): the drug habit, capital punishment, pornography, the chewing gum market, the abortion market, prostitution, marriage, advertising, the all-volunteer army, pollution, zero population growth, the multinationals, the property rights of trespassing cattle, the behavior of administrative agencies, the bail system, the optimum enforcement of laws, crime and punishment, the brain drain. Economists usually deduce some relationships: if the revenuers become more effective, the price of bootleg whiskey will rise; if potential murderers are rewarded for not committing murder, there will be fewer murders; if crime is made less economical there will be less crime. If a man's cows graze on another's land, the free market is ready, willing, and able to deal with the problem. "The amount of crime deterrence that a chief of police can attain will be *maximized* with a given budget if, and only if, the marginal amount of crime deterrence made possible by $1.00 is the same for every input used in his crime preventing firm."[5]

One should not deny that the understanding of the role of prices and incentives may be useful. Certainly, the concepts of demand, supply, and price are meaningful concepts. And the businessperson had better have some intelligent understanding of cost. Concern about profits may have an appropriate place. The businessperson may and should use all the information obtainable as intelligently as possible. All that is not in question here.

Ayres has written: "To question whether the operations of the market—that is the whole operation of buying and selling—mean what they have been traditionally alleged to mean is not to argue against buying and selling. . . . The whole point to the Veblenian criticism of the classical tradition is that the economy is not regulated by the price system. It is regulated by the institutional structure of Western society, of which the market is at most only a manifestation."[6]

There are situations where the solution of maximizing problems may be useful at the microlevel—in helping with decision making by firms or industries. The firm, appropriately, may try to maximize profit in the next planning period as effectively as it can, given the prevailing ground rules. In this setting, to solve the maximization problem, the executives may appropriately make some simplifying assumptions. They may well assume some "constant" parameters: certain prices and costs will remain the same during the planning period, tax rates will remain the same, and so on, at least for a while. On the basis of this information, they decide how much to produce in the next planning period and at which prices to sell, probably influenced also to a considerable degree by some rules laid down by the government. These calculations might well involve the methodology of linear programming, but generally they do not. Actually, businesspeople customarily do not use the analytical procedures of the price theory of economics. They use some rules of thumb, some rough calculations relating guesses about costs and receipts in the event that various possible alternative policies are followed, hoping they have taken into account the factors that will in fact be important and then opting for one of the policies frequently, figuratively speaking, after flipping a coin and offering a short prayer to whatever god the businessperson happens to believe in.

Price comparisons are meaningful. As a pretty good general rule, a lower price is more desirable from the viewpoint of a buyer and a higher price is more desirable from the viewpoint of a seller. What does not stand up, out of price theory and general equilibrium analysis, is the allegation that market price (or consumer or producer surplus) can be equated to "social value." Nor does the conclusion that the government should not ever intervene or regulate stand up. The proof that pure competition, involving the absense of regulation, maximizes welfare with more certainty than does regulation is unsubstantiated. This is true in spite of a recent statement to the contrary by an equally recent winner of the Nobel Prize in economics: "The 'wealth of nations' is maximized when persons are 'free to choose.' This instrumental relationship between liberty or freedom and economic welfare emerges directly from the conventional theory of economic interaction."[7]

Similarly, there is *something* to be said for competition, at least competition of some sort and kept in its place. Competition, in the sense of two companies competing for sales, may result in lower prices and better merchandise than would be the situation if there were only one firm serving the market. Customers of private enterprise *may*, not necessarily, get more courteous service, lower prices, and a better product than some government enterprise *might* provide. They may not. But this is not exactly the economist's world of pure competition where there are so many sellers and buyers that no single one can affect price.

In any event, demand, supply, and price influences work their way through the system in such a highly institutionalized way that it stands to reason that economists concerned about prices should bestir themselves to understand that those behavior patterns are an important aspect of their activity, rather than eschewing understanding while having fun modeling mathematically. H. H. Liebhafsky says of market prices:

> Instead of being an ultimate standard of valuation to which the social order *ought* to conform, *actual* market prices are in reality a reflection of that social order which does exist. To accept *actual* market prices as a measure of social valuations is thus to accept the *status quo* in markets; and to argue that a particular configuration of prices *should* exist is tantamount to arguing that the social order which will produce that configuration *should* exist.[8]

Alfred Marshall also wrote, longer ago:

> The Statical theory of equilibrium is only an introduction to economic studies. . . . Its limitations are so constantly overlooked, especially by those who approach it from an abstract point of view, that there is a danger in throwing it into definite form at all.[9]

NOTES

[1]This comment is not entirely fair to Alfred Marshall, *Principles of Economics* (London: Macmillan, 1890). But it would seem not too unfair to latter day price theory texts: George J. Stigler, *The Theory of Price* (New York: Macmillan, 1942); Milton Friedman, *Price Theory* (Chicago: Aldine, 1962). The less said the better about such mathematized versions as Hal R. Varian, *Microeconomic Analysis* (New York: Norton, 1978). A competently done price theory book, but with tongue in cheek, is: H. H. Liebhafsky, *The Nature of Price Theory* (Rev. ed.; Homewood, Ill: Dorsey, 1968[1963]).

[2]Such lists abound in the elementary texts. See, for example: Edwin Mansfield, *Microeconomics* (New York: Norton, 1970), pp. 223-4.

[3]*The Houston Post*, Sept. 11, 1986, p. 2D.

[4]John Platt, "Social Traps," *American Psychologist* 28 (August 1973), pp. 641-51; B. F. Skinner, *Contingencies of Reinforcement: A Theoretical Analysis* (New York: Appleton, 1969); Thomas Schelling, "The Ecology of Micromotives," *Public Interest* 25 (1971), pp. 61-98.

[5]Several of these arguments, including the last a propos of the budgetary problems of a chief of police, are found in: Roger Leroy Miller, *Economics Today* (San Francisco: Canfield Press, 1973), pp. 437-444. *The Journal of Political Economy* is also replete with arguments along these lines. Authors involved include Isaac Ehrlich, Richard A. Posner, William Landes, George Stigler, Gary Becker, and Ronald H. Coase.

[6]C. E. Ayres, *Toward a Reasonable Society* (Austin: University of Texas Press, 1961), pp. 27-28.

[7]James M. Buchanan, "Towards the Simple Economics of Natural Liberty: An Exploratory Analysis," *Kyklos* 40 (fasc. 1, 1987), p.3.

[8]H. H. Liebfhafsky, *American Government and Business* (New York: Wiley, 1971), p. 15.

[9]Marshall, pp. 460-1.

Chapter XI

Implications for Macroeconomics

Macroeconomics uses as its analytical components total or overall measures of economic activity. These include national income and production, investment, savings, exports and imports, and consumption. In addition, macroeconomics is concerned with indicators of economic well-being such as employment, unemployment, price inflation, and growth.

THE NATURE OF KEYNESIAN THEORY

National income, or Keynesian, macroeconomic theory acquired prominence during the Great Depression of the 1930s. The chief influence was *The General Theory of Employment, Interest and Money* written by John Maynard Keynes in 1936, which set much of the practice of President Franklin Roosevelt's New Deal in a theoretical framework.[1]

The theory was, at least initially, a useful antidote to price theory, especially to the idea that pure competition and free enterprise, if let alone, could be counted on to deal effectively with the business-cycle problem. The theory was depression theory, and its chief useful insights had to do with the unemployment problem. Increased investment and increased government spending could be useful policies, Keynes showed, to raise employment and stimulate output and growth.

The Basic Model

In its simplest form the Keynesian argument is illustrated in table 11-1. In Case I it is assumed that $1,000(000,000)$ of additional, new, "autonomous," real investment occurs. (One may assume that about six zeros have been dropped from the numbers in what follows.) Perhaps businesses borrow the sum from private savers or from the banking system and use it to hire unemployed labor, buy raw materials,

161

and produce new capital equipment and thus create new productive capacity. Perhaps the government does much the same thing, financing the activity by running a deficit and increasing the public debt.

TABLE 11-1
Effect of New Investment on Income, Consumption, and Saving

CASE I: Assumptions: 1. New Investment of $1,000 (I)
                   2. Marginal propensity to consume (mpc) of ¾
                   3. The multiplier (m) = $[1/(1 - mpc)]$

Investment	Resultant Increase in Income (ΔY)	Resultant Increase in Consumption (ΔC)	Resultant Increase in Savings (ΔS)
1,000	1,000	750	250
	750	562.50	187.50
	562.50	421.88	140.62
	and so on	and so on	and so on
Totals 1,000	4,000	3,000	1,000

So: $\Delta Y = [1/(1 - mpc)]\ I = [1/(1 - ¾)]\ 1,000 = 4,000$
or $\Delta Y = 4 \times 1,000 = 4,000$

CASE II: Assumptions: 1. New Investment of $1,000 (I)
                    2. Marginal propensity to consume ½

Investment	Resultant Increase in Income (ΔY)	Resultant Increase in Consumption (ΔC)	Resultant Increase in Savings (ΔS)
1,000	1,000	500	500
	500	250	250
	250	125	125
	125	62.50	62.50
	and so on	and so on	and so on
Totals 1,000	2,000	1,000	1,000

CASE III: Assumptions: 1. New Investment of $1,000 (I)
                     2. Marginal propensity to consume of 9⁄10

Investment	Resultant Increase in Income (ΔY)	Resultant Increase in Consumption (ΔC)	Resultant Increase in Savings (ΔS)
1,000	1,000	900	100
	900	810	90
	810	729	81
	729	656.10	72.90
	and so on	and so on	and so on
Totals 1,000	10,000	9,000	1,000

In the first round of using the new investment (I), those funds become an addition to the income of the worker or the raw material producer who receives them. It is assumed, in Case I, that the recipients of such increases in income spend three-fourths (the marginal propensity to consume, mpc) and save one-fourth (the marginal propensity to save, mps). As indicated in the table, this throws (3/4) × 1000 = 750 of further increase in income back into the "resultant increase in income" column. The 750 becomes an increase in income for whoever receives it. And the 750 is subsequently also divided three-fourths to spending and one-fourth to saving and so on.

This process goes on through many rounds until the cumulated total of (1) resultant increase in income is 4,000, (2) resultant increase in consumption is 3,000 (three-fourths of 4,000), and (3) the resultant increase in saving is 1000 (one-fourth of 4,000). This corresponds with the formula: $\Delta Y = [1/(1 - \text{mpc})]\,I$, where $[1/(1 - \text{mpc})]$ is the Keynesian multiplier, m. And this resultant increase in saving of 1000 equals the initial spurt in investment of 1000. And one of the standard equalities of economics holds: saving equals investment $(S = I)$. But equality holds not because saving must occur before investments can be made but because an amount of saving equal to the amount of autonomous investment is automatically drawn out as a result of the way the process works.

This reversal of the cause and effect relation in the $S = I$ equality is one of the major contributions of Keynes, if not the major contribution. It takes the luster off the argument that great inequality in the distribution of income is necessary to facilitate investment because investment can only occur if it is preceded by voluntary, personal saving and only the very rich are in position to save in substantial amounts.

Cases II and III illustrate that pronounced effort to save and be abstemious is not necessarily the most helpful way to increase national income. The effort to save half of income in Case II results in a given autonomous investment increasing income by only $2000, a figure which is less than is the $10,000 of Case III where people are much more of a mind to spend and spend nine-tenths of the increases in income. But in both cases the actual amount of saving is the same in the end and equals the autonomous spurt in investment of $1,000 that began the process. The effort to save has not affected the amount of saving but the given and equal amount of investment has increased income less in the second case.

In Keynesian theorizing, new investment is a development that can be generated by a policy decision. Saving cannot be an initial stimulus, because saving as a percentage of income is more or less constant. The proportion of savings at a given level of income is thus an institutionalized behavior pattern. An original decision is not made by a society to save a certain amount, which decision then determines the total amount of new investment and the size of the resultant increase in income.

Created funds can put the unemployed to work during a depression, and production and employment can improve at the same time with little if any inflationary impact. In this process the relevant, important decisions must be made, not at the level of the individual firm, but rather by the executive branch of the federal government or Congress.

Government investment (or deficit financing) is a rough-and-ready possibility for improving matters during a depression. But it may not work. It will not work if business chooses to alarm itself as to the socialistic implications of such government spending and cuts back private investment by enough to offset the increase in government spending. This is more or less what happened in the United States in 1936.

Also, pretty clearly, this is not a process that can be fine-tuned. One cannot say that a $351 million increase in government spending will increase gross national product by $843 million and create 240,000 jobs. Yet, econometric models trying to forecast this sort of thing have become the meat and drink of macroeconomists. Economists have tried to superimpose this pseudoprecision on the basic Keynesian argument. The result has not been particularly helpful; and, they have tried to play the game during periods of more or less full employment, and inflation has been the result. This sort of policymaking, practiced rather unimaginatively, but with much calculation of econometric models, has sometimes been the chief activity of the President's Council of Economic Advisers.

So, Keynesian theory was depression theory, and its chief useful insights had to do with curing depressions and unemployment. The theory does not have much to say that is useful for dealing with full employment, overfull employment, inflation problems, and growth.

Currency Devaluation

Currency devaluation is a reduction in the value of a nation's currency relative to foreign currencies. Currency valuation has been a favorite field for the use of national income theory and one of the principal applications of that theory has been in the international trade field.[2]

In the international field the chief modification of the basic model is that one has, instead of saving equals investment (S = I), a fundamental equality that is more complex: S + Imports (M) = I + Exports (X). It takes consumption plus savings plus imports, or consumption plus investment plus exports, to equal national income. Exports are assumed similar to investment in playing an active role, and imports are similar to savings in playing a passive role.

Research in this area commonly supports the proposition that currency devaluation tends to "improve" the balance of trade of the devaluing country, that is, to increase exports relative to imports. It is almost an article of faith, even, that devaluation improves the trade balance, that an improved or favorable balance of trade is desirable, and that such a development will improve national income and welfare. The model is:

$\Delta Y = (1/[1 - \text{mpc}]) \times I$
but instead of $(1/[1 - \text{mpc}]) = 1/\text{mps}$
the international multiplier is now:
$m = (1/[1 - \text{mpc}]) = 1/ (\text{mps} + \text{mpm})$,

where mpm is the marginal propensity to import or the percentage of a change in income that is spent on imports. Mpc, mps, and mpm and consequently the multiplier (m) need to be constants if this analysis is to be readily tractable.

A trouble with this analysis is that the very nature of currency devaluation is such that it is likely to change the values of these allegedly constant propensities, precisely at the time the devaluation occurs and because it is occurring. For example, whether currency devaluation is going to be successful in improving the trade balance of the devaluing country (so that it can recoup its foreign-exchange reserves) is going to depend upon whether people believe that the action of the government in devaluing was statesmanlike, believe that the devaluation was of approximately the right percentage, and believe that the problems that led to the loss of foreign exchange reserves (that led to the devaluation) have been solved. And believing so will help make it so. If, on the contrary, people interpret the devaluation as evidence of the financial weakness or incompetence of the government, they are likely to believe that one devaluation will lead to another and they are likely to engage in precisely the currency speculation operations which will force a subsequent devaluation. Either of these very different results might occur in spite of the possibility that in the two cases the estimates of pre-devaluation propensities were the same. So, the propensities may not take into account all the important factors and they may be changeable rather than constant. Especially in a time of crisis, they may mislead.

So far as many aspects of the problem are concerned, hindsight is going to be the best prophet. But maybe, at least, something can now be said on the basis of some fairly crude historical data with regard to whether devaluation is reasonably likely to improve a trade balance after either eighteen months or two years or four or five years.

Data have been compiled for about 188 devaluations. Commodity trade balances have been computed for the year preceding the devaluation, the year of the devaluation, and for each of the six following years (insofar as available). Two comparisons have been made. First, the trade balance in each of the six years following the devaluation (measured in the local currency) has been compared with the trade balance of the year of the devaluation. Second, the trade balance in each of the six years following the devaluation has been compared with the trade balance of the year preceding the devaluation. Was the trade balance "improved" in the year in question by comparison with the year of the devaluation or by comparison with the year preceding the devaluation? Table 11-2 presents the data.

Covered in the figure of 188 devaluations are all of the devaluations (or appreciations) since about 1920 for which it was possible, fairly readily, to find data. Situations, such as have been known in Chile, Brazil, Argentina, and a number of other countries, where there has been ongoing devaluation almost every year for many years, have been omitted. No doubt many devaluations have been overlooked, and there are other problems with the data, but the sample is large enough to place the burden of proof on one who alleges results contrary to those indicated by these data.

TABLE 11-2
Devaluations and Trade Balances

	Change in Balance in Indicated Year by Comparison with Year of Devaluation			Change in Balance in Indicated Year by Comparison with Year Preceding Devaluation		
	Improve	*Worsen*	No. of Cases	*Improve*	*Worsen*	No. of Cases
First Year After	100	88	188	91	94	185
Second Year After	80	102	182	77	103	180
Third Year After	67	113	180	64	112	176
Fourth Year After	70	102	172	65	103	168
Fifth Year After	72	89	161	66	94	163
Sixth Year After	52	101	153	53	99	152

Sources: International Financial Statistics, 1972 Supplement; Board of Governors of the Federal Reserve System, *Banking and Monetary Statistics,* Washington 1943; United Nations, *Yearbook(s) of International Trade Statistics,* New York; League of Nations, *International Trade Statistics,* Geneva, various years.

For all of the twelve comparisons, only in the one case of the comparison of the balance in the year following the devaluation with the balance in the year of the devaluation were there more examples of "improvement" than of "worsening." This "conventional" result is for the first year after a devaluation with 100 cases of improvement and 88 cases of worsening.

The conventional wisdom to the effect that devaluation improves the trade balance of the devaluing country is suspect. And the "new conventional wisdom" to the effect that the process may take a bit longer than was formerly supposed is even more suspect. Such improvement as is likely will be temporary and occur quite promptly after the devaluation. Beyond that, worsening is about as likely as improvement, or slightly more so. But, on the whole, the correlation between devaluation and improvement (or worsening) in the trade balance is about as poor a correlation as one could find. In the absence of more particular knowledge of the circumstances of the particular devaluation, the planner would do well not to count on a predictable relationship between the devaluation and the trade balance.

These relations argue that there is no clear relation between devaluation and an increase in national income. An increase in exports, or an "improvement" in the trade balance (if a policy produces that result) may accompany an increase in national income that is due to a monetary phenomenon; yet, real wealth is being lost in the form of the net export trade balance.

LATER VARIATIONS IN MACROECONOMICS
Monetarism

The quantity theory of money holds that if the supply of money is increased substantially there will be some inflation. This rough and ready likelihood was noticed by a Spanish priest at Salamanca about 1550, and maybe by Aristotle before that.

The proposition was seized upon by Milton Friedman about 1950. It was made to carry a burden in terms of precision that was more than the approach should have been asked to carry. Friedman argued that there was a strict, proportional, and mechanical relation between the percentage rate of increase in the money supply and the percentage rate of inflation. Thinking in these terms, and quite reasonably believing that inflation is undesirable (at least ceteris paribus), Friedman made the policy recommendation that the money supply be increased automatically each year by a definitely set small percentage in the range between three and five percent.[3]

Effort to control inflation is desirable. But is this proposal the appropriate policy? It is not easy to imagine the administrative machinery that would control the issuance of the money and would determine who would get it. The proposal that it be dropped from airplanes hardly seems serious.

One of Milton Friedman's favorite objects for denunciation is the central banker. He is, therefore, not willing to use central bankers to make policy judgments controlling who will get the money.

An additional Friedman pronouncement: "Money matters," has also had a tremendous appeal to the American people, whom one would have guessed hardly needed any arm twisting to be convinced of the truth of that adage. Certainly Keynesians, in general, had never denied that money mattered. It is desirable that governments should be reasonably discreet in issuing money. It is not the principle that is at stake, it is the practice. A perhaps interesting side issue in connection with Friedman's role in "money matters" is the aspect that the Friedman argument essentially is that money does not matter. The Friedman argument is to the effect that the price level will change in close proportion with the change in the supply of money, regardless. Thus change in the supply of money, according to Friedman, has no appreciable effects on real income and welfare, except perhaps in the short run. So, why all the fuss?

Rational Expectations

Another recent vogue in the macroeconomics area has been rational expectations. The core of the matter is the hypothesis put forth by John F. Muth to the effect that "expectations, since they are informed predictions of future events, are essentially the same as the predictions of the relevant economic theory."[4] He goes on to say: "The hypothesis asserts three things: (1) Information is scarce, and the economic system generally does not waste it. (2) The way expectations are formed depends specifically on the structure of the relevant system describing the economy. (3) A 'public prediction' . . . will have no substantial effect on the operation of the economic system (unless it is based on inside information). *This is not quite the same thing as stating that the marginal revenue product of economics is zero,* because expectations of a single firm may still be subject to greater error than the theory."

Just what was Muth saying? At a given time the people of a society subscribe to a theory as to how things are and behave in a manner that is a rational expression of that theory. At least this is the general result, even though individual firms may make mistakes. Then the future behavior of the system as a whole accurately reflects this prevailing theory and condition. The future can accurately be forecast except for the possible disturbing effect of unanticipated events. Included here is the comforting, but probably erroneous, opinion that society will not be effectively misled by lying politicians or other sources of misinformation. "A 'public prediction' . . . will have no substantial effect on the operation of the economic system. . . ."

The only influence that can affect or modify the course of events is unanticipated change, outside disturbance, or a natural catastrophe.

Jacob Frenkel and Michael Mussa have attempted to apply the method to explain foreign exchange rate determination. Their conclusion is: "The actual change [in the foreign exchange rate] is this expected change plus the (necessarily unpredictable) unexpected change due to 'new information' that alters expectations. . . . The bulk of exchange rate changes appears to be due to new information."[5] So, one is entitled to ask: how useful is an approach that ends up telling us that the only influences that matter are unanticipated events?

Nobody is quarreling with the proposition that the relevant theory should be used if one can figure out what the relevant theory is. With regard to the issue as to expectations depending on the structure of the system describing the economy, one may well also say: How true! Then the chief criticism of the rational expectations practitioners may well be with their conception as to what the relevant structure actually is. At this point a new difficulty arises. One might think there would be a major amount of discussion in the rational expectations literature as to the nature of the relevant economic theory and structure and as to the meaning of rationality. There is, in fact, precious little. What there is, in abundance, is econometric methodology. The two volume work edited by Robert E. Lucas, Jr. and Thomas J. Sargent entitled *Rational Expectations and Econometric Practice* has much more to say about econometric procedures and mathematical modeling than it does about rationality and the underlying social structure that the approach is attempting to elucidate.[6] There are some presumptions made about social structure such as that there is a natural rate of unemployment. But there is little substantive discussion of the implications of such a presumption or the justification.

All in all it is difficult to understand the vogue that rational expectations has enjoyed.

Supply-Side Economics (Reaganomics)

Rational expectations was popular with professional economists in the early 1980s, but it was something a bit different, supply-side economics, that became the new wave in Washington in 1981. Those associated with supply-side economics include Arthur Laffer, George Gilder, Bruce Barlett, Paul Craig Roberts, Jack Kemp, and legions more.[7]

There is disagreement, but the supply-side argument runs something like this: It is desirable to lower taxes in a process that especially favors the wealthy, not so much because the wealthy are more meritorious, although the typical supply-sider might well be prepared to argue that they are, but because the wealthy save a larger proportion of their income than do the poor. An increase in saving is desirable because saving equals and creates investment. (Typical macroeconomics relations are being manipulated here, but they are turned around from the orthodox Keynesian argument.) More investment is desirable because investment generates capital and productive capacity and the ability of the economy to supply more goods.

The savings-investment-output relation provides the rationale for calling the approach supply-side economics. The argument is concerned with how to increase the supply of goods. Increased production means a larger gross national product and a higher national income. With a higher national income, taxpayers will pay more taxes *even at the lower rates that initiated the process.* In their initial exuberance at the beginning of the Reagan administration, supply siders were alleging that this consequence would be sufficiently powerful in raising additional new taxes to eliminate the federal deficit by fiscal 1983-84. That this result was not attained is now notorious. Nevertheless the country was prosperous in 1984 and 1985. But, since the supply-side scenario had not worked, supply-side economics or Reaganomics would hardly seem entitled to take credit for the prosperity. If explanation for the prosperity is to be found in macroeconomics at all (which may well not be the case), it is that ordinary, old-style Keynesian deficit financing caused the prosperity, such as it was. Deficit financing was certainly practiced on a large scale during the Reagan administration.

ECONOMETRIC MODELS
The Validity of the Constancy Assumption

A general characteristic of macroeconomic model building is the assumption that constant relationships may be found which will describe with reasonable accuracy the connections among the economic forces at work. Such constant relations (generally stated as constant marginal propensities) play a role in macroeconomic theory similar to constant demand and supply elasticities in price theory.

It makes a good deal of difference, when a crisis comes along, whether these constants accurately describe real relations that will remain the same after the onset of the crisis. If the constants hold, the econometric model involved can be used to tell the planners how much to cut taxes, or raise tariffs, or increase investment in order to deal with the difficulty, which may be unemployment or a fall in the value of the dollar. The economy can be "fine tuned." But if the "constants" are inconstant, after the inception of the difficulty, planning on the assumption of their reliability will fail.

If an economist (on a light teaching load and with a large grant) can identify one of these constants and establish that the constancy really holds through thick and thin (that is, after the storm clouds have gathered) and can, in consequence, do some reliable predicting or responsible planning, a professional reputation is made and something worthwhile has been accomplished. But, to use Milton Friedman's example of the attraction of gravity, the marginal propensity to consume needs to have somewhat the constancy of the attraction of gravity.

Econometric forecasting is important, the work should be attempted, and it is desirable to find these constant relations if they exist—but only if they exist. And the economics journals should stop publishing the results of inconclusive econometric studies. But the foundations (the National Science Foundation, the Ford Foundation, and so on) love to finance activity of this sort. They want published articles as a demonstration that their grant money was not wasted. (We are now in the area of Thomas Kuhn's normal [and sterile] science.)

Presumably the key constant in national income theory is the marginal propensity to consume, which in most of the writing on the subject is presumed to be constant at a figure of about 75 percent. It is not possible to test the magnitude of this figure empirically in a theoretically satisfactory way. To be theoretically satisfactory one would have to have hard numbers as to how much would be consumed at a given moment (or during a given year) at all possible levels of income. The only "hard" number one has, of course, is the estimate of the consumption and national income that actually occurred that year. One dot is a poor basis for drawing a line.

Among the second-best procedures for estimating the marginal propensity to consume, the most common involves time series data. The change in consumption between successive years is compared with the change in income during the corresponding time period (the statistical series actually used is personal income for the United States). Then one compiles all of these year-to-year changes for all the year pairs from 1929 to 1984 and gets 55 estimates of the marginal propensity to consume. If the marginal propensity to consume is really a constant over time, these numbers should vary but little from year to year.

The actual situation indicated in table 11-3 is that the average (arithmetic mean) marginal propensity to consume for the United States was 83.87 percent. Casual inspection of the numbers in the marginal propensity to consume column might be enough to convince one that 83.87 is not a reliable constant for representing the marginal propensity to consume. That the standard deviation of the marginal propensity to consume is extremely large at 58.52 is evidence of a more technical sort. A 58.52 variation relative to a norm of 83.87 gives a coefficient of variation

TABLE 11-3
Average and Marginal Propensities to Consume, United States

	Personal Consumption Expenditures C (Billion $)	Personal Income PY (Billion $)	Average Propensity to Consume C/PY	Marginal Propensity to Consume ΔC/ΔPY
1929	77.2	85.9	89.87	
1930	69.9	77.0	90.78	82.0
1931	60.5	65.9	91.81	84.7
1932	48.6	50.2	96.81	75.8
1933	45.8	47.0	97.45	87.5
1934	51.3	54.0	95.00	78.6
1935	55.7	60.4	92.22	68.7
1936	61.9	68.6	90.23	75.6
1937	66.5	74.1	89.74	83.6
1938	63.9	68.3	93.56	61.9
1939	66.8	72.8	91.76	64.4
1940	70.8	78.3	90.42	72.7
1941	80.6	96.0	83.96	55.4
1942	88.5	122.9	72.01	29.4
1943	99.3	151.3	65.63	38.0
1944	108.3	165.3	65.52	64.3
1945	119.7	171.1	69.96	196.5
1946	143.4	178.7	80.25	311.8
1947	160.7	191.3	84.00	137.3
1948	173.6	210.2	82.59	68.2
1949	176.8	207.2	85.33	−106.7
1950	191.0	227.6	83.92	69.6
1951	206.3	255.6	80.71	54.6
1952	216.7	272.5	79.52	61.5
1953	230.0	288.2	79.81	87.3
1954	236.5	290.1	81.52	342.1
1955	254.4	310.9	81.83	86.1
1956	266.7	333.0	80.09	55.7
1957	281.4	351.1	80.15	81.2
1958	290.1	361.2	80.32	86.1
1959	311.2	383.5	81.15	94.6
1960	325.2	401.0	81.10	80.0
1961	335.2	416.8	80.42	63.3
1962	355.1	442.6	80.23	77.1
1963	375.0	465.5	80.56	86.9
1964	401.2	497.5	80.64	81.9
1965	432.8	538.9	80.31	76.3
1966	466.3	587.2	79.41	69.4
1967	492.1	629.3	78.20	61.3

TABLE 11-3 *(Continued)*
Average and Marginal Propensities to Consume, United States

	Personal Consumption Expenditures C (Billion $)	Personal Income PY (Billion $)	Average Propensity to Consume C/PY	Marginal Propensity to Consume ΔC/ΔPY
1968	536.2	688.9	77.83	74.0
1969	579.5	750.9	77.17	69.8
1970	617.6	808.3	76.41	66.4
1971	672.2	859.1	78.24	107.5
1972	737.1	942.5	78.21	77.8
1973	812.0	1,052.4	77.16	97.0
1974	888.1	1,154.9	76.90	74.2
1975	976.4	1,265.0	77.19	80.2
1976	1,084.3	1,391.2	77.94	85.5
1977	1,204.4	1,540.4	78.19	80.5
1978	1,346.5	1.732.7	78.29	73.9
1979	1,507.2	1,951.2	77.24	73.5
1980	1,668.1	2,165.3	77.04	75.2
1981	1,849.1	2,429.5	76.11	68.5
1982	1,984.9	2,584.6	76.80	87.6
1983	2,155.9	2,744.2	78.56	107.1
1984	2,341.8	3,012.1	77.75	69.4

Statistics relevant to Average Propensity to Consume:

Sample Size:	56
Arithmetic Mean ($\bar{x}$):	81.53
Standard Deviation (σ):	6.88
Standard Error of the Mean ($S_{\bar{x}}$):	0.92
Coefficient of Variation ($V = \sigma/\bar{x}$):	0.0844

Statistics relevant to Marginal Propensity to Consume:

Sample Size:	55
Arithmetic Mean ($\bar{x}$):	83.87
Standard Deviation (σ):	58.52
Standard Error of the Mean ($S_{\bar{x}}$):	7.89
Coefficient of Variation ($V = \sigma/\bar{x}$):	0.6977

Sources: *Historical Statistics of the United States; Economic Indicators.*

(a measure of dispersion) which is an extremely high 0.6977. There is every reason for saying that the marginal propensity to consume is not a constant, at least when computed from time series data.

In table 11-4 a similar computation is made for another one of the much-used propensities, the marginal propensity to import. Reasonably accurate data for this "constant," computed from time series data, are available for the United States

TABLE 11-4
Import Propensities and Elasticities, United States

	I Marginal Propensity to Import $\Delta M/\Delta NI$	II Income Elasticity of Demand for Imports $\%\Delta M/\%\Delta NI$		I Marginal Propensity to Import $\Delta M/\Delta NI$	II Income Elasticity of Demand for Imports $\%\Delta M/\%\Delta NI$
1900	19.3	4.2	1943	1.9	1.0
1901	− 2.6	− .5	1944	4.4	2.2
1902	6.3	1.3	1945	−15.6	− 7.9
1903	10.7	2.1	1946	−48.3	−21.8
1904	− 6.9	− 1.3	1947	4.6	1.7
1905	9.5	1.9	1948	5.6	1.9
1906	6.3	1.1	1949	9.2	2.8
1907	16.7	3.2	1950	9.4	3.1
1908	25.4	4.3	1951	5.7	1.5
1909	3.9	.8	1952	− 2.0	− .5
1910	11.4	2.3	1953	1.1	.3
1911	−40.4	− 6.5	1954	17.0	4.7
1912	9.6	1.7	1955	6.4	1.5
1913	7.9	1.4	1956	4.4	1.9
1914	−33.7	− 6.4	1957	3.1	.9
1915	−16.6	− 2.8	1958	− 5.5	− .1
1916	11.6	2.3	1959	2.4	2.1
1917	7.3	1.2	1960	− 4.2	− 1.0
1918	.7	.1	1961	− 7.5	− .6
1919	14.6	2.7	1962	2.4	1.6
1920	25.0	4.1	1963	3.2	.9
1921	23.6	3.1	1964	6.5	1.3
1922	125.8	30.2	1965	4.3	1.7
1923	.8	.1	1966	7.3	1.75
1924	−13.6	− 2.2	1967	3.6	.87
1925	20.2	3.8	1968	10.5	2.56
1926	5.9	1.0	1969	5.4	1.16
1927	−55.5	− 9.2	1970	12.0	2.55
1928	− 4.8	− .8	1971	9.9	1.98
1929	8.6	1.6	1972	11.0	2.06
1930	11.1	2.2	1973	11.4	1.94
1931	6.1	1.5	1974	41.4	6.39
1932	4.5	1.3	1975	− 7.4	.84
1933	− 5.3	− 1.7	1976	17.5	2.19
1934	2.3	.6	1977	16.2	1.80
1935	4.8	1.4	1978	11.5	1.18
1936	4.8	1.3	1979	17.4	1.74
1937	7.6	2.0	1980	25.2	2.34
1938	18.6	4.4	1981	6.2	.52
1939	6.9	2.4	1982	−13.1	− 1.18
1940	3.5	1.1	1983	6.8	.67
1941	3.1	.8	1984	21.2	2.16
1942	− 1.8	− .6			

TABLE 11-4 *(Continued)*
Import Propensities and Elasticities, United States

Statistics relevant to Marginal Propensity to Import:

    1900-1929: Sample Size: 30
                 Arithmetic Mean ($\bar{x}$): 6.57
                 Standard Deviation (σ): 29.30
                 Standard Error of the Mean ($S_{\bar{x}}$): 5.35
                 Coefficient of Variation ($V = \sigma/\bar{x}$): 4.46

    1930-1984: Sample Size: 55
                 Arithmetic Mean ($\bar{x}$): 5.25
                 Standard Deviation (σ): 11.74
                 Standard Error of the Mean ($S_{\bar{x}}$): 1.58
                 Coefficient of Variation ($V = \sigma/\bar{x}$): 2.24

Sources: *Historical Statistics of the United States; Statistical Abstract of the United States; National Income* (Supplement to *Survey of Current Business*); National Industrial Conference Board, *Studies in Enterprise and Social Progress; Economic Indicators.*

from 1900. For purposes of comparison with the marginal propensity to consume, the time period is broken down into 1900-1929 and 1930-1984. For the period 1900-1929 the average marginal propensity to import was 6.57 percent, but the standard deviation of this figure was an almost unbelievable 29.30, giving an extremely high coefficient of variation of 4.46. For the period 1930-1984, the average of 5.25 percent has a standard deviation of 11.74 and a coefficient of variation of 2.24, also extremely high figures.

The variation in the marginal propensity to consume is considerable. The variation in the marginal propensity to import is almost an order of magnitude greater. The amount of these variations makes one wonder about the relevance of assuming that these numbers are constants. (The authors made these computations and are not prepared to guarantee the result. But direct check of the numbers should be enough to confirm that there is very considerable variation in the marginal propensities, enough to make suspect an argument to the effect that they are constant.)

There are several points that those interested in saving the approach can make. They can say that one should compare marginal propensities only at similar phases in the business cycle, and there are other possibilities. But, really, no amount of manipulation of the data will salvage the assertion that the key marginal propensities of national income theory are constants. They are not. And especially in times of crisis they are not.

This conclusion taints not only the application of national income theory by the Keynesians but also the other uses of national income relations by the monetarists, the rational expectations people, and the supply siders. This is not the point where these contestants have disagreed. All manipulate models that assume the internal marginal propensities are constants.

The post-World War II Keynesians have abused Keynes in developing these models mathematically in ways that assume strong constancy. A rereading of the *General Theory* confirms that Keynes was not making strong claims for the constancy of the marginal propensities. Keynes's position was moderate and defensible. Tendencies, directions of change, and rough orders of magnitude were discussed not strong constancy and the possibility of fine tuning.

Keynes wrote:

> Too large a proportion of recent "mathematical" economics are mere concoctions, as imprecise as the initial assumptions they rest on, which allow the author to lose sight of the complexities and interdependencies of the real world in a maze of pretentious and unhelpful symbols.[8]

The search for constant parameters is not entirely invalid, but, at best, it represents a half truth. Some economic relationships are probably more or less constant for substantial periods of time, and it is worthwhile to have some awareness of what these numbers actually are during periods of stability. In institutional theory, one might say that as long as a social institution is set in its ways its behavioral relationships will be quite constant. People at a certain income level in suburbia in the 1960s, or the 1990s, will probably, on the average, save a fairly constant percentage of their incomes during the boom phase of the business cycle. It is useful to identify such a constant, but hardly of earthshaking importance. The trouble is that during times of crisis, when the really important economic decisions are made, the constants will not hold. This is just the time when the institutions and their "fixed" relations are subject to flux. A major fault with present-day mathematical economics is its emphasis on identifying constants which turn out not to be constants when it is a matter of importance that they are. And yet these constants are necessary if economic relations are to be set up in mathematical models.

Other Aspects of the Methodology

It is fun to build up a complicated model and identify the significant variables, and the parameters one would like to estimate. Careers are often made on this basis. But whether one does the dirty statistical work oneself or not, it is very often true that the statistical data needed for computing one or another of the variables cannot be obtained. Confronted with this difficulty the econometrician, instead of going off somewhere else to make an honest living, is likely to use a proxy variable. One says that some other concept, for which one is able to get data, represents about the same influence as the variable in which one is interested. So, one puts into the model these other data, says a short prayer, and alleges it does the same job as the data one needed. This is what Milton Friedman has done in trying to test his permanent income hypothesis. Since data on what people's permanent income will actually be is not obtainable, Friedman has used as his proxy "present and previous disposable personal income with geometrically declining weights"—or something like that.

Another term that is less likely to "give the show away" is "surrogate." For example one might say that the capital/labor ratio "is estimated in surrogate form as the installed horsepower capacity per person engaged."

NOTES

[1]New York: Harcourt, Brace, 1936. See also: Alvin H. Hansen, *A Guide to Keynes* (New York: McGraw-Hill, 1953); Lawrence R. Klein, *The Keynesian Revolution* (New York: Macmillan, 1948); United Nations, *National and International Measures for Full Employment* (New York: Lake Success, 1949). A standard national income textbook has been: Thomas F. Dernburg and Duncan M. McDougall, *Macroeconomics* (New York: McGraw-Hill, 1960). An example of a later and highly mathematical text is: Thomas J. Sargent, *Dynamic Macroeconomic Theory* (Cambridge: Harvard University Press, 1987).

[2]Joan Robinson, *Essays in the Theory of Employment* (2nd ed.; Oxford: Blackwell, 1947), p. 142; Fritz Machlup, *International Trade and the National Income Multiplier* (Philadelphia: Blakiston, 1943); or see standard texts such as those by Charles Kindleberger or Richard E. Caves and Ronald W. Jones.

[3]Milton Friedman, *Capitalism and Freedom* (Chicago: University of Chicago Press, 1962), p. 54.

[4]John F. Muth, "Rational Expectations and the Theory of Price Movements," *Econometrica* 29 (July 1961), p. 316.

[5]Jacob A. Frenkel and Michael L. Mussa, "The Efficiency of Foreign Exchange Markets and Measures of Turbulence," *American Economic Review* 70 (May 1980), pp. 374-381, esp. p. 374.

[6]2 vols.; Minneapolis: University of Minnesota Press, 1981.

[7]If one would like at least one citation, a possibility is George Gilder, *Wealth and Poverty* (New York: Basic Books, 1981).

[8]John Maynard Keynes, *General Theory of Employment, Interest and Money* (New York: Harcourt, Brace, 1936), pp. 297-8.

Chapter XII

Implications for Marxism

The present economic orthodoxy does not seem to be working very well. Happily, it has a whipping boy that most people can love to hate. Many economics departments congratulate themselves on giving a voice to heterodoxy by hiring an in-house Marxist, who will make the right noises and keep things reasonably interesting. There are other heterodox approaches that have intellectual credibility but do not enjoy the status of Marxism: underconsumption, the single tax, the economic doctrines of the various religions, libertarianism, Ayn Rand objectivism, and institutionalism.

Karl Marx, in the nineteenth century, attacked classical economics in its own frame of reference. This involved working with most of the Ricardian assumptions and analytical tools. The procedure both strengthened and weakened his position. If he was to have significant scholarly impact this was probably good judgment. Professional economists could understand and be stung by his criticism. Beside that, in the world of scholarship and science, for institutionally controlled reasons, scholars usually work with the analytical tools and methods on which they were brought up. So, even Marx was bound into the institutional constraints imposed by the classical economics tradition he was attacking. But his use of this procedure meant that his theory incorporated many of the weaknesses of classical economics.

Marx assumed pure competition, Say's law of markets, and the labor theory of value. (At least it seems that Marx adhered to Say's law [supply creates its own demand] in connection with the development of his core argument, although in his discussion of business cycles, this may not have been the case.)[1]

THE ORGANIZATION OF SOCIETY
Superstructure and Substructure

Marx divided society into a superstructure and a substructure. The superstructure included the noneconomic institutions, such as religion, ethics, the law, government, etiquette, and so on; the (economic) substructure encompassed the economic base and included the "modes" of production. The modes of production were divided into the "forces" of production and the "social relations" of production.

Forces and Relations of Production
(Especially Private Property)

The forces of production in Marx are the material powers of production or the means of production; these include technological understanding as well as real capital—machines, equipment, factories, and so on.

There is an apparent closeness between Marx's forces of production and technology as conceived in institutional theory. Likewise, Marx's social relations of production are at first glance analogical to the institutions governing economic activities in institutionalism. In institutionalism, however, institutions have non-economic dimensions such as attitudes and values. Marx separated such non-economic matters from the economic, thus dividing society into two parts or levels. It was the non-economic realm that he called the superstructure. Institutionalists thus see society as made up of institutions with economic and non-economic features, while Marx split society and its institutions into the economic relations of production and the superstructure. Because of these differences Marx's analysis of institutions is different from, and does not anticipate, the position of the institutionalists.

Although Marx himself was quite vague about the matter, one listing of the institutions of capitalism as perceived by Marxists is:[2] (1) the labor market, (2) private property and the legal relations of ownership, (3) private ownership and control of the means of production, and (4) the economic man.

This is a rather limited list. Two of the items involve the institution of property, which is no doubt an important institution. In fact, the institution of private property, for the Marxists, overshadows, almost to the point of exclusion, all others. Ownership of property rights in capital, they say, provides the leverage that permits capitalists to exploit labor. Workers need tools to work effectively. If they do not own them themselves, they have to work for those who do. The role of property is made basic in the Marxist explanation as to how exploitation occurs. And yet there surely are many other ways in which some people can acquire the leverage or power to manipulate and "exploit" their fellows: strategic positions in the money changing process (bankers), strategic positions in the marketing process (middlemen), and social status (which strangely is not the essence of "class" for the Marxists, despite their class struggle theme).

Marxists are not criticizing capital when they criticize capitalism. Capital, in the form of capital goods, is used under socialism, and the more the better. It is the manner in which, in the West, the *private* ownership of capital permits the exploitation of labor that is being focused on and is the basis for calling the system capitalism.

The Technology-Institutions Dichotomy

Marx wrote in *Wage Labor and Capital (Lohnarbeit und Kapital)* during the 1847-1849 period:

> These social relations into which the producers enter with one another, the conditions under which they exchange their activities and partici-pate in the whole act of production, will naturally vary according to the character of the means of production. With the invention of a new instrument of warfare, firearms, the whole internal organization of the army necessarily changed; the relationships within which individuals can constitute an army and act as an army were transformed and the relations of different armies to one another also changed.
>
> *Thus the social relations within which individuals produce, the social relations of production, change, are transformed, with the change and development of the material means of production, the productive forces.*[3]

Marx was anticipating the Veblenian explanation of institutional change as being forced as a by-product of the implementation of the use of new technology. He had this insight early in his career. It is regrettable that he did not pursue the implications of this argument rather than spending most of his later energy dissecting the process by which surplus value is accumulated by the capitalists, to the exclusion of studying other processes such as unfair dealing by middlemen and wealth-extracting financial leverage.

THE LABOR THEORY OF VALUE AND ITS CONSEQUENCES

The Labor Theory of Value

Marx devoted most of the time and energy of his mature years to describing a process by which the capitalists appropriate surplus value and thus exploit the workers. Marx's argument starts with the labor theory of value, stated in much the same form as Ricardo had used fifty years earlier. Marx felt a compelling need to pin down and quantify (or at least theoretically be able to quantify) the amount of exploitation of labor by capital. Marx thought that exploitation and the expansion of capitalism would lead to a falling rate of profit and this would contribute to the collapse of the capitalist system. If the falling rate of profit is a nonexistent phenomenon and if the homogeneous, socially necessary unit of labor time (Marx's starting point) are defective concepts, then his whole chain of reasoning rests on weak foundations.

To quantify surplus value or the exploitation practiced by capitalists, Marx needed to start with a quantifiable unit of measurement. Marx conceived the appropriate unit to be the homogeneous, socially necessary unit of labor time. He wrote:

> To measure the exchange-value of commodities by the labor-time they contain, the different kinds of labor have to be reduced to uniform, homogeneous, simple labor, in short to labor of uniform quality, whose only difference, therefore, is quantity.
>
> This reduction appears to be an abstraction, but it is an abstraction which is made every day in the social process of production. The conversion of all commodities into labor-time is no greater an abstraction, and is no less real, than the resolution of all organic bodies into air.
>
> This abstraction, human labor in general, *exists* in the form of average labor which, in a given society, the average person can perform.
>
> It is, however, clear that the reduction is made, for, as exchange-value, the product of highly skilled labor is equivalent, in definite proportions, to the product of simple labor; thus being equated to a certain amount of this simple labor.
>
> The exchange value of a commodity is not expressed in its own use-value, but as materialization of universal social labor-time, the use-value of one commodity is brought into relation with the use-values of other commodities.[4]

A criticism of the homogeneous, socially necessary unit of labor time as a yardstick is the same as the criticism of the efforts in general equilibrium analysis to identify a maximum optimum, or even a unique solution (in chapter 9, see figure 9-4, for example). Assume that the only factors of production, instead of being capital and labor, are two qualities of labor, manual and skilled. Then, depending on the relative demand patterns for the two products, efficient production calls for manual and skilled labor to be combined in varying proportions. One then has the same difficulty in identifying either a unique solution or a maximum as was observed in the case of general equilibrium analysis in chapter 9, figure 9-4. Marx does not have a clear-cut yardstick that can be used to quantify exploitation, either theoretically or practically.

There is another criticism of the labor theory of value, aside from the fact that the socially necessary unit of labor time is a slippery, non-quantifiable concept (and that the value of raw materials cannot be satisfactorily handled).

Involved is the role of accumulating scientific and technological knowledge in influencing the quantity of production. Radovan Richta, a Czech, has pointed out that the influence of improved technology on the quantity of product overshadows the implications involved in trying to add up and homogenize units of labor time. Richta mentions that Marx, even, had argued that "the product of mental labor— science—always stands far below its value, because the labor-time needed to reproduce it had no relation at all to the labor-time required for its original production." Richta goes on to say that "the process of extended reproduction and priority accumulation of capital ceases to be essential for all-round industrial advance."[5]

What is important, according to Richta, is to be in a leadership position in the accumulation of technical knowledge. He grants that the capitalist countries have, in the past, occupied this leadership position but goes on to claim that "the social groundwork capable of carrying out the scientific and technological revolution . . . is to be found in the advance of socialism and communism."

Strange, that Marx, who was prophetically appreciative of the role of technology in some contexts, should have failed to appreciate the power of technology for warping the accuracy of attempts to measure the socially necessary unit of labor time.

Then, in relation to the Marxist argument, there is the additional qualification to the effect that in Western, developed-country economies workers are actually paid more than the cost of reproducing them. (But that is another story and involves the role of labor unions and social legislation such as the minimum wage laws, rather than the inherent characteristics of a purely competitive, laissez-faire economic system.)

Accumulating Surplus and the Reserve Army of the Unemployed

In Marxian theory, the prices or values at which goods are exchanged are presumed to be controlled by the relative amounts of the homogeneous, socially necessary labor time which it took to produce them. And the laborer receives a total wage corresponding to the amount of labor time it took to produce the amount of goods necessary to provide some level of low or customary sustenance to that laborer. This procedure for paying labor tends to produce a surplus when the capitalist sells the product for more than enough to cover the subsistence wage and is in a position which permits appropriating this surplus value for self. The capitalist then reinvests the gains in additional capital and the stock of capital grows and the ability of the economy to produce goods grows.

The wages of labor were kept low because the workers had little bargaining leverage. Marx made the argument stronger: "It follows, therefore, that in proportion as capital accumulates, the lot of the laborer, be his payment high or low, must grow worse."[6]

Marx also argued that the capitalists used their power to discharge workers as their economic positions dictated and thereby generate more and more unemployment, especially in depression phases of the business cycle. Marx was a pioneer analyst of the business cycle. The unemployed constituted an increasing, so-called reserve army of the unemployed, a handy labor pool from the viewpoint of the capitalists. Its existence further increased the leverage of the capitalists in dealing with labor.

The Falling Rate of Profit and Revolution

So, there were supposed to be at least two tendencies pointing to future trouble: falling profit rates and increasing unemployment. Profit rates were falling because productive capacity was rising while purchasing power was lagging. These tendencies were destined to lead to the collapse of the capitalist system. Marx was ambiguous regarding just how this collapse was to come about. Was the "revolution" to involve a violent uprising, or was the system just going to fall apart on its own because capitalists cannot function without profits? "The Communists openly declare that their ends can be attained only by the forcible overthrow of all existing social conditions. Workers of the world unite, you have nothing to lose but your chains." This sounds like a clarion call for violent revolution. But those sentiments were expressed in the *Communist Manifesto* in 1848, not in *Capital* in 1867.

Marx did say in a letter to Weydemeyer in 1852: "What I did that was new was to prove: (1) that the existence of classes is only bound up with particular historical phases in the development of production, (2) that the class struggle necessarily leads to the dictatorship of the proletariat, (3) that this dictatorship only constitutes the transition to the abolition of all classes and to a classless society."[7]

The language of the later *Das Kapital* was much more restrained, and the work ends without describing the process by which the capitalist system is actually supposed to fall. Today, there is a significant contingent of self-styled Marxists who do not believe in definitive revolution at all.

One may wonder, since falling profits and massive unemployment were Marx's explanation of the forces that get the capitalist system into trouble, why the Russians adopted a policy of cold war and repeatedly created international crises following World War II. Such policies kept the United States nervous, stimulated Congress to support heavy military expenditures, generally operated to keep the United States economy active and profitable, and kept the profit rate up and the unemployment rate down. According to the Marxist scenario, such developments would be calculated to save the capitalist system from collapse—hardly a Russian goal.

Another question with regard to the implication of the falling rate of profit is this. Why would a falling *rate* of profit have such a deleterious effect on capitalists since the *total amount* of capital is rising? The possibility would exist that the amount of profit would be larger even though the rate was lower. The question would then become as to which influence was stronger in the long run. Definitive research on this point has not been done.

FIGURE 12-1
Yield on British Consols/Long-Term Government Bonds

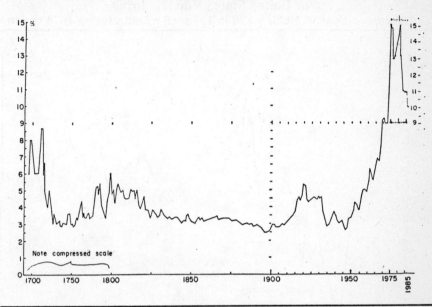

Sources: George F. Warren and Frank A. Pearson, *Prices* (New York: Wiley, 1933); Sidney Homer, *A History of Interest Rates* (New Brunswick, NJ: Rutgers University Press, 1963), pp. 156, 161, 409; International Monetary Fund, *International Financial Statistics, passim.*

Some Statistical Tests on Profit Trends

With regard to the existence of a declining profit rate, it is not possible to obtain the data needed for purposes of testing the trend by using the definition of profits in Marx. At any rate, it is glaringly obvious that Marxists have failed to do so, although the burden of proof should be on those who wish to establish the existence of a secular downward trend in profit rates in the advanced capitalistic countries. Figure 12-1, for example, hardly pictures a long-run trend downward in the yield on British government obligations. And figure 12-2 hardly demonstrates the existence of a secular trend downward in United States corporate profits.

All this is very strange. The sophisticated Marxist argument points to falling profit rates. But much of the indignation of run-of-the-mill Marxists is directed against high profit and interest rates. Marxist dogma gets the capitalist system into trouble because the profit rate is falling, not because it is high or rising. Those who express a concern about high profits may be expressing a very legitimate, but non-Marxist, concern. A lot of self-styled Marxists might not be Marxists at all if they really understood Marx's position on profits and profit trends.

FIGURE 12-2
Percent Return on Net Assets (Worth) After Taxes
For United States Manufacturing
(1,205 corporations in 1925, 2,136 in 1973, all manufacturing 1974 to date)

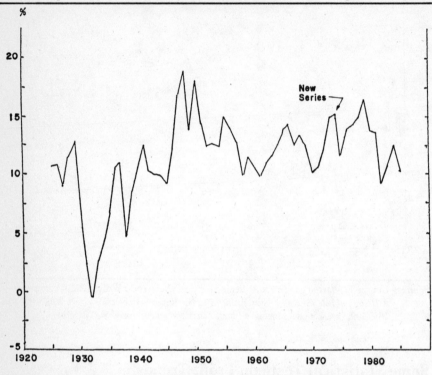

Sources: Citibank, *Monthly Economic Letter; Economic Report of the President* (Annual).

Critique of the Labor Theory of Value and its Consequences

It is true that those in a position of power can appropriate relatively higher returns to themselves. These power positions may be a result of ownership of capital but also they may be a result of control over capital one does not own or a result of the fact that some people are better endowed with the money-making skills called for by the capitalist system than are other people. Marx wasted a good deal of effort unnecessarily trying to construct a logical framework based on assumptions which represented only part of the story.

Marx argued further that the surplus value accruing to the capitalists was used to create an increase in the capital stock. The resulting abundance of capital stock was supposed to result in a secular decline in the profit rate. Apart from the question as to whether the profit rate has declined, there is the question as to whether the gains of those in a position to appropriate relatively higher returns actually use them to increase the capital stock. The wealthy may, certainly, use their gains to finance the accumulation of real capital. They may also use them to finance luxurious consumption, to bid up the price of land and condominiums or to finance inflation, to acquire numbered accounts in Swiss banks, in "building pyramids," or in rearing people who do not live very long.[8] And there may well be other possibilities.

The importance of those different uses of the high returns may vary from culture to culture, institution to institution, and time to time. Relatively great effort may have gone into capital accumulation in Scotland circa 1800, in the American Northeast circa 1900, and in Japan circa 1980. Relatively more funds may have gone into conspicuous consumption, foreign bank balances, and such like uses, in Latin American and other underdeveloped countries over the past hundred years or so.[9]

IMPERIALISM

As early as about 1900, Marxists were elaborating additional arguments to take into account the fact that events were not moving in the manner or as fast as forecast by Marx. The cleavage between the workers and the capitalists was not unambiguously becoming more pronounced. If anything, instead of the economy polarizing into worker and capitalist groups, an unanticipated middle class was growing in relative importance. There was some basis for saying that the standard of living of the mass of the population was rising, at least in the developed countries where the Marxian argument was supposed to be most relevant. Profit rates were not obviously falling as a long-run trend; neither was unemployment rising. There were sporadic depressions, which had been described by Marx, but were they getting worse? Unemployment rates were fluctuating. But were they becoming higher? The supporting evidence was not there.

V. I. Lenin (and others) embellished Marxist theory with international imperialism as an explanation of the delay. That most of the essential ideas in Lenin's 1916 *Imperialism* had already been expressed in the bourgeois John Hobson's 1902 *Imperialism* might suggest that the ideas were not entirely dependent on Marxian logic. Be that as it may, Lenin argued that the capitalists in the capitalistic countries were desperately exporting (a) commodities, because of the low returns from domestic sales, and (b) capital, in the hopes of obtaining higher profit rates abroad. He also argued that the capitalists were using their power to extract raw materials from the backward countries at ruinously low prices and were increasing their profits thereby.

Marx believed that a feature of the capitalist system involved desperate efforts to export more goods in order to maintain profits. This attitude may readily be documented in the *Communist Manifesto:* "The need of a constantly expanding market for its products chases the bourgeoisie over the whole surface of the globe. It must nestle everywhere, settle everywhere, establish connections everywhere. The cheap prices of its exports are the heavy artillery with which it batters down all Chinese walls."[10]

That capitalists export at cheap prices is respectable Marxist doctrine only half the time; and it is "gut reaction" Marxism virtually none of the time. K. Izmailvo probably is speaking for a view more commonly held by emotional, self-styled, poorly indoctrinated Marxists when he says: "The capitalist monopolies sell their products in the underdeveloped countries at very high prices."[11]

For Lenin, the export of capital as distinct from the export of commodities, or at least the allegation of such a distinction, became of dominant importance: "Export of capital as distinguished from export of commodities becomes of particularly great importance."[12] It is clear that he believed that the export of capital was imperative, from the viewpoint of the capitalists, in order to hold up profit rates in the developed countries, which would then have a reduced glut of capital holding down interest and profit rates.

Lenin wrote, on the subject of profit rates: "In these backward countries profits are usually high, for capital is scarce, the price of land is relatively low, wages are low, raw materials are cheap. The necessity for exporting capital (from the developed countries) arises from the fact that in a few countries capitalism has become 'over-ripe,' and, owing to the backward stage of agriculture and the impoverishment of the masses, capital lacks opportunities for 'profitable' investment."[13]

There are several difficulties with this argument. For one thing it is not true that the price of land is relatively low, at least by local standards, in the underdeveloped countries. On the contrary, at least in many of them, there is a high premium on land ownership.

For another thing, Lenin's argument requires that profit rates or interest rates, on the average and in real terms, be higher than in the developed countries. It is by no means certain that this is the situation. Generally, nominal interest rates have been relatively high in underdeveloped countries. After allowance has been made for inflation, however, it is less than clear that real interest rates are higher in the underdeveloped countries, especially after one averages profit and interest rates over all economic activity, including subsistence agriculture, and observes that the rates of return in some areas are abysmally low. Lenin's argument does require speaking of national averages to justify the generalization that the net movement of capital is in a given direction because of the influence of profit-rate considerations.

Also, in the way that Lenin presents the process of foreign investment as "export of capital as distinct from export of goods," there is an implication that capital migrates internationally by magic or immaculate conception. In fact, for a transfer of capital to occur it must be a counterpart of a net goods flow in the direction in which the capital is moving, and the distinction between net goods flows and net capital flows is artificial.

Lenin argued that capitalists were busy exploiting underdeveloped countries by using their power and leverage to extract (a) raw materials and (b) profits from them.

(a) No doubt the capitalist countries have been interested in obtaining raw materials from underdeveloped countries at prices as low as possible. Whether they have been any more anxious to buy them than the underdeveloped countries have been to sell them is much less certain. Of course, the underdeveloped countries have been interested in getting high prices. But there are at least two difficulties in asserting that all this implies exploitation (in the sense of net goods imports) by the developed countries and creates unfavorable price trends for the underdeveloped countries. For one thing, it is not clear that the capitalist countries want to receive net goods imports and run unfavorable balances of trade. Witness the developed-country efforts to use trade restrictions to hold down imports. Developed countries frequently have an obsessive desire for *export* (so-called favorable) not *import* trade balances. Also, if exploitation is viewed as price or terms-of-trade exploitation (as an effort to buy cheap and sell dear), it is not clear that the developed countries have consciously had such a terms-of-trade policy. Export dumping (a practice observed by Marx) has been a common characteristic of the international trade behavior of capitalist countries. So, it is difficult to make a case that there is a systematic effort at terms-of-trade exploitation. Also, such statistical evidence as we have with regard to the long-run movement of the terms of trade is ambiguous about whether there has been a long-run worsening from the viewpoint of the underdeveloped countries.[14]

There is a whole range of rich capitalist country behavior that poor underdeveloped countries can complain about, but this is not what theoretical Marxism is concerned with. (Such behavior includes putting restrictions in the way of the import of textiles, clothing, and shoes from poor countries; overlending to poor countries and then demanding repayment; or, fighting Cold War battles with paid mercenaries on poor country turf.)

THE CLASS STRUGGLE AND THE DIALECTIC
The Class Struggle

The identification by Marx of the institution of private property as the crucial ingredient in the capitalist system implied a class struggle. There were, on the one hand, the capitalists, with the power and leverage that property ownership gave them, and on the other hand, the rest of the population, the proletariat, at a disadvantage because they did not own the tools they needed. Marx made this dichotomy into a "class" distinction. This is not the same distinction as that between a hereditary social elite and the rest of the population. In particular, it is not the differentiation made in nineteenth century England between the nobility and gentry and the rest of the population. The rising group of capitalist-industrialists which Marx set against the workers in the class struggle was actually engaged in bitter contest for hegemony with the nobility and gentry during much of the century. The fight over the repeal of the Corn Laws in the 1840s was one aspect of that conflict of interests. The struggle between capitalists and laborers began before the capitalists had disposed of the gentry.

According to the class struggle argument, the cleavage between the capitalists and the workers was supposed to become ever more polarized as the population was forced to ally with one side or the other. When the final confrontation—which Marx thought was imminent in 1867—actually occurred, the workers would overwhelm the capitalists.

That this did not happen is one of the notable failures of the Marxist argument. If anything, a middle class, not obviously committed to either the capitalists or the workers, gained in importance. This development complicated the evolution toward the anticipated definitive confrontation between capital and labor.

The Dialectic and the Economic Interpretation of History

Marxism has a strong teleological aspect. The Marxian dialectic, which is the core of Marx's theory of history, is teleological in the sense that it involves an argument describing a process that leads to an intended or preordained result. There is design in nature. Ends are immanent in nature. Phenomena are the result of design or purpose beyond human control.

Marx's argument is that, at any given time in a society, a dominant group (the nobility, the bourgeoisie, the Establishment) exploits the rest of the population. This was the thesis of the dialectic argument (thesis, antithesis, synthesis). Then, with the passage of time, the exploited (slaves, serfs, workers, college students) form a nucleus of opposition to the dominant group or elite, and this nucleus of opposition becomes larger and stronger. This development corresponds to the antithesis in the dialectic. Eventually the exploited group becomes strong enough to seize power from and to eliminate the formerly dominant group. Thus, those who had previously been exploited come to be the whole of society. This is the synthesis in the thesis-antithesis-synthesis sequence and the process is the class struggle.

In the standard development of this argument, the synthesis arrived at will become a new thesis against which there will develop a new antithesis, and so on. For Marx this process was, for example, reflected in the argument that the medieval nobility (a thesis) was eventually opposed by a new class of bourgeois capitalists (an antithesis). The bourgeois capitalists eventually took power away from the nobility and became a synthesis, of sorts. But the bourgeois capitalists then became a thesis as worker opposition developed, the workers being the new antithesis.

According to this sequence, the workers would eventually come to dominate and become the new synthesis. At this point the scenario changes and the historical-evolutionary process comes to an end. There is no new thesis and antithesis. The workers (after the dictatorship of the proletariat) establish the ideal society: communism (with a small "c"). This is the promised land, Nirvana, the Garden of Eden, paradise, Utopia. This is the final outcome of natural, historical processes directed to this end. It is not a result that follows from the efforts of well-intentioned people trying to improve society. Marx held in contempt the Utopian socialists who thought they could imagine an ideal society and by reasonable argument induce people to implement such a society. Marx claimed he was describing a process inevitably leading to a result. This is the reason for saying that Marx's argument is teleological. That Marx may also have desired the result in question is presumably beside the point.

What basis is there for changing the nature of the argument at the stage where the workers take over from the capitalists? Why should the dialectic not be repeated? Given human nature, is it overly optimistic to expect that everyone will be happy with the Utopia provided by the workers? How is it going to be determined who does the work, and especially the more demeaning work, in paradise? Who will "wait table?" Who will fix the broken toilets?

There is a hint of an answer to this question in Marx, but it is hard to find. One may argue that he believed that technology will have improved to the extent that it will be possible to provide abundance for all with no trouble. Just why this happy development should occur with timing corresponding to the takeover by the workers is not explained. So, this is an article of faith rather than a proposition with much analytical substance.

A partial explanation is found in the "Critique of the Gotha Program" in 1875: "In a higher phase of communist society, after the enslaving subordination of the individual to the division of labor, . . . after the productive forces have also increased with the all-round development of the individual, and all the springs of co-operative wealth flow more abundantly—only then can the narrow horizon of bourgeois right be crossed in its entirety and society inscribe on its banners: From each according to his ability, to each according to his needs!"[15]

So, there is considerable parallel between the communism of Marxian socialism, the heaven of various religions, and so on. This is a point of difference between classical Marxist socialism and institutional-instrumental theory. The latter theory does not envisage an ideal society that can, now or ever, be described definitively or to which we are evolving. Rather, institutional theory conceives that people's ideas of what is desirable will change as time passes and circumstances change, and nature has no particular interest in the result. A teleological process is not involved.[16]

Another implication of the dialectic is more objectionable. The dialectical argument points to bilateral confrontation and violent revolution in which the antithesis destroys the previous synthesis, the proletariat destroys the bourgeoisie. This violent confrontation is devoutly hoped for and worked for by Marxists in general and latter-day, gut-reaction Marxists in particular, but perhaps, not on the part of the new generation of Marxist intellectuals, some of whom believe that class struggle forever will be more fun. At any rate, *Das Kapital* does not conclude with a ringing: "Long live *violent* revolution." But, almost the last words in the earlier *Communist Manifesto* declare: "The Communists . . . openly declare that their ends can be attained only by the forcible overthrow of all existing social conditions."

Kenneth Boulding has written of this aspect of dialectic process:

A dialectical philosophy, however, whether nationalistic, racist, or Marxist, which stresses victory rather than problem solving, beating down the enemy rather than cooperating with him (and which therefore tends to justify and excuse the immoral behavior which dialectical processes always produce), is likely to intensify the dialectical processes themselves to the point where they will become damaging to all parties, and unfriendly to human welfare and development.[17]

Dichotomizing

The world is not going to be made into an ideal society merely by replacing the capitalists by the workers. In fact, that particular "revolution" is not going to do away with the necessity that somehow somebody has to perform the management function in production operations and in consequence will be occupying a central position that permits the personal appropriation of special perquisites. There is no way the human race is going to solve the problem of special privilege. Dealing with that situation will remain an ongoing struggle after this revolution and after the next one. To be brutally frank about it, there are always going to be ongoing struggles along all the battlelines involving all the different institutions and groups. People will always use what leverage they have to maneuver for an improved position. Better to understand this than to be deluded with the idea that one grand and glorious uprising against capitalists is going to solve all problems permanently.

Instead of trying to dichotomize society into capitalists and workers, a better way to look at the functional relations in modern industry might be synthesized as the "pecking order" approach. The factory has a hierarchy, not a dichotomy. Each worker or employee is located in the hierarchy or in the pecking order in a position where one takes orders from some and gives orders to others. Everyone is resentful of some and resented by others. One is looked on as a benevolent leader by some, but at the same time one is looking up to one's own benevolent leader in the next higher echelon. What is not going on is a polarization process in which the hierarchy is reducing itself gradually to two layers that will then square off and reduce the number of layers to one, and a satisfactory one at that. That scenario is a Marxist pipe dream.

The inherent complexity of industrial society (and of the post-industrial society, if there is such) is enough to guarantee that understanding and trying to reconcile the problems of complicated structure is the essence of policymaking. Forget the tempting mirage of black and white, right and wrong, and no middle ground. No easy solution to our problems will appear in the form of a well motivated rebel storming over some barricade.

CONCLUSION

The Marxist paradigm is overly logical, complicated, and misleading; furthermore, its predictions about the falling rate of profit, the expansion of the reserve army of the unemployed, and increasingly severe business cycles have not been borne out.

Perhaps the well intentioned people of the world, who genuinely desire improvement in the human condition, should realize that we are dealing with the on-going task of making things better in small steps. There are distribution-of-income questions, equity questions, and fairness questions. Capitalists and workers have their interests, but so do shopkeepers, white collar professionals, farmers, government workers, and scientists. Life is full of continuing problems and endless contest over how to resolve them; there is no neat, definitive, and final solution to be had.

NOTES

[1] Karl Marx, *Capital* (3 vols.; Chicago: C. H. Kerr, 1906 [1867ff]), Paul Baran and Paul Sweezy, *Monopoly Capital* (New York: Monthly Review, 1966); Emile Burns, ed., *Handbook of Marxism* (London: Gollancz, 1935); Harry Cleaver, *Reading "Capital" Politically* (Austin: University of Texas Press, 1979); Bertell Ollman, *Alienation* (Cambridge, Eng.: Cambridge University Press, 1971); Joan Robinson, *An Essay on Marxian Economics* (London: Macmillan, 1942); Howard Sherman, *Radical Political Economy* (New York: Basic Books, 1972).

[2] Richard Edwards, Michael Reich, and Thomas E. Weisskopf, *The Capitalist System—A Radical Analysis of American Society* (Englewood Cliffs, N.J.: Prentice-Hall, 1972), p. 89.

[3] Karl Marx and Frederick Engels, *Selected Works* (Moscow: Progress Publishers, 1968), p. 81.

[4] Karl Marx, *Contribution to the Critique of Political Economy* (Moscow: Progress Publishers, 1970 [1859]), pp. 30-31, 38.

[5] Radovan Richta, *Civilization at the Crossroads* (White Plains, New York: International Arts and Sciences Press, 1969), pp. 33, 37, 39, 59.

[6] Karl Marx, *Capital* (Chicago: Encyclopedia Britannica, 1952 [1867]), p. 320.

[7] Marx and Engels, *Selected Works*, p. 679.

[8] Wendell Gordon, *Political Economy of Latin America* (New York: Columbia University Press, 1965), p. 215.

[9] Raúl Prebisch, "Cinco Etapas de mi Pensamiento sobre el Desarrollo," *Comercio Exterior* 37 (May 1987), p. 350.

[10] Karl Marx and Friedrich Engels, *The Manifesto of the Communist Party* (New York: International Publishers, 1948[1848]), pp. 12-13.

[11] K. Izmailvo, *Voprosy Ekonomiki* (September, 1954), p. 96; *Mezhdunarodnaya Torgovlya* (Moscow: Vneshtorgizdat, 1954), p. 359; Academia de Ciencias de la U.R.S.S., *Manual de Economia Politica* (2nd ed.; Mexico: Editorial Grijalbo, 1957), p. 239.

[12] V. I. Lenin, *Imperialism: The Highest Stage of Capitalism* (Revised translation: New York: International Publishers, 1933[1916]), p. 81.

[13] Ibid., p. 58.

[14]Wendell Gordon, *International Trade: Goods, People, and Ideas* (New York: Knopf, 1958), pp. 64-70, and ch. 17, "International Price Relations."

[15]Marx and Engels, pp. 324-5.

[16]It is not certain that Veblen would agree with this interpretation of teleology. See Thorstein Veblen, *Veblen on Marx, Race, Science, and Economics* (New York: Capricorn Books, 1969), pp. 75-76. The material is a reprint of the article: "Why is Economics Not an Evolutionary Science?," *Quarterly Journal of Economics XII* (July 1898).

[17]Kenneth E. Boulding, *A Primer on Social Dynamics* (New York: Free press, 1970), pp. vi-viii.

Part III

Applications

Chapter XIII

Research Methods

Institutional or evolutionary economics consists of a theory of economic change, a value theory, and implications for research, planning, and policy. Research, planning, and policy applications may take many forms. In fact an important consideration is that they not be forced into a stylized mold. Despite this implication of flexibility, which derives from the nature of the institutional value theory itself, it is desirable to try, in some degree, to indicate the nature of institutionalism's handling of problems.

First, there are three areas for research which involve somewhat different research methods: (1) study of the behavior patterns of institutions, (2) study of the working out of the institutional response to the appearance of a new technology, and (3) the analysis of policy making.

THE STUDY OF INSTITUTIONAL BEHAVIOR

The Problem

A typical industry study, in the form now prevailing in the scholarly journals, might involve an effort to determine the relation between the degree of industrial concentration and the percentage of domestic consumption (of, say, cement) which is imported. The degree of concentration in several domestic marketing areas may be estimated and statistical correlations computed as to the percentage of each market served by imports. The conclusion may be reached that: "Import share rises with increasing concentration. This is predicted by theory and confirmed by our empirical investigation."[1] Yet, the reader may be left wondering. How many of these firms are operating in more than one domestic market and also operating overseas? Which are the large cement companies anyway and how do they relate to each other? What is the nature of the institutionalized understandings that exist among the dominant firms as to appropriate behavior? How would one react to a study of the oil industry that uses this methodology and never

195

mentions OPEC, and which concluded: "Import share rises with increasing concentration. This is predicted by theory and confirmed by our empirical investigation." Is not a study somehow incomplete that does not take institutionalized behavior into account?

What are the problems when one attempts to do this?

There are difficulties in identifying institutionalized behavior norms. One can do justice (or half justice) to an institution's governance of behavior only after living with the institution for a long time and observing its influence on behavior under many circumstances. Yet those who have lived with an institution long enough to have this sort of insight may feel a degree of loyalty to the institution that prevents their being objective about much of what the institution does. They feel such a loyalty or they should not likely have remained with the organization. If one knows enough about an institution to write wisely about it, one will not, except in some circumstances, expose its inner mechanisms. Denouements by insiders (or, more likely, former insiders who have had a falling-out) will usually reflect special pleadings or personal spleen rather than accurate reporting. A scholar, working from the outside, may get at the truth by obtaining special pleadings from various parties involved and then engaging in judicious questioning and weighing. This was the method of the Ervin Committee of the United States Senate in studying the workings of the White House in connection with the Watergate episode in 1973. Meaningful study of cartel practices was made possible by insider disclosures in the early years of World War II. Walton Hamilton's *Price and Price Policies* and George Stocking and Myron Watkins's *Cartels in Action* are models of what can be done with the information made available under such special circumstances.[2]

In rare cases conditions may make it feasible for the investigator to pursue an inquiry in an impersonal manner; but, in most circumstances, this is not possible. Most of the time it is impossible for the outsider or scholar to get a real feel for the workings of an institution.

Competent, muckraking reporting in the tradition of Ida Tarbell, Lincoln Steffens and, more recently, Anthony Sampson in some degree fills the gap.[3]

Professional economists should try to do more probing of institutions in a responsible way. Be the difficulties as they may, the study of the behavior patterns of institutions should be the meat and drink of economics (and of sociology and the other social sciences). Understanding the behavior patterns of institutions should be helpful in the formulation of public policy. And the complexities of institutional patterns are not grasped by reasoning from a simplistic profit motive assumption. Nor is intelligent understanding of oil industry behavior gotten from models which relate a certain change in the price of crude to a resultant effect on the discovery of new petroleum reserves. A ten percent rise in the price of crude may be predicted by the model to result in an increase in crude reserves of thirteen percent. Such models abounded in the middle 1970s as the economics profession's spontaneous reaction to the oil crisis. The profession used the analytical tools it had, but those tools were not appropriate.

Behavior in the oil industry may, not too unfairly, be belabored a bit more. The oil industry is an example of an industry with some rather stridently expressed, and internally inconsistent, behavior norms. On the one hand there is a frequently expressed, chest-beating display of self reliance and the demand that the government leave the industry alone to make profits. On the other hand there has been the fostering by the industry of a level of government regulation of production which has extended to specifying how much oil can be produced from each well during each month. The industry has always briskly claimed that the risks involved in the oil industry justified special tax treatment by the government in the form of depletion allowances that were larger than those granted to most minerals. It is not enough to be self-reliant. The oilman or oilwoman is entitled to a reward for self-reliance. Also the industry has been quite capable in certain circumstances of demanding governmental regulation of the international trade in oil by the use of tariffs, quotas, and other devices.

Probably the quaintest institutionalized behavior norm in the oil industry is the proposition that ownership of oil is established by the same "rule of capture" that has been applied to establish the title of the individual landowner (who shoots a rabbit while it is crossing through the landowner's property, or the hunter who shoots a deer on land he has leased) to the dead animal. If you can pump the oil out from under your neighbor's land, it is yours.

Agriculture is another example of an industry that blows hot and cold on the matter of government regulation. During periods of falling and low agricultural prices (for example, 1985, 1986, 1987), the industry, with a mighty voice, demands that the government do something about low prices. In periods of high and rising prices the government is a burden that should get off the farmers' backs and let the market work. The shortness of farmer memories as to whether or not they want the government to concern itself with farming is matched only by the ability of their city cousins to be equally opportunistic. Ask any city-bred individualist whether the government should fix potholes in the street and whether it should tax people to do it.

There are other aspects of the farm culture that influence production in ways not commonly captured by standard price theory. Farmers may believe in timing planting by the phases of the moon, the appropriate days of the month, or the shaman's blessing. There may be some real merit in planting during the appropriate phase of the moon. Or such practices may epitomize ignorance. Are you sure you know? Maybe the chief problem with rain dances used to be that they did not make enough noise. It always rains toward the end of open-air rock concerts. Or does it?

A standard proposition in price theory is that producers react to falling demand by reducing prices and quantity of production. That is the necessary implication of the upward–sloping–to–the–right supply curves that are necessary if the standard price theory demand and supply equilibrium story is to work out. Yet, there is considerable evidence that producers in many situations react to falling demand by raising prices. The line of thinking of the producer is that, with falling demand, for gross receipts and profits to be held up, prices must rise. This will work if the conviction of the businessperson that the demand for one's own product is inelastic is correct. There is considerable evidence, for example, that over the history of the steel industry in the United States this has been a standard behavior pattern. Steel industry people believe the demand for steel is inelastic whether it is or not. The extent to which this sort of thing goes on can be checked fairly effectively by economists with information that is frequently in the public domain.

There is a quotation from Kenneth Boulding which runs:

> I have argued for years that bankers were a savage tribe who should
> be studied by the anthropologists rather than by the economists, and
> I once tried to persuade Margaret Mead to do a book on "Coming of
> Age in the Federal Reserve," with, I regret to say, no response at
> all! The culture of bankers, indeed, is more mysterious than that of
> the Dobuans or the Chuk-Chuks. The Navaho indeed may have a
> Harvard anthropologist in every family, but the Federal Reserve Board
> has, to my knowledge, never allowed a single one to attend the cere-
> monials in its marble hogan. Nobody really knows what bankers are
> like, what kinds of images of the world they have, what they talk
> about, what kind of gossip they follow, what taboos they have, and
> how their decisions are made. The economics of money and banking
> is almost entirely a matter of the analysis of published statistics and
> the attempt to find correlations among them. It is pure "black box"
> analysis with practically no attempt to pry off the lid to see what are
> the actual processes which produce the often very peculiar outputs.[4]

Any enterprise or industry will have its idiosyncrasies. How does the "good old boy" network work? Or is there a "good old boy network" where the fraternity brothers and kinfolk or whatever, look after each other? Maybe instead, the institutional climate involves mutual distrust and callous efforts to upstage one's peers, and a climate of secrecy and maneuvering prevails. Or maybe the setting is one featuring "the good life," camaraderie, and even some promiscuity. Or maybe the setting emphasizes stodgy respectability, with or without a skeleton in the chest. Maybe loyalty to the firm prevails; maybe the setting is permeated with friction between the workers and management. Maybe the guiding attitude is 8 to 5 and let us get out of here as fast as we can when the whistle blows, perhaps trampling on a few dawdling customers on the way to the door. Maybe the company enjoys a reservoir of goodwill with the employees, maybe not. Maybe a work setting is pleasant, maybe churlishness prevails, or maybe sexual innuendo abounds.

The enterprise may hire all kinds of efficiency experts to snoop around and then make reports suggesting ways to improve productivity. Maybe some of the suggestions are appropriate, and are implemented graciously and successfully; maybe they are resented and matters are worse. Efficiency experts may rub people the wrong way, or they may be glib and innocuous, or they may be pleasantly helpful, or they may come around too often. Psychologists may aid in the understanding of problem situations with useful results. Or the psychologist may have internal psychological hangups to a degree that places that person in the wrong profession.

Some of the employees may be getting a free ride or a free lunch, without management apparently knowing or caring. Others may do more than their share of the work, without management showing any appreciation of the situation. Or management may have a reputation for trying to be evenhanded in these matters.

Economists could well make more use of the insights of anthropology, sociology, psychology, and political science as they try to understand better the behavior of economic institutions. Analysis based on an oversimplified assumption that "effort to maximize" profits or individual income can explain or motivate behavior may lead to wrong answers—even though "the effort to gain higher profits" actually is an important and highly institutionalized influence in the economy, but only one among many.

How can one conduct research on the behavior norms of institutions, especially when one is approaching the problem without prior knowledge of the workings of the institution? As a preliminary step one can read as much as is available about the institution. Working, at least for a time, in the company, or agency, or industry, if feasible, will be helpful. Sample questionnaires may be used; however, the difficulties involved in preparing the questions, selecting the sample, extracting the responses, and then evaluating them may well be considerable. Such activity is an art or a profession, or both, involving a knack of a very high order. And the questionnaire procedure should not be used unless one understands the difficulties.

Interviewing members of the institution is an obvious, but not necessarily easy, procedure. Introductions to the "right" people may not come easily, and such people may or may not respond to a direct request for an interview. One can request permission from high-level officials to look at the "books" or to interview the personnel, although the chances are extremely good that an economist will be denied permission to look at accounts or records which are at all sensitive. An economist working for a congressional committee, or for a prestigious research organization such as the Brookings Institution or the National Bureau of Economic Research, may have better luck—or worse. It may well take a subpoena before the congressional committee can get access. The recipient of a substantial research grant may use that as leverage. But, after all is said and done, some people are just naturally better at this sort of investigation than are others.

It is a mystery how Wassily Leontief obtained access to corporate accounts in the early days of his work with input-output matrices. Perhaps the corporate realization that Leontief was not muckraking may have helped. But, when economists give adequate assurance to the corporation that they will not rake muck they may also pretty well have gutted the usefulness of their research.

In any case, one is looking for indications of standardized behavior and indications that the institution will respond in some particular way in a given situation. The loan officer of a bank spontaneously reacts negatively to loans in a certain part of town or to certain types of people. During a certain period, society's favorite cliché is "separate but equal"—the more separate and the less equal the better. Or we may find a setting where the members really choose to believe that "there is no such thing as a free lunch," and act accordingly. Some such behavioral regularities may be of a type that can be picked up by regression analysis, but most are not—or are identified as well or better by direct observation.

Example: An Academic Department

In general, the program offered the undergraduate major in economics is designed to prepare the student to become a graduate major rather than a good citizen. It does not matter that most students are not going on to graduate school and that most of what matters in economics is independent of calculus and matrix algebra, constant coefficients, and multiequation models. The esoteric price theory and national income theory courses, frequently required as a prerequisite to other advanced courses, involve levels of mathematical and geometrical sophistication which are not required to make the worthwhile points. Such courses do provide useful methodology if one is going on to graduate theory courses of an equally sterile type. As a result, the undergraduate major with a real concern for society and an abhorrence for artificial mathematical models runs from economics like the plague.

One of the stranger aspects of this process is the role of the younger faculty members in insisting on increasing the requirements involving the more abstruse theory at both the undergraduate and graduate levels. The more interesting aspect of this operation is not the ability of the young to wield power in such decision making but, at least in economics, their insistence on making the degree program standardized, esoteric, and highly mathematical and theoretical (just like it was back at the prestige graduate school from which they came).

The attitude of the young in insisting on the requirement of some pretty sterile theory in degree programs may be explained somewhat as follows. Young Ph.D.'s have a major stake in the methodology to which they were exposed as they struggled for their Ph.D.'s. We have a vested interest in what we know. What else are we equipped to teach? So, young Ph.D.'s react by believing everybody else should undergo an initiation that is painful and involves the same hazing techniques they survived. Also, for their own self-respect, they have an interest in proving that what they know is not useless. So, there results a situation where, to some degree, it is the oldsters who, these days, are the chief defenders of a liberal curriculum—a curriculum that will permit the student a respectable range of experimentation in searching out problem areas that seem important and in developing methods of research appropriate to the problem. A less complimentary explanation of the oldsters' behavior is that they do not understand the new, sophisticated methodology. They are the ones avoiding the new.

Example: International Banking

Jack M. Guttentag and Richard Herring have compiled a list of the institutionalized behavior norms that led the international bankers to overlend to the underdeveloped countries during the 1970s and early 1980s. Disaster myopia on the part of the bankers is alleged to involve a situation where prudent decision makers are driven from the market because "a bank that attempts to charge an appropriate default premium for low-probability hazards is likely to lose business to banks that are willing to disregard the hazard"; cognitive dissonance "is a psychological mechanism designed to protect the decision-maker's self-esteem when information arises that casts doubt on the wisdom of past decisions"; inadequate analysis of covariances involves failure to appreciate that, although each loan in isolation might appear safe, there was a systematic linkage among the loans which meant that when trouble started it was likely to mushroom; the short-leash fallacy involves the perception that if the loans involve short maturities they are likely to be safe; "the practice of pricing syndicated country loans on the floating-rate basis is a practice that *seems* to transfer interest rate risk from bank lenders to country borrowers"; and misemphasis on accounting values involves confusion between accounting values and "true economic values."[5]

THE STUDY OF THE TECHNOLOGY-INSTITUTIONS INTERRELATION

The Problem

A case study in the field of institutionalism might involve (1) identification of a major technological discovery, (2) discussion of the reaction of those controlling the prevailing institutional arrangements as they become aware of the possible implications of the new development (this being the, so-called, initial reaction to the "technological imperatives"), (3) discussion of the process by which the new technology was allowed to become operational or of the influences that may have frustrated its use, and (4) identification of the institutional changes that occur as a result of the introduction of the new technology. If the introduction of the new technology aborts in step (3), there, obviously, is no step (4).

The information that is needed for conducting such studies is difficult to come by. The identification of technological change and the appreciation of its significance in the context of the general sweep of the history of technology are not tasks for which economists are particularly well qualified. Nevertheless, major technological changes have such an impact that, at least, a particular important discovery may be fairly readily identified: the internal combustion engine, or the vacuum tube, or the computer chip. With a particular technology in mind, economists should be able to learn enough about it from the scientific and technological literature and from history of science material so that they will not "accidentally" reveal themselves later as practical ignoramuses.

A reading of the history of some major inventions may help to give a feel for the starting point in this process. Most of us, after a little meditation, can identify ways in which various of these inventions have modified institutions, affected our lives, and influenced economic attitudes.[6]

A real effort is called for on the part of economists to understand the implications of the technique involved in the industries they are studying. The uniqueness of each invention and the study of the implications should not be swept under the rug by economists making use of assumptions such as the concept of the homogeneity of capital. This cavalier attitude toward the uniqueness of each discovery is observable in neoclassical growth models which involve simply assuming that technology has quantity but not quality and accumulates at a constant percentage growth rate. The discussion of the influences that stimulate the innovation, again, involves penetration by the investigator of the inner workings of the institution. In this case, however, the difficulties involved in getting the facts and identifying the influences may be ameliorated by the fact that, after the event, the successful innovator may like to talk. This is a starting point, even though some double checking is in order. At least, one has an allegation to check which is probably checkable. This is not always the case in connection with the identification of the static behavior norms of an institution, especially when one of those norms may be on the borderline of legality.

Identification of the institutional changes and the new institutions that come into being as a result of the new technology is likely to involve a mixture of some pretty obvious developments with some others where the cause and effect relation, although important, may not be quite so obvious. Who was trying to freeze out whom in arguments over patent rights? Who was really entitled to claim priority in the discovery? Who makes the money, and as a result of what maneuver, and who gets left? The innovation may have deleterious effects. Who gets blamed?

The effect of new technology (supertankers resulting in oil spills) on the ecology (coastlines and wildlife) is an example of the early impact of new technology. The Wilderness Society and the Sierra Club are institutions with behavior norms calculated to protect nature from the impact of new technology. These are institutions called into being by the influence of technical change on ecology, but they are not designed to foster the technology.

An obvious, but important, example of the effect of new technology on institutional organization involves the internal combustion motor and the development of suburban shopping centers.

Another example of the effect of new technology on institutionalized arrangements involves the radio and television.[7] It is not merely that the radio and television have supplanted conversation—however much or little of that there may have been on the front porch in the evening in earlier times. There is a wholly different dimension in terms of what is being bought and sold for what. It is not that the listeners and viewers, for the most part, are paying a price for a program that they want to hear or see. The listeners and viewers are not paying anything for the programs. They have probably paid for the radio set or the television set, but the manufacturers and merchandisers of quite unrelated products who hope that the captive and unhappy audiences, anxious to block out the advertisements, can be enticed into buying the products that have no substantive relation to the program. This is, to put it mildly, a strange market and a strange demand and supply interrelation. One might say that the broadcasts themselves are externalities so far as this market process is concerned.

The Industrial Revolution

The Industrial Revolution itself may be looked on as a case study in the technology-institutions interrelation. It began in northwestern Europe, and more particularly in northern England and southern Scotland during the eighteenth century. The major technological advances that were prime movers in initiating the process included in the background: gunpowder, printing, Arabic numerals and the concept of zero, paper, eyeglasses, the casting of iron, the astrolabe and the magnetic compass, the mechanical clock, and Viking ships with keels and the sternpost rudder capable of sailing the open ocean, and not to forget the lowly screw. In the foreground the major discoveries were (a) Newton's physics, (b) Darby's coke, (c) Watt's steam engine, and (d) the major inventions in spinning and weaving, beginning with John Kay's flying shuttle about 1733.[8]

These inventions did not all occur in northern England and southern Scotland, but they were put together there into the Industrial Revolution. Why there, instead of somewhere else? Why then, instead of some other time? An attempt to answer requires backtracking in history to explain why English institutions were less resistant to change than were the institutions of other areas which were technically at least as advanced as England at the time. The attempt to answer also involves consideration of the relative availability of the appropriate neutral stuff (resources).

The older civilizations which were the prime repositories of the technological knowledge of the world in the fifteenth century, Italy, Byzantium, China, India, the Arab-Islamic area, were also operating under the dead hand of powerful, ancient institutionalized constraints: the Catholic Church in Italy, the Eastern church (until the 1450s), the Koran around half the Mediterranean, the system of writing in China, the Inquisition in Spain (by the sixteenth century), Hinduism in India.

England, as a frontier region which had been part of the Roman Empire (and had had fairly free access to the technology of the civilized ancient world), had not evolved into a highly stylized culture, set in its ways, by the fifteenth century. "A frontier is a greater breeder of ingenuity."[9] And the Protestant Reformation of the sixteenth century, even more, freed northwestern Europe in general and England in particular from the institutionalized behavior patterns, fortified by the Inquisition, that were stymieing development in southern Europe.

Thanks to one of the provisions of the Magna Carta, England was, by the later Middle Ages, one of the largest areas in the world that was substantially free of internal trade barriers. In the 1500s the English Merchants of the Staple had succeeded in wresting control of England's trade from the German merchants of the Hanseatic League. England was taking positive measures to attract technical knowledge by overtly hiring foreign artisans. At the same time potential rivals Spain and France were rejecting skilled labor. In Spain there occurred the expulsion of the Jews in 1492, and in France the massacre of the Huguenots in 1572. Another favorable factor for England was the fact that her trade policy featured an *export* tariff on raw wool, to encourage woolen textile manufacture in England (it is strange that more modern countries desiring to develop have not featured export barriers on raw commodities; instead they have generally used import barriers against manufactured goods. The export tariff on raw materials favors the country's standard of living during the transition period. The import tariff on manufacturers is detrimental to the standard of living during the transition period.)

Then too, during the period from 1500 to 1750, the enclosure movement freed a substantial labor supply for work in the factories. This is by no means the whole story as to the pros and cons of the enclosure movement, but . . . .

At all events, by the eighteenth century, English industry was receptive to the implementation of new technology in the textile industry. England was not straightjacketed into prevailing practices in the manner that the Inquisition was fostering across the Channel.

The humidity of the climate of Manchester, a city in northwest England, created a natural advantage that encouraged the location of spinning and weaving in the city. The moist air made it easier to control cotton fibers during production. It is important to have raw materials and natural conditions peculiarly appropriate to the needs of the evolving new knowledge. So, readily available coal and iron also facilitated the English development.

The institutions that evolved to permit effective use of the technology of the Industrial Revolution were (1) the corporate form of business organization, allowing limited liability of owners and consequently the tapping of the "savings" of large numbers of people, (2) the factory system, a not unmixed blessing,[10] (3) commercial banks, constrained somewhat by central banks, and the power to create money against fractional reserves, and (4) the conceptions of free competition and laissez faire (keep the government out of business) as the appropriate machinery for managing and running the economy. The (5) profit motive itself may be visualized as an institutionalized arrangement that acquired its present role and meaning in influencing the behavior of people as a by-product of the pressures and needs created by the technological developments of the Industrial Revolution.

The most important new phenomenon was probably (6) the industrial city, with its transportation problems, its ghettos, and its filth. Institutional arrangements that were forced into retirement included the guild system and the putting-out system. Cottage industry and the rural farmer-artisan, to whom handicraft work had been "put out," lost importance. "By-employments" became less available to country dwellers. And the nature of family life changed drastically as the worker, often a child, instead of being employed at home, or nearby, customarily left home for a very long day to work in the factory. The nature of family and home life was substantially transformed. The factory, an institution quite apart from the home, became a major part of life. Its smoke, and its great fires, and its grime and din produced a very different sort of condition than had existed with cottage industry, although the "deserted village" was probably not as idyllic as Oliver Goldsmith claimed. Surely, the twelve, fourteen, and sixteen hour working days in the factories were no fun.

The rise of the industrialists to power in England between 1750 and 1850 was strenuously resisted by the land-based nobility. One manifestation of this contest between the entrenched interests of the landlords (the nobility) and the rising industrial class was the struggle over the repeal of the Corn Laws, tariffs protecting British-grown grain from the competition of imported grain. The industrialists wanted cheap imported grain to lower the price of bread so they could pay their workers less (as Ricardo assured them would be possible if they could get the tariffs on grain repealed). The landlords resisted the loss of their tariff protection with tenacity and perseverance, but in the 1840s they lost the battle.

Mining the Ocean Floor and the Law of the Sea

Techniques have been developed that will permit mining the deep ocean floor for minerals such as manganese, nickel, and cobalt. Mining companies are interested in knowing what the rules will be that will control such mining. They are also interested in influencing what those rules will be. United States mining companies would like rules fairly similar to the rules that applied to staking mining claims in the Old West in the United States. Ownership titles to the ocean floor have not yet been formalized, so the companies cannot yet talk about the sanctity of property rights with the almost religious zeal expressed in defending property rights domestically in the United States.

Also there are other interests at stake. Landlocked countries such as Bolivia and Switzerland would like to share in the proceeds from the ocean wealth. They are most reluctant to see countries that accidentally have long seacoasts, such as Chile, get most of the gain. Bolivia is especially emotional on this issue because Chile took a good deal of Pacific coast from Bolivia as a result of the War of the Pacific back in the nineteenth century.

At all events it is clear that these new technologies, permitting mining the deep ocean, call for new institutionalized behavior norms to guide the process.

In response to this need there has been a series of international conferences in which the participating governments have attempted to formulate a new legal code to control the ownership and exploitation of the ocean.[11]

The process of drafting new rules is not easy. The old rules involving three mile limits, and ten mile limits, and even 200 mile limits do not deal with the problem. The whole open ocean is involved. The general rule calling for the free right to sail the open seas and even narrow straits connecting large bodies of water does not deal with the new issues either.

So, as a result of the series of conferences a proposed draft treaty was drawn up and was ready for submission to national governments for possible adoption by 1980. But the whole matter was thrown into limbo, when the Reagan administration objected to the proposed arrangements. It seems that United States mining companies thought they were not given enough freedom of action in staking binding claims *early in the process* to much of the ocean floor. The treaty provided for an international consortium to control who could mine where, to regulate the marketing process, and to see to it that the gains were divided generally, including among countries without seacoasts. All this, the advocates of free private enterprise, who permeated the Reagan administration, found offensive.

So, it is difficult to establish the new rules. Especially, United States insistence on its view has inhibited worldwide consensus. But there will be some new rules eventually. Too much gain is involved. After the next (or the one after) international alarm that the world supply of minerals is about to run out, there will be action on this front. Perhaps rules will be established as a result of meaningful international cooperation, perhaps rules will be established as a result of the arbitrary action of the powerful.

THE ANALYSIS OF POLICY MAKING

Then there is the analysis of policy making. That matter is important enough to be the concern of the next two chapters.

NOTES

[1]David I. Rosenbaum and Steven L. Reading, "Market Structure and Import Share: A Regional Market Analysis," *Southern Economic Journal* 54 (January 1988), pp. 694-700, and esp. p. 699.

[2]See as examples of studies of institutional behavior: Walton Hamilton, *Price and Price Policies* (New York: McGraw-Hill, 1938); John D. McDonald, *The Game of Business* (Garden City, New York: Doubleday, 1975); Gustavus Myers, *History of the Great American Fortunes* (New York: Modern Library, 1936 [1970]); Michael Maccoby, *Gamesman* (New York: Simon and Schuster, 1976); Edward S. Herman, *Corporate Control, Corporate Power* (Cambridge, England: Cambridge University Press, 1981). Adolf A. Berle, *The Modern Corporation and Private Property* (New York: Macmillan, 1933); George W. Stocking and Myron W. Watkins, *Cartels in Action* (New York: Twentieth Century Fund, 1946); Jane Knodell, "Open Market Operations: Evolution and Significance," *Journal of Economic Issues* XXI (June 1987), pp. 691-699; Kozo Yamamura, "Caveat Emptor: The Industrial Policy of Japan," in Paul R. Krugman, ed., *Strategic Trade Policy and the New International Economics* (Cambridge, MA: MIT Press, 1986), pp. 169-209. Much such writing involves practical common sense on the part of people who are quite unaware of institutionalism.

[3]Ronnie Dugger, *Our Invaded Universities: Form, Reform, and New Starts* (New York: Norton, 1974); Joseph Lincoln Steffens, *The Shame of the Cities* (New York: P. Smith, 1948 [1904]); Ida M. Tarbell, *The History of the Standard Oil Company* (New York: Macmillan, 1925 [1904]); Anthony Sampson, *The Sovereign State of ITT* (New York: Stein and Day, 1973); Anthony Sampson, *The Money Lenders: Bankers and a World in Turmoil* (New York: Viking, 1981).

[4]Kenneth Boulding, "Toward the Development of a Cultural Economics," *Social Science Quarterly* 53 (September 1972), p. 270.

[5]Jack M. Guttentag and Richard Herring, "Commercial Bank Lending to Developing Countries . . . ," in Gordon W. Smith and John T. Cuddington, eds., *International Debt and the Developing Countries* (Washington: World Bank, 1985), pp. 129-150.

[6]Michael Bliss, *The Discovery of Insulin* (Chicago: University of Chicago Press, 1982); James D. Watson, *Double Helix* (New York: New American Library, 1968); Daniel J. Boorstin, *The Discoverers* (New York: Random House, 1983).

[7]Stewart L. Long, "Technological Change and Institutional Response: The Creation of American Broadcasting," *Journal of Economic Issues* XXI (June 1987), pp. 743-749.

[8]C. E. Ayres, *The Theory of Economic Progress* (Chapel Hill: The University of North Carolina Press, 1944), ch. VII; see also, A. E. Musson, ed., *Science, Technology, and Economic Growth in the Eighteenth Century* (London: Methuen, 1972), esp. p. 40: and Joseph Needham, *The Grand Titration* (Toronto: University of Toronto Press, 1969); Arnold Toynbee, *Lectures on the Industrial Revolution of the Eighteenth Century in England* (2nd ed.; London: Rivingtons, 1887 [1884]); Harry Elmer Barnes, *An Economic History of the Western World* (New York: Harcourt, Brace, 1935).

[9]C. E. Ayres, *The Industrial Economy* (Boston: Houghton Mifflin, 1952), p. 74.

[10]Charles Dickens, *Martin Chuzzlewit:* "Bethink yourselves . . . that there are scores of thousands breathing now, and breathing thick with painful toil, who . . . have never lived at all, nor had a chance of life. Go ye . . . teachers of content and honest pride, into the mine, the mill, the forge, the squalid depths of deepest ignorance, and uttermost abyss of man's neglect, and say can any hopeful plant spring up in air so foul that it extinguishes the soul's bright torch as fast as it is kindled." John Stuart Mill: "It is doubtful if all the mechanical inventions yet made have lightened the day's toil of a single human being." *Principles of Political Economy* (6th ed.; London: Longmans, Green, 1904 [1848]), p. 455.

[11]Tom Alexander, "The Reaganites' Misadventure at Sea," *Fortune* 106 (Aug. 23, 1982), pp. 128-144; Elisabeth Mann Borgese, "The Law of the Sea," *Scientific American* 248 (March 1983), pp. 42-49; *New Directions in the Law of the Sea*, 2 vols. (Dobbs Ferry, NY: Oceana Publ., 1973); Bernard H. Oxman and L. O. Buderi, eds., *Law of the Sea: U.S. Policy Dilemma* (San Francisco: Institute for Contemporary Studies, 1983); Norman J. Padelford, *Public Policy for the Use of the Seas* (Cambridge: MIT Press, 1970).

Chapter XIV

Policy Making, Choice, and Planning

This discussion will probably not offer fully satisfactory answers as to how to make policy. Nevertheless, it is worthwhile to go over the matter.

SOCIAL DECISION-MAKING PROCESSES

Types

The following catalog of possible processes has five items: The first four are the oft-repeated items in Kenneth Arrow's list,[1] (1) voting, (2) the market mechanism, (3) dictatorship, and (4) convention. An added possibility might be called (5) osmosis, or ongoing interaction. It involves the technology-institutions interaction process of institutionalism combined with the self-correcting value judgment process of instrumentalism.

Perhaps readers are already convinced that the market mechanism, although it may play, and in fact does play, an important role, is not a desirable final arbiter. Perhaps also they are willing to rule out dictatorship. Then, in the Arrow schema, one is left with a mixture of democratic voting process and convention, that is, democratic process plus habit and tradition (which is to say institutionalized behavior). We are not going to improve anything by following the precepts of habit and tradition. So, the choices, *in the Arrow setup*, reduce to the innumerable options as to how the democratic voting process may be arranged, and there is, in addition, ongoing interaction.

Inconsistent Choices in Voting (Arrow)

An example of the problem involved in making logically consistent choices via the voting process involves Arrow's (or Condorcet's, circa 1785) paradox of voting:

A natural way of arriving at the collective preference scale would be to say that one alternative is preferred to another if a majority of the community prefer the first alternative to the second, i.e., would choose the first over the second if those were the only two alternatives. Let A, B, and C be the three alternatives, and 1, 2, and 3 the three individuals. Suppose individual 1 prefers A to B and B to C (and therefore A to C), individual 2 prefers B to C and C to A (and therefore B to A), and individual 3 prefers C to A and A to B (and therefore C to B). Then a majority prefer A to B, and a majority prefer B to C. . . . If the community is to be regarded as behaving rationally, we are forced to say that A is preferred to C. But in fact a majority of the community prefer C to A [count them]. So the method just outlined for passing from individual to collective tastes fails to satisfy the condition of rationality, as we ordinarily understand it.[2]

Arrow has not proven that the democratic voting process should be abandoned because of its inability to guarantee a consistent solution. He has merely demonstrated that democracy is a somewhat more subtle process than pure logic in this form can encompass. It is likely that Arrow would now say that his subsequent thirty, or so, years of effort to make mathematical, general-equilibrium-type sense out of this paradox leaves the matter pretty much where it was in 1951.

One may agree with Arrow about the possibility of getting inconsistent results out of a succession of majority votes on a group of interrelated issues. Probably most of us have participated in public assemblies functioning under Robert's Rules of Order and have seen the parliamentary procedures work out in a sequence of events that makes it impossible for the group ever to vote on some issue in the form in which we would really like to see the vote taken. We vote on an alternative choice. We make our choice by a majority vote, and we go home and grumble.

Perhaps we find that, after all, we can live with the imperfect result of the majority vote. It turns out not to have mattered too much. Or perhaps it does matter, and we try again, perhaps even effecting a change in the procedural rules (doing something about the congressional seniority system, for example) in the meantime. Often, the result after the next hassle is, we believe, better.

There are more important difficulties with the democratic process than Arrow's demonstration of the possibility of inconsistent results. Especially there is the frequency of erratic, capricious, and arbitrary action. But dictatorship is even more likely to generate erratic, capricious, and arbitrary action.

The problem with the democratic process is to make it work in a manner the people can halfway respect, not to make it always regurgitate consistent results or theoretically precise maxima or optimal growth paths. Imperfect as the democratic process may be, it is the best we have, and it is the best we are likely to have. Also, it is a process permitting many variations. Improvement is an ongoing possibility. We do not, once and for all, devise an ideal world by a succession of national majority votes. We are not going to devise a definitive ideal world. Period! Arrow is correct about isolated episodes, but it does not matter. We are not talking about isolated episodes, we are talking about ongoing process.

Democracy is a process that permits popular, peaceful participation in the rule-changing process. It may be a muddled process, but it is not a static logical exercise.

Who Can Vote

Judgments as to who can vote (or who can control) are social decisions being made and reconsidered in the self-correcting value judgment process. The most influential parties in this process at any given time are those who already have the vote (or the leverage or power). The dead and the unborn are only heard from through those proxy variables: the relatively influential living. Of course, all of the living are not particularly influential either. Issues such as the appropriate minimum voting age remain. There may be other limitations on the vote, such as lack of property ownership, of failure to pay a poll tax, or race, or status as a convicted criminal. Large segments of the population may be intimidated, or bribed, by the power structure. One may make a value judgment that some who do not have the vote should have it. Perhaps the voting age should be eighteen instead of twenty-one. Concerned people may argue the pros and cons. One argument for giving the young the vote may not be that they are exploited without representation so much as that they just might vote pretty intelligently. At any rate, the rules may be changed as the contestants use the leverage available to them at any given time.

This is the self-correcting value judgment process at work and such changes come with difficulty. Those who already have the vote are not interested in having their relative influence diluted. And the fact that they are making the decision as to whether the voting right will be extended, lessens the likelihood that the change can be readily made. Established institutional arrangements tend to be inhibitory of change. This is a fact of life.

Another Type of Decision-Making Process (Osmosis)

Arrow's list of four procedures that may be employed in making social choices is an incomplete list. In fact it leaves out the most important procedure: the technology-institutions ongoing interaction combined with the self-correcting value judgment process, a process called osmosis in the earlier listing.

Individuals, conditioned by their evolving biology and by the institutionalized behavior norms that flavored their upbringing, have an awareness of the possibilities presented by evolving technology. Individuals have this awareness because it is in the human mind that the process of technological evolution goes on. People have a certain sum of knowledge at a moment. The brain, perhaps stimulated by nothing more than "idle curiosity," perhaps stimulated by some of the institutionalized behavior norms such as the profit motive, ruminates about the available knowledge and perhaps the thought processes involved in the ruminations generate some new knowledge. The individual then speculates as to possible uses to which the new knowledge may be put, takes into account one's attitudes (one's current values), takes into account resource availability (meaning evolving aware-ness of the resource availabilities), and attempts to make meaningful use of the new knowledge—probably being influenced to change some institutionalized be-havior norms in the process. One may be satisfied as to the serviceability of the new knowledge and continue to use it or one may reject it. This is the self-correct-ing value judgment process going on at the individual level, the individual-institution interaction level, and the institution-institution interaction level.

At any rate here is a decision-making process which goes on (and on) of its own momentum and which overshadows all the others in importance. It is a feedback process involving continual interaction among people (with their mental processes and attitudes), technology, institutions, and resources. It does not involve the solution of a maximization problem or a marginal cost equals marginal revenue problem—except sporadically where, in particular situations, highly con-straining assumptions may be used, and appropriately used, to make the formu-lation of a maximization problem feasible. More commonly we are riding off into the sunset in an interesting, ongoing process. We are backing and filling, readjust-ing, and following intriguing new possibilities.

In this setting much meaningful decision making occurs without our even being aware of the process. Questions are answered, decisions are made, you might say, by osmosis, or as a by-product of other decisions. For example, there was never any conscious decision made that it was desirable for American cities to spread all over the map in contrast with the more compact European cities. But also there is much thoughtful effort going on to influence policy. Discussion of those efforts follows.

INFLUENCES ON SOCIAL CHOICE
The Relative Strength of Pressure Groups

In the private enterprise economy in many sectors, there exist a limited number of producers or sellers. This is the oligopoly phenomenon. This is true in automobile production, petroleum, or steel, or barbering (in a given residential area), or grocery shopping (only a few stores are reasonably available to a family). The number of producers is generally sufficiently limited so that it is feasible for them, if they choose to do so, to cooperate in setting production and pricing policies. Even if they have no formal agreement as to how to behave, they are quite likely to work under a tacit understanding as to how best to behave for the general good of their group. People in a line of business have continuing occasion to discuss industry problems and to acquire a common feeling for those problems. Formal instruments of such cooperation include the trade associations such as the National Association of Manufacturers, the American Petroleum Institute, the Iron and Steel Institute, as well as similar organizations at the local level.

On the consumer side, such interchange and cooperation are generally not feasible. All the potential buyers of automobiles cannot organize to tell Ford or General Motors that no one will buy a car unless the prices are lower. In general, sellers can and do confront buyers with prices on a take it or leave it basis. Sellers certainly are influenced by the state of the market. But there is not symmetry between sellers and buyers in terms of their roles in the market.

The difficulty is organizational. It is not practicable as a matter of organization, generally, for buyers as a group to confront sellers with a reservation price. There are too many of them and they are too widely dispersed. Also, their interest in the price of any particular commodity is too small a proportion of their total purchases for it to be worth their while to spend a large amount of time trying to set a commonly agreed-on, take it or leave it price for, say, No. 2 cans of early June peas.

On the producer side, the tendency to cooperate does not debar the possibility of occasional price wars, bitter inter-company struggles, and a bit of judicious non-price competition. But the chief lesson learned from the forays in the area of major conflict is that cooperation is the desirable standard pattern of behavior. They all have a stake in a more orderly and profitable industry. And competition is likely to make the industry less profitable. (Of course, each has an interest in a larger share of such profits and gains as there are.)

So, the economy is more effectively organized to raise prices and costs in the interest of higher profits and wages than it is organized to promote lower prices and greater goods availability. Things happen this way in spite of the fact that the population as a whole has just as much interest, in its role of consumer, in getting more goods at lower prices as it has, in its role of producer, in charging higher prices and getting higher wages and profits. It misrepresents the problem to say that there is a conspiracy by a little group of producers (the Establishment) to exploit consumers (the great exploited masses). We are all producers and we are all consumers, but we are all more effectively organized to push our interests as producers than as consumers.

Note the difference between the nature of this cleavage of interests and the cleavage emphasized by the Marxists. Marxists emphasize the cleavage between capitalist and worker interests. But in the situation looked at here, it is the relation between producer and consumer interest that is relevant. In this setting, capitalists and workers (people in general in their role as workers) have a common interest in raising prices and costs (costs including both wages and profits).

Self Service versus Society Serving

A major theme of orthodox economics involves the allegation that if individuals operate in a self-serving manner the result will turn out to be for the best, a maximum, so far as society is concerned. Such an attitude might result from comparing the competitive market system with other economic systems on some sort of impressionistic basis and making a judgment in favor of the competitive market system. Or the attitude may result from some sort of a logical demonstration such as general equilibrium analysis unsuccessfully attempts. Or, some people may simply relish the type of competition that prevails in the market, whether it is precisely pure competition or not. Or, yet again, one may simply have faith that an invisible hand is at work to insure the maximization result. One feels this in one's bones even if one cannot prove it.

As an additional article of faith, although this is stretching faith pretty far, one may advance the ambiguous argument that markets that are characterized by oligopoly or monopolistic competition in fact operate as though they were purely competitive despite the fact that they are not. Milton Friedman, for example, is endowed with this additional faith. Friedman wrote: "But as I have studied economic activities in the United States, I have become increasingly impressed with how wide is the range of problems and industries for which it is appropriate to treat the economy as if it were competitive."[3] As to the nature of the evidence supporting this conclusion Friedman is noncommittal. Offhand, one would probably surmise that there is no presumption that self-serving behavior on the part of individuals contributes to the welfare of others. There would seem to be a burden of proof on those alleging this identity of interest. And in the absence of compelling evidence on this score, it is rather silly for society blithely to assume that the general welfare is being appropriately looked after by a system in which the only regulator is competition among individuals struggling for personal gain.

A system which allocates votes on a one dollar-one vote basis is going to favor those who have the most dollars or the most aptitude for acquiring dollars in the setting of the prevailing institutionalized behavior norms. Such people will almost certainly use their leverage to perpetuate a system oriented to favor those who have more money and more aptitude as they operate in the setting of a competitive market—those with most skill in making money in the capitalist system. Is this the sort of system people really want? Maybe it is and maybe it is not. And maybe, people will change their minds on this score, making self-correcting value judgments, as time passes.

Widespread and uncompromising poor mouthing of government and deprecating governmental employees are hardly useful when government is the instrument society has for fostering the general interest. This is different from occasional appropriate bursts of indignation that result from particular examples of abuse. Individual citizens do well to be concerned about government, and individual governmental employees who are abusing their position represent a serious problem, as do private businesspeople who use their leverage to exploit their position. Rules and regulations are not desirable just for the sake of having rules and regulations. But the problem is how to establish desirable and workable rules that foster the general interest and how to maintain an administration that enforces the rules in an evenhanded and constructive way. "Eternal vigilance is the price of freedom" is no idle platitude. And it is a lot easier to gripe about the government than to contribute constructively to its working.

Constrained Choice (Power and Leverage)

Power or leverage may be used by some to control the behavior of others. Perhaps one does not express a choice merely reflecting habit or accident or rational purpose or thoughtfulness. Perhaps one expresses a choice, votes, or buys something, because one is forced or leveraged by someone else to do it. Kidnapping for ransom imposes a choice, and it is an unpleasant option among choices, on someone. There is a good deal of literature on the subject of power and the use of power.[4]

Certainly crude power and the threat to use crude power have been making life unpleasant for much of the human race throughout its history. Crude power was the essence of Nazi procedure. It exists and is used by the dictatorships that prevail today in many countries. Also a sort of reverse use of power can be exercised by the weaker to intimidate the stronger in some situations. The United States is very sensitive to the possibility that access to the Middle Eastern oil might be cut off. Terrorism is quite lacking in discrimination in terms of who suffers and in terms even of which terrorists risk more than do other terrorists. "Setting others up" to do the dirty work or "take the rap" has been a useful skill all through history.

But to turn to a more mundane aspect of the problem, the most important single fact in understanding the working of the economies of the Western countries may well be awareness that the process is being strongly influenced by those in strategic positions in the money-changing process much more so than by those whose leverage derives from direct ownership of capital. The Marxists have the wrong scapegoat.

One may speculate on what is going on in terms of a phenomenon which has become important in the 1980s: the corporate takeover, friendly or unfriendly. Until recently, the institutional arrangements involved in the divorcement of ownership from control in corporations meant that the ingroup in a corporation had the leverage to perpetuate itself in power even though it owned but a microscopic percentage of the corporation's stock. But recently, enterprising "takeover artists" have discovered that this same characteristic of corporations, the ability to control even though one owns little stock, gives determined outsiders the ability to take over by means of skilled manipulation of rival blocks of minority stock. Ownership (or control of the votes) of $2 or $3 billion of stock may permit one to take over control of a $100 billion corporation from a group of insiders who only own $500 million of stock. But, still and all, $2 or $3 billion is a lot of money. And most of the takeover artists do not actually have that kind of money themselves. They borrow it. Also, the ingroup conceivably may also be able to defend itself by borrowing. So, in the background are the moneychangers. And one can believe that they are not supporting first one and then another of the central figures in the takeover efforts out of charity.

Another phenomenon, that might better be called leverage than power, involves the use of funds and the making of investments by trust officers (perhaps the trust officers of banks) managing the funds of widows and orphans. In Western society, a very high proportion of all the funds invested in an enterprise from outside the firm are funds whose use is controlled by insurance companies or trust officers. Actually, a microscopic proportion of the genuine new investment is made by risk-taking private savers, those legendary heroes of the free private enterprise story. Schumpeter's innovator is not financing innovation out of personal funds. Back to the insurance companies: they have the investable funds and the leverage, but they do not enforce their will with storm troopers who wake people up in the middle of the night, kick their doors down, and beat them up. What is that more or less anonymous vice-president in the insurance company, who is actually making the meaningful decision, thinking about? Whatever it is, he is certainly in a position to leverage a lot of other people.

Another slant at the power and leverage issue involves the relation among people at different levels in a hierarchy. Most of us are involved in a hierarchy. In some sense we are "over" some people and "under" some other people. Some people are or try to be benign in relation to the people under them. Some may have underlings who are challenging them all the time, others have underlings who "know their place." There is a myth, especially prevalent in Western society, that the successful career involves starting at the bottom of the hierarchy ladder and working to the top, at which summit there is nobody over one. One is finally out from under and has it made. One has power. But really there is no such summit. The president of a corporation has a good deal of leverage, some having more than others and some using more skillfully what they have. But there is no summit. The president of the university answers to the chancellor (depending on the structural jargon). The chancellor answers to the board of regents. The board of regents answers to the governor and the legislature. The governor and the legislature are interested in getting re-elected. The president of the corporation is looking one way at a board of directors, another way at rivals for the presidency, another way at the takeover artists. And the president wants to make sure that some one of the vice-presidents does not upstage the boss.

In a given situation, is the chief executive officer of a corporation more concerned with defending a status quo, with profit, with growth, or with something else? Who is leveraging whom and to what end?[5]

Depending on one's own characteristics and the characteristics of one's associates, a given individual may make it to the top of one hierarchy and not to the top of another. "Ability" in some homogeneous sense, is not only not determining, it is not identifiable. One's success depends on one's aptitudes in relation to the behavior norms prevailing in the setting where one is operating. There is no such thing as a definitive intelligence scale, either in terms of individual rankings or in terms of the relative superiority of races. Some may thrive in a market economy. A somewhat different type of individual may thrive in a socialist economy. One tourist may have a digestive tract that resists Montezuma's curse more effectively than does the digestive tract of someone else. One person may make straight As. And someone else may make a million dollars.

It is not just bankers who are in a position to take advantage of strategic position in the economic process. Middlemen in the distribution and marketing process are frequently in a similar position. A favorite complaint of farmers is that it is likely to be the middlemen rather than the farmers who are the chief beneficiaries during periods of relatively high consumer prices for the products of agriculture. One may select a small scale, earthy example applying to the growing of barley for the purpose of making malt, in the high valleys of the states of Tlaxcala, Puebla, and Hidalgo in Mexico. According to a calculation, the middleman can make as much money in one trip in which he collects barley as the typical campesino makes from farming a twelve-acre plot for a year.[6]

Political position may also provide the leverage for extracting some gain in the economic process. It is interesting that Ayn Rand extended her denunciation of government to include businesspeople who profited from exploiting their connections with government. Presumably she would not have approved of Lee Iacocca. An example of the mixing of politics and business dealing involving a former mayor, Louie Welch, of Houston has been described.[7]

These miscellaneous situations involving leveraging, finagling, and the use of power do not fit very well into the simplicity of mathematical and econometric models.

Many of the complaints of underdeveloped countries against foreign investors can be put in terms of strategic position in the economic process. Especially when raw commodity production is involved, the difference between the price at the point of production in the underdeveloped country and the price at which the materials or the semiprocessed or finished products are sold in other countries is a major part of the story. The leverage possessed by individuals in the underdeveloped countries for participating in this price differential may be slight or it may be considerable. Awareness of this relation has provided a good deal of the motivation for nationalization of mining and petroleum producing properties in underdeveloped countries.

Levels of Decision Making and Decentralization

A possible classification in the decision-making process involves the level at which decisions are made. Apart from individual and corporate and other types of non-governmental decisions, governmental decisions may be made (1) at various low levels of government such as counties, municipalities, and school districts, (2) at state or provincial levels, (3) at the level of the "sovereign" state, and (4) at international and especially at the United Nations level.

There are various possible criteria as to the desirability of making decisions at different levels. One criterion might be: the nearer to the people the better, that is, the lower the level of government involved the better. Another criterion might be that, in a given society, for historical reasons, some particular level of government is sacrosanct. In the United States the states' rights fetish led some to believe (or did before the Civil War) that the state government is the preferred decision-making level.

In most countries, however, the "sovereign" nation has functioned as the decision-making level of overshadowing importance since the sixteenth century.

In a world where world society effectively controlled the general situation, world society might be expected to be the residual authority in the decision-making process. Incidentally, this might not imply a massive movement of the bureaucrats from national government payrolls to the United Nations payroll. This is possible because much nation-level bureaucracy (armies and customs officials, for example) are part of the apparatus by which nations challenge each other. A more effective United Nations might make it possible to dispense with much of such nation-level bureaucracy and armed forces without the need for replacement at the United

Nations level. This would represent a desirable development from the viewpoint of those opposed to bureaucracy and from the viewpoint of those believing that it would be desirable for the United Nations to be in a position to exercise prestigious leadership in the world unintimidated by the armies of great powers.

In spite of the ardent states' righters, it just has to be true that, in case of conflicts among policies adopted by various governments at the lower levels, conflicts, which the parties are not willing to resolve by themselves, are going to be resolved somehow, combat not being a particularly happy alternative. A world in which there are orderly procedures for referring disputes to the next higher level of government would seem a happy alternative.

If we recognize the principle that the next higher level of government resolves conflicts, and if the spoiled child (nation or ruler) is not allowed to impose its views on others, it may well turn out that relatively few problems actually have to be resolved at the level of the world authority. Much more good-citizen-type local decision making might then naturally occur and the whole atmosphere be more pleasant.

Interdependence versus Nationalism

The history of the aftermaths of revolutions since World War II is not encouraging. Mostly the post World War II period has seen macho, charismatic leaders of revolutions and founders of new countries taking advantage of their initial power position to entrench themselves in control of their country—for life. The tough, successful leader of a revolution or of an independence movement does not seem generally to have the understanding, the tolerance, or the willingness to make the effort to engage in the give and take and conciliation necessary if a society is to be open, free, and genuinely democratic. Instead the successful revolutionary reacts to criticism with a revival of repression.

Also, it is an institutionalized behavior norm of the Marxists that moderate, reformist, halfway democratic governments should never be given a meaningful chance to succeed. And it is an institutionalized behavior norm of the United States government to insist that new governments who are in any way beholden to the United States should take a pledge of allegiance to the free enterprise system, whether or not that is their inclination.

Following the armed overthrow of a government, the new leaders temporarily have unprecedented opportunities for constructive reworking of the institutional arrangements of the society, for feathering their own nests, or for botching up and creating a new repressive regime. The United States was unbelievably lucky in George Washington, who was willing to participate long enough to assist the new country in establishing durable institutional arrangements and who was then willing to bow out graciously.

Small, underdeveloped countries, which have the greatest stake in an interdependent world and in an effective United Nations, have been doing their best since 1945 to render the United Nations impotent and to assert their own national sovereignties and prerogatives, rights which can hardly protect them against the superpowers in the absence of an effective United Nations. In spite of everything, we have seen the United Nations in recent years, frequently, in response to small country pressure, resolving in favor of irresponsible national sovereignty: "The full exercise by the developing countries of permanent sovereignty over their natural resources will fulfill an important role in obtaining the objectives of the United Nations Second Development Decade."[8]

For youth who are interested in fighting for great and noble causes, it may be of interest to know that there is a cause, world order, that is worth the candle. We need leadership that speaks for interdependence rather than for nationalism, for the human race rather than for national or state sovereignty. It bears saying several times: The world needs fewer declarations of independence and a few more declarations of interdependence.

Revolution, Dictatorship, and Democracy

Historically the possibility of violent revolution has existed and people have exercised this option against autocratic power many times in the history of the human race. But in our time the underprivileged might well be a little bit slow to use violence in order to frustrate the working of the rather imperfect democracy that we have. People in general, especially the underprivileged, had better take a long second look at their demagogues and inquire if they really want them as dictators. Whites in the United States should be a little more appreciative of the extremely high level of black statesmanship that was expressed in the nonviolent movements of the Southern Christian Leadership Council and the National Association for the Advancement of Colored People.

The rebellious, in their insistence that they are put upon and in their concern to destroy the system and the Establishment, should also be concerned that they not destroy civilization itself.

John Dewey wrote of democracy:

The keynote of democracy as a way of life may be expressed, it seems to me, as the necessity for the participation of every mature human being in formation of the values that regulate the living of men together. . . . Universal suffrage, recurring elections, responsibility of those who are in political power to the voters, and the other factors of democratic government are means that have been found expedient for realizing democracy as the truly human way of living. They are not a final end and a final value. They are to be judged on the basis of their contribution to end. It is a form of idolatry to erect means into the end which they serve. Democratic political forms are simply the best means that human wit has devised up to a special time in history. But they rest back upon the idea that no man or limited set of men is wise enough or good enough to rule others without their consent; the positive meaning of this statement is that all those who are affected by social institutions must have a share in producing and managing them. The two facts that each one is influenced in what he does and enjoys and in what he becomes by the institutions under which he lives, and that therefore he shall have, in a democracy, a voice in shaping them, are the passive and active sides of the same fact.[9]

PLANNING

Societies may try to guide their economies by organized planning, rather than letting them fend for themselves as the whims of the free market might dictate. Planning would also be distinct from a situation, such as that more or less prevailing in the United States, where there is quite a range of miscellaneous laws and regulations and institutionalized behavior norms controlling or influencing behavior, but where there does not exist an organized effort to plan for the total economy in a coordinated way.

The Nature of Planning

A plan is a program of action involving the establishment of goals, policies, and procedures for a social or economic unit. The program may well be presented in considerable detail and accompanied by supporting data.[10] The time periods that plans are drawn up to cover may be of varying lengths, one year, five years, seven years, shorter, longer, or in between.

In any event the preparation and discussion of the plan represent a very useful opportunity for taking stock as to the state of the economy. In the United States, the annual economic report of the Council of Economic Advisers represents such an exercise. The Humphrey-Hawkins Act of 1978 went much further and provided for a national planning machinery and an annual economic report that would specify planning goals; however, this planning program has not been effectively implemented.

Thoughtful organized effort by government to anticipate the problems that lie ahead, especially in the next year or so, is surely called for. And the effort prevailing in the early 1980s to extol deregulation and deprecate public effort to understand and plan for the future, has surely not been constructive or helpful. It is desirable to have programs on hold that can be called into operation rather quickly if certain difficulties arise. Having desirable public works programs on hold or proceeding slowly can be useful if private enterprise enters a period of falling production and lays off workers. The public works projects that are on hold can be initiated or expanded to deal with the unemployment situation. This is a far better procedure than having to create the public works jobs from scratch after unemployment has suddenly escalated. Whatever the advocates of the market system may say about the ability of that system to solve all economic problems, in fact society is not going to allow the federal government to stand idly by during a period of major unemployment. Better to have constructive production programs on standby instead of relying on ad hoc leaf raking and unemployment insurance.

We are going to regulate and plan; we are going to interfere with the economy from time to time, or most of the time. The important question has to do with the criteria and the methods that are going to be used in this activity and the degree of honesty that is practiced as we recognize or fail to recognize what we are actually doing.

Beyond the issue as to whether there should be some degree of government regulation of the economy is the question as to whether there should also be occasional efforts to look at the economy as a whole and discuss or plot the future. Almost incredibly, a popular attitude has grown up in the United States that such planning should not be practiced, at least in this country. The prevalence of this attitude is especially remarkable in view of our repeated insistence that underdeveloped countries receiving foreign aid from the United States should engage in comprehensive planning: witness that insistence in President John Kennedy's Alliance for Progress program.

The people want future problems anticipated and yet they object to the planning that would coordinate reasonable efforts to deal with the assortment of likely upcoming problems.

Indicative or Binding Planning?

It may be some comfort to people who automatically react negatively to the idea of planning that there is the possibility of planning which is indicative as to what it would be desirable to do but which involves no constraint on people to act in particular ways. Planning may involve study of the overall situation, attempt to assess future development, make recommendations as to what is desirable, and suggest or *indicate* what the appropriate procedure for the participants may be during the period being planned for. Then it is up to the thoughtful judgment of the people involved to decide what they actually will do. The additional information that is made available by this process may well be helpful all around even though compliance is not mandatory and the plan is not implemented in precise detail.

Binding planning compels or tries to compel conformity on the part of the participants. The planning agency, if it is engaged in binding planning, uses legal or other leverage to enforce compliance. If all this is handled reasonably, if participants observe such strictures as "to plant more soy beans and less cotton," the population may be satisfied with the procedure. If there is a considerable amount of arbitrariness and unpleasantness involved, that is another story.

The truth of the matter is that there are features of an obligatory nature in much regulation, features that are strongly endorsed by people who, in general, present themselves as strong opponents of planning, big government, and arbitrary controls. At least from the 1930s on, in the oil industry, the dominant industry leadership has desired governmental control of the quantity of production and obtained it through such agencies as the Texas Railroad Commission, which set ceilings on Texas well output. In agriculture, much of the time, the dominant voice of the farmers has demanded that production, and such like controls, be enforced by the government, and the Department of Agriculture enforced compliance. And local industry frequently has loudly demanded quotas on the imports of competing commodities. But the United States has not had a binding *overall* plan such as the Soviet Union has had.

The all or nothing rhetoric, which has dominated much of the discussion of planning, has not been conducive to the judicious use of planning, mixed with private initiative, in ways that might generally be very helpful.

Two things are probably certain: that the people are not going to care for complete regimentation nor are they going to care for a libertarian order where everyone is free to do one's thing. But this choice is not really the issue when one is discussing the desirability of planning.

Plans and planning involve an effort to take the total picture into account and understand the alternatives. This might be called a holistic approach to problems. Such effort is desirable. Whether or under what circumstances particular aspects of plans will be made legally binding is a matter for the self-correcting value judgment process.

A little more light and a little less heat in discussion of these issues would be helpful.

The Tinbergen Approach

An approach to the planning problem, which has enjoyed considerable prestige, involves the argument that all problems can be solved simultaneously if the planner has available as many policies as problems. This idea contributed to winning a Nobel prize for Jan Tinbergen.[11] The approach involves rationally assigning policies to the particular problem that the particular policy is most effective in dealing with. And the planning works through the pattern of policy assignments, assigning policies to problems in some sort of reasoned order, and gets all the problems dealt with.

The logic involved in this argument was merely the algebraic proposition that, with various reservations, values for all the unknowns in a system of linear simultaneous equations can be found, provided there are as many equations as there are unknowns.

You might think this proposition, as an effective tool for planning, would be laid to rest or deposited in file 13, by the understanding that we have 10,000 problems and we really are incapable of lining up 10,000 policies and working out a neat ordering that assigns each policy successively to the problem with which it is best equipped to deal. But even if the initial ordering of problems and policies were possible, which it is not, the solution of the system of equations would be, in all reason, quite impossible. For one thing it is unreasonable to believe that all the equations in the system would be linear, and one is almost immediately in an area where the likelihoods are that the system has no unique solution. It is not that the mathematics is difficult and bigger and faster computers are needed. The difficulty may well be fundamental. There is no unique solution, just as there is no unique solution to Arrow's voting paradox problem.

The Ad Hoc Problem

In fact governments are likely to be denounced by the citizenry in times of crisis when it develops that the government has not planned ahead to anticipate what it would do in such and such a situation. Sometimes such criticism is a bit unfair, especially if the public has been loudly demanding deregulation and lower taxes. Perhaps the problem could not have been anticipated. It could not reasonably have been anticipated that Iranians would take over the United States embassy in Teheran in 1979. But hurricanes are a different sort of issue. Even though the time and place and severity of individual hurricanes cannot be anticipated, planning as to how to deal with hurricanes is a most worthwhile activity, and includes steps that people may well be ordered to take under certain circumstances. In the economy, it is not possible to anticipate exactly the timing and characteristics of the next depression, but it is possible to be fairly sure that there will be one, and it is desirable to formulate reasonable plans for dealing with various of the usual depression problems. The job guarantee for dealing with the unemployment problem is an example.

Decisions without Rules (Discretionary Authority)

Problems, both ad hoc problems and more or less regularly recurring problems, may be dealt with in predetermined ways or they may be dealt with by the use of discretion by a decision maker who is not bound by predetermined rules. Depending on how the decision maker may have been selected, such decision makers may have acquired their power as a by-product of dictatorships or through democratic processes. Or, in either case, decision making and implementation may be delegated to subordinates, and in general will be. In this process superiors may or may not be conscientious in their supervision. Or they may be overly interested in creating a situation where they will be in position to deny responsibility (deniability) if the policy goes sour. For their part the subordinates may or may not practice a good deal of independence, or free wheeling, in making and implementing policy. And nice questions involving buck-passing and assumption of responsibility may be involved, such as were revealed in the Iran-Contra hearings in 1987. Ad hoc decision making may be well and conscientiously done, or it may be an irresponsible mess.

As an example of the discretionary use of authority, the Board of Governors of the Federal Reserve system may vary the rediscount rate or the reserve requirements or engage in open market operations as its judgment dictates as it more or less continually resurveys the economy and is concerned about national income trends, inflation, unemployment, the balance of payments, and so on. The Fed, over the years, has taken considerable pride in combining secrecy and discretion, although fairly recently it has begun to tie its discretionary hands slightly by announcing that it is trying to contain the growth of the money supply within certain limits during subsequent planning periods. So, there is a bit of predictability as to Fed policy that was formerly not present, but still not much.

Nevertheless, in general, governments and bureaucrats seem to relish discretionary decision making without rules. It gives decision makers more flexibility and more opportunity for self-expression, perhaps in furthering their interpretation of the general interest or their own interest.

Thus, if fiscal policy is to be used as a measure to fight unemployment, Congress may debate (and even debate interminably) the merits of different tax and spending and debt and deficit policies. The interminable nature of this process may lead well-intentioned people to advocate that discretionary authority be delegated to bureaucrats rather than to legislators. Such delegation may work reasonably well, or it may not, or it may be an early step on the road to autocratic government. In any event, monetary policy is a far more flexible tool than fiscal policy because of the nature of the institutional arrangements controlling the use of the two tools.

Ongoing Automatic Decision Rules

Milton Friedman and the Chicago advocates of pure competition very adroitly stole the National Bureau of Economic Research from the institutionalists during the period at the close of World War II. More recently they have continued their success by pioneering the advocacy of ongoing automatic decision rules, a policy more appropriate to institutionalism than to the advocates of laissez faire. If it were really true that the free market can satisfactorily regulate the economy and "free to choose" is the best general policy, automatic decision rules should be unnecessary. But for the institutionalists, decision rules should be appropriate when the self-correcting value judgment process so indicates. Be that as it may, Friedman and other advocates of the free market have been leaders in developing the concept of automatic decision rules.[12]

All the problems that may come up are not going to be resolvable by means of "in place" automatic, ongoing decision rules. Many really important decisions will involve new and unforeseen difficulties. Nevertheless, it is desirable, where feasible, to deal with the innumerable, recurring problems that can be dealt with in that way by means of standardized rules. A whole lot of uncertainty, hardship, and speculative profiteering may be avoided. It is desirable to have stand-by procedures, that everyone knows will be used, to deal with the ever recurring and continuing problems, such as what to do when a hurricane is coming in. If those problems are dealt with by bureaucrats making ad hoc and often late decisions, then there will be traffic jams on the Galveston causeway as the storm arrives. Get decisions out of the realm of the short-run and the ad hoc when it is feasible to do so. Deal with the unemployment problem with an ongoing job guarantee program rather than with an improvised public works program.

Rules about Decision Rules

A decision rule establishes what the policy measure will be when a certain problem arises. The policy measure is not selected on an ad hoc, discretionary, or authoritarian basis by an individual. But any old decision rule will not necessarily be better than ad hoc decision making, merely because it is a rule. In the light of the problem, the decision rule needs to be reasonable, useful, effective and *doable*. One problem with Milton Friedman's famous rule for expanding the money supply by a certain percentage every year is that it is not doable.

Various criteria may be applied to decision rules. One is that it is preferable to underdo a stimulus rather than to overdo it. Undershooting rather than overshooting may be a good general rule. If one is, for example, indexing wages to the cost of living index, the decision rule might well be to correct for 90 or 95 percent of the inflation only. The thought is that this practice will deflate the inflation rate.

Another procedure that may be useful in a substantial number of cases is gearing the rule to a constant annual percent change in the instrument for as long as the problem continues. Do not allow planners to play with the numbers. Suggested rules on agricultural prices and eliminating tariffs are examples of such practices. They are discussed in the next chapter.

There should be the general rule that all market interventions will be designed to slow down rates of change, but not to turn around the direction of movement. Give the people who are going to be affected half a chance to mesh with the process. To know roughly what the nature of the planner's action is going to be is a good idea. For example, interventions in foreign exchange markets should be designed to slow down the pace at which rates are changing, not to reverse the direction of change of the rates.

Another fairly general rule is that the policy measure involved should have an impact directly on or at least relatively close to the activity which it is desired to influence. One of the problems with the protective tariff as a device to encourage production, especially in the case of the infant industry argument for tariffs, is that the primary impact is so far removed from the productive process that it is desired to promote. This is the reason that a production subsidy (paid in correspondence to the amount of production) is likely to work better as a policy tool in economic development than is the protective tariff. About all that can be said in favor of the protective tariff (quota, license, or embargo) is that it salves the egos of the producers who thereby are helped in maintaining the illusion that it is competitive free private enterprise that is doing the job. The production subsidy (not a subsidy on goods as they move through the channels of trade) is a more honest policy tool, even though it does not cater to the producer's self-esteem and ego.

Decision rules which deal satisfactorily with one problem must not have significant undesirable side effects. Better no rule or a different rule, if the possibility of pernicious side effects is plausible. But also ostensibly reasonable decision rules, once in being, are entitled to a chance to demonstrate their continuing merit before being discarded as a result of fairly trivial side effects or as a result of not working immediately.

In the next chapter there is a discussion of various possible problem situations and of possible policies for dealing with those problems. Several of those policy suggestions provide examples of workable decision rules.

CONCLUSION

Planning and plans that involve some historical background, a description of the current state of the economy, and some suggestions as to policies for dealing with the observed problems are worthwhile. The plan itself and the publication of its text provide useful perspective and a point of departure for businesspeople, the citizenry in general (even those who like to complain about the government), and the government itself. This is true whether or not most, any, or all of the recommended policies are implemented, or whether the plan is indicative or mandatory.

If the plan is halfway reasonable, however, surely many of the provisions will be worth implementing. Over time the extent to which the plans are binding will, no doubt, be subject to the self-correcting value judgment process.

NOTES

[1] Marie Marquis de Condorcet, *Essai sur l'Application de l'Analyse à la Probabilité des Décisions Redue à la Pluralité*, cc. 1785.

[2] Kenneth Arrow, *Social Choice and Individual Values* (2nd ed.; New Haven: Yale, 1963 [1951]), pp. 1-2.

[3] Milton Friedman, *Capitalism and Freedom* (Chicago: University of Chicago Press, 1982 [1962]), p. 120.

[4] Warren J. Samuels, ed., *The Economy as a System of Power* (New Brunswick, New Jersey: Transaction Books, 1979); Edward S. Herman, *Corporate Control, Corporate Power* (Cambridge, Eng.: Cambridge University Press, 1981), esp. pp. 17-52; Wallace Peterson, "Power and Economic Performance," *Journal of Economic Issues* XIV (December 1980), pp. 827-870; and the list is hardly begun.

[5] Michael Maccoby, *The Gamesman: The New Corporate Leaders* (New York: Simon and Schuster, 1976).

[6] Rodrigo A. Medellín E., in *Comercio Exterior* (September 1980), p. 932.

[7] Mimi Swartz, "The Louie File," *Texas Monthly* 13 (October 1985), pp. 152-155, 247-250.

[8] United Nations (Resolution 2626 of the General Assembly, approved October 24, 1970), "International Development Strategy for the Second United Nations Development Decade," *Cemla, Boletin Mensual* XVI (December 1970), p. 596.

[9] John Dewey, *Intelligence in the Modern World: John Dewey's Philosophy* (New York: The Modern Library, 1939), pp. 400-404.

[10] The important institutionalist Allan G. Gruchy has written extensively on planning. See especially his: *Contemporary Economic Thought* (Clifton, New Jersey: Augustus M. Kelley, 1972), pp. 237-285; and "Institutionalism, Planning, and the Current Crisis," *Journal of Economic Issues* XI (June 1977), pp. 431-448.

[11]Jan Tinbergen, *On the Theory of Economic Policy* (Amsterdam: North Holland, 1952), p. 100. An example of an attempt to use this approach is: Robert A. Mundell, "The Appropriate Use of Monetary and Fiscal Policy for Internal and External Stability," *IMF Staff Papers* IX (March 1962), pp. 70-77.

[12]Ralph C. Bryant, *Money and Monetary Policy in Interdependent Nations* (Washington: Brookings, 1980), pp. 243-250, 309-333, 485-487; Friedman, p. 51; Finn E. Kydland and Edward C. Prescott, "Rules Rather Than Discretion: The Inconsistency of Optimal Plans," *Journal of Political Economy* 85 (June 1977), pp. 473-491; Alexander Lamfalussy, *Rules versus Discretion: An Essay on Monetary Policy in an Inflationary Environment* (Basle: Bank for International Settlements, 1981); Henry C. Simons, *Economic Policy for a Free Society* (Chicago: University of Chicago Press, 1948), pp. 160-183; Henry C. Simons, "Rules vs. Authority in Monetary Policy," *Journal of Political Economy* 44 (February 1936), pp. 1-30.

Chapter XV

Policies

Institutionalism does not provide a methodology capable of proving that one rule or policy is preferable to another; nor does it seek to, or see the merit in so doing. What institutional economists try to do is to explain the process by which rules and policies are formed. Institutionalists, like other individuals, are free to envisage policy improvements and try to get society to adopt them. This chapter presents possible policies for dealing with problems currently facing society. Policies are suggested and arguments for them are presented, but these arguments may or may not be convincing to all. Even other institutionalists, on the basis of institutionalism, may or may not advocate any particular one of these policies. Whether or not these policy recommendations obtain meaningful support in the short-run future, it is hoped that their discussion is stimulating and constructive.

The arguments are not here presented in detail, but they are presented in enough detail to provide a basis for consideration. There is no claim that, even if these policies were adopted, all the problems of the human race would be solved. This is not a complete blueprint for society; presented here is merely a selection of possible policies. After all, we are caught up in an ongoing process in which conditions are changing. And thank goodness for that.

THE REGULATION OF BUSINESS

The American or Western business system (sometimes, not particularly appropriately called: capitalism, the competitive system, the market system, the free private enterprise system and, perhaps, more appropriately, a mixed system) is eulogized by many for providing a fantastically high standard of living. It is reviled by others for being exploitative of workers. This discussion of capitalist business practices is not intended to pass a judgment on the system. What is attempted is to identify problem areas in the system and to advocate changes that may be helpful in dealing with particular difficulties. Since corporations, and especially the giant corporations, are pretty much the heart of the system, these suggestions particularly apply to large corporations. The number of business enterprises in the United States is about 15 million. Three million of these are corporations. Of this three million, the largest 500 industrial corporations had, in 1984, sales of $1.8 trillion and net profits after taxes of $86 billion. Net profits after taxes of all corporations were $188 billion (1983), and the gross national product of the country was $3.7 trillion (1984) and $4.5 trillion in 1987. The largest 500 companies thus accounted for 46 percent of all corporate profits.[1]

Then, as one takes into account the phenomenon of the divorcement of ownership from control in the large corporations, one can well wonder about the credentials of the small number of business people who dominate those large corporations and are thus in position to dominate the economy. It is fairly notorious that stockholder-owners are not in a position to exercise meaningful control over corporate policy.[2]

In general, corporations are effectively controlled by a self-perpetuating ingroup whose motivation likely includes a bit of interest in personal gain. The role of self-perpetuating ingroups in this situation has been modified in recent years by the development of the arts of hostile takeover and threatened hostile takeover engineered by a breed of corporate raiders operating chiefly with the funds obtained by the issue of junk bonds. This new development has not produced any demonstrable benefit to the stockholders, the general public, or the cause of production efficiency. But it has been an enthralling game involving much of the country's business talent while the Japanese and Germans have worried more about product quality, productivity, and exports.

The insiders, including now the successful takeover people, may well be more interested in empire building by plowing back profits rather than in distributing them as dividends to the stockholders. In any event, corporate insiders, rather than stockholder-owners make the important decisions in the American economy as to where and when investments will be made, a lot of free private enterprise mythology to the contrary notwithstanding. (This is not to say that decisions would necessarily be ideal from the viewpoint of the society as a whole even if they were actually made by stockholder-owners. Nevertheless, in view of the mythology as to the way the capitalist system is supposed to work, motivated by the profit motive, it is of some importance that this is not exactly the way the process operates.)

Perhaps, in spite of all the rhetoric about the desirability of the government leaving private enterprise alone with the profit motive, a few controls may be desirable. In what follows, a few controls will be very sketchily alleged, without much supporting justification being offered.

One policy might well be to limit the additional degree of concentration of corporate power that results from the circumstance that corporations own a lot of stock in each other. (Conceive of a situation where all corporate stock might be owned by other corporations.) Just maybe it would be a healthy change to prohibit the ownership of corporate stock by other corporations. Given the magnitude of what would be involved, the divestiture would probably need to be accomplished slowly over a period of years. And it might well be that the initial step along this line should merely involve prohibition in the future of the purchase of stock by any but physical individuals (no new purchases of corporate stock by other corporations.)

At this late date one can still regret that, in the early days of the corporate system in the first part of the nineteenth century, the ownership of corporate stock by corporations was permitted. It is a practice which could rather painlessly have been prevented in the beginning. It will now require major and difficult measures to undo the situation.

What is to be done to corporations when they violate the law? There is hesitancy about sending those individuals involved in white-collar crime to jail. As a minimum sanction against individuals so involved, it might be desirable to have regulations requiring the removal from boards of directors of individuals who voted for the illegal behavior. And if it proves difficult to pinpoint the individuals especially involved, the salubrious procedure might well be to purge the whole board of directors plus perhaps the company president (chief executive officer) and the relevant vice-presidents until and unless some are willing to talk. A little more turnover in boards of directors, such as would cut into the ingroup's power position at least a little bit, should provide a breath of fresh air.

Another possibility might involve the requirement that the corporation distribute virtually all profits after taxes as dividends to the stockholder-owners. And the stockholders would then decide whether or where to reinvest their earnings, instead of this function being performed for them by the corporate ingroup.

Modern technology requires large business enterprises. So, even though large corporations may use their market power to price gouge consumers, the problem cannot be dealt with satisfactorily by trying to enforce smallness on corporations. Nor can it be dealt with by giving the workers a role in the management of the corporation. The workers have the same interest management has in price gouging the public. And, beside that, management is a specialized job. It is by no means clear that workers coming in off the factory floor are in any better position to make meaningful decisions or decisions in the public interest than is the present type of management. Worker participation in management may not especially serve the public interest. But public representatives on the boards of large corporations might be a good idea.

Corporations should not be chartered by levels of government too low effectively to control the overall activities of the entities. In the United States, corporations active in production in several states should be chartered by the federal government, not by the individual states. Corporations operating internationally should be chartered by an appropriate unit of the United Nations system. Probably this principle should not apply to enterprises which merely merchandise, buy and sell, beyond the limits of their primary producing area, although what is desirable on this score should well be studied further.

As long as procedures are not in place to force corporations to distribute all of their profits as dividends this change in chartering criteria would permit more meaningful corporate income taxes by levels of government that have jurisdiction over all of the activities of the corporation. Certainly at present the taxation of multinational corporations is an unsatisfactory muddle.[3]

Deregulation does not necessarily result in stable, market-clearing prices. It frequently results in violent ups and downs, marketing gimmicks such as frequent flier bonuses, bankruptcies, mergers, price uncertainty, and marketing chaos. Witness almost any industry that has been deregulated, such as the airlines and banking. Rules and regulations should only exist if there are reasons for the rules and regulations. But, spare us blind deregulation as the core policy of the government for dealing with business.

THE JOB GUARANTEE

The most important of the decision rules may well be the job guarantee for dealing with the unemployment problem. Detail on the issue is belabored elsewhere, but some comments should be made here.[4] Everyone ready, willing, and able to work should be guaranteed a job. It should be a meaningful job, not a workfare, trash-pick-up type assignment such as is becoming a feature of some unemployment compensation programs. If there is going to be a meaningful job guarantee there has to be an employer of last resort with the obligation to hire all of the ready, willing, and able in genuine jobs. Perforce this employer of last resort would be the central government. (All levels of government should stop making depressions worse by firing people during hard times.) To insure that the nature of the work offered in the program be meaningful, the program must be continuing. Ad hoc job creation in quickly established public works programs cannot be a satisfactory way to deal with the situation.

It is to be hoped that private enterprise, in general and most of the time, will prove capable of providing all or most of the jobs. But the sticky problem involves the policy to follow when private enterprise fails to provide jobs for all of those ready, willing, and able to work. The resources of the employer of last resort must include a sufficient variety of job possibilities so that a reasonably accommodating individual is not forced to take a distasteful job which is out of line with that individual's capabilities and legitimate interests. But whether this means that the government role in the economy will be large or small depends on the resilience of private enterprise. Private enterprise can operate satisfactorily and constructively and play the major productive role in such a system, or it can choose to be uncooperative, moan about the government, and force the government to play a larger and larger role. There is no particular gain from trying to forecast ahead of time for certain what the balance will be between the roles of government and private enterprise. In fact, with the passage of time the balance will probably shift back and forth.

A question that will occur to some involves the cost of such a program. It is easy and probably correct to say that the program would be costless since it would create a situation in which more people are engaged in useful production than would otherwise be the case. But of course, that remark does not dispose of practical problems involving the actual funding of the program.[5] Hiring all the presently unemployed at the minimum wage would probably not cost more than the present welfare costs of unemployment. If you doubt it, get a copy of the budget, do some guessing about the real role of various programs, and do some addition. No econometric modeling is necessary. The gains in terms of saving on unemployment insurance and in terms of production in lieu of idleness have to be reckoned as major gains. And the maintenance of worker purchasing power that is involved should be good for business and mean that the government will actually have to provide fewer jobs than might seem to be the case at first glance.

Another problem that may occur to people involves the handling of the dead-beats, the malingerers, and those who are positively offensive or dangerous, who will trip old people or ridicule skinny or fat people. It may sound anomalous, in the setting of a program that calls itself a job guarantee program, to say that employers should be free to discharge such people on the spot when the offensive behavior occurs. (But certainly there should be procedures which, after the event and if the firee protests, would permit impartial judgment on whether the employer's action has been reasonable.) The present proposal is that people discharged for offensive behavior should then remain without benefit of the job guarantee protection for some period such as six weeks or two months, giving them a little time to think things over, after which the individual would again be entitled to take advantage of the job guarantee. Then, if the individual repeats objectionable behavior, there comes a time when that person is reclassified out of the ready, willing, and able to work category into the category of the handicapped. And the handicapped, those entitled to sympathy and those who are not, for better or worse, are going to be an ongoing problem to which the job guarantee does not address itself. To say that the job guarantee program is highly desirable is not the same thing as saying that it will solve all the world's problems. Programs to help the handicapped and deal with difficult people will still be desirable.[6]

DAY CARE

A policy to which the women's movement can and does give high priority is day care for children. Given the difference between the sexes, free day care for children is *the* feasible policy which offers most possibility for helping women operate effectively in the business world in competition with men. There are problems, of course, including how to keep child molesters out of the day care centers. But one of the problems should not be that the country cannot afford an adequate day care program.

PUBLIC FINANCE
Estate and Inheritance Taxes

Higher rates on estate and inheritance taxes are no panacea, but they are one of the best ways to reduce the inequality in opportunity that exists. In 1987, in the United States, estates of up to $600,000 were completely exempt from the federal estate tax. The inheritance of such large estates virtually free from taxation is not even particularly helpful to the heirs, who are likely to be already in their forties and well established financially. A stage when people really need financial support is when they are completing their education, going to work, and establishing families. At that stage the offspring of the affluent are likely to be getting such support from their parents and the offspring of the poor are not.

Perhaps the proceeds from the estate tax could be used to support a program involving one-time-only financial subsidies to young people as they are just getting started in life.

The appropriateness of doing something about wealth distribution in the United States may be indicated by the following information: ". . . the richest one percent [of the families in the United States] . . . own half of the country's wealth. . . ."[7]

The Gift Tax

At present a gift tax is paid by the giver on gifts of over $10,000 per year to any one recipient. The rates are quite high, being so designed in order to prevent avoidance of the estate tax by the use of gifts made during the lifetime of the donor. Perhaps it would be better if gifts were visualized as an increase in the income of the recipient and were taxed as though they were part of the recipient's income, rather than the donor being taxed. This procedure would correspond with the concept that the prime recipient of the benefit should be the one to pay. Exemptions on gifts under, say, $500 or $1000 should keep this procedure from placing a damper on Christmas and birthday festivities.

In its present form, the gift tax is a rather strange concept—inhibiting people from giving money away.

The Income Tax

Studies of the overall tax burden in the United States in terms of how heavily it falls on the rich and the poor indicate that it is surprisingly close to proportional. The federal income tax was almost the only tax that contributed to keeping the system from being somewhat regressive, that is, that took a larger proportion of the income of the poor by comparison with the rich. This was possible because the wealthy save a higher proportion of income than do the poor and are therefore not affected so much by the pervasive sales taxes which burden the poor more. The reductions in income tax rates and the tendency to proportionality in the rates which have gone into effect in the 1980s can only make this tendency toward regressiveness more pronounced. In fact, major studies (for example by the Congressional Budget Office) are beginning to show that the income gap between rich and poor has widened during the Reagan years, presumably largely as a result of a tax reduction pattern that has favored the wealthy.

Surely, this is an undesirable trend. It would be desirable to return to greater progressivity in the income tax structure, along with continued elimination of complications in the tax structure. The tax reform of 1986 left a lot to be done along the line of simplifying that structure.

Now that economists are relatively better paid than was the case thirty or forty years ago, they have lost some of their pristine enthusiasm for social causes and in particular for progressivity in the income tax.

The Cyclically Balanced Budget

The cyclically balanced budget could be made subject to a decision rule procedure. The formula could be that following any year when the real per capita gross national product fell by more than some amount, the projected deficit for the coming fiscal should be increased (or the surplus reduced) by some fixed multiple of that figure, and vice versa.

Provisions forcing budget balancing may well be appropriate at the level of state and local governments. But annually balanced budgets should not be forced on the federal government. There needs to be one level of government with the additional flexibility that goes with the ability to run, at least in the short- and medium-run, deficits and surpluses. These deliberate imbalances can be useful policy measures for stimulating depressed economies and for slowing down over-heated economies.

Given the difficulty Congress has in saying "no" to pressure groups, decision rules that regulate the budgetary process are probably desirable.

AGRICULTURAL PRICES

Reasonable decision rules are probably feasible in order to manage agricultural prices. But the agricultural price support system that has existed in the United States since the 1920s is not an example. This parity price support approach has involved an attempt to maintain "parity" between the prices farmers pay for what they buy and the prices farmers receive for the things they sell. The system has not worked well. There is no good reason for believing that it is appropriate for the price of one item to bear a fixed relation with the price of another item over a long period of time, or even over a short period of time. Also, the way the system has worked, the chief beneficiaries and recipients of payments under the programs have been the more affluent farmers. And the program has not prevented the recurrence of crises, violent price fluctuations, and waves of farm foreclosures in agriculture.

If there is to be an effort to influence commodity prices by a decision rule, it needs to be a different decision rule from the parity price approach that has been basic in the United States scheme of things. It is desirable that there should be such an effort because agricultural prices do tend to fluctuate more violently than do prices in general and their fluctuations do constitute an especially serious problem for agriculture.[8]

A decision rule that would be reasonable for dealing with price instability affecting commodities sold on major public markets such as the Coffee and Sugar Exchange or the Chicago Bureau of Trade might work as follows in the case of falling prices. The decision rule would be that the growers and producers would be guaranteed by the government a price at least 90 percent (or some such percent) of the price of the preceding year. So, prices could fluctuate 10 percent without remedial action being called for. The real problem in agriculture has involved price fluctuation much more violent than this, short-run fluctuations of 30 or 40 percent or more in a year. In this concept the price of a commodity tending to fall relative to other prices as a natural long-run trend would be permitted to do so; it could fall up to 10 percent a year indefinitely with no remedial action being taken. Unpopular or inefficiently produced articles would thus be permitted to pass into limbo without expensive salvage operations being attempted.

If the price falls by more than 10 percent during a short period of time, however, the producer would be entitled to a check from the appropriate government agency for the value of the amount of the excess price drop beyond 10 percent. Thus, if the price of some commodity fell from $1.00 a bushel to $0.80, the producer would be entitled to a $0.10 a bushel payment. To guard against a certain type of chicanery, the relevant price controlling such payment would be the price on the public market on the day of the sale, not the price the buyer and seller alleged was set in the contract. This is the reason why such a program is probably only feasible for application to commodities which are sold in large quantities through public markets.

An associated action involves the handling of rising prices as distinct from falling prices. There would probably be serious difficulty in establishing workable procedures for taking gains away from producers by a similar procedure. For better or worse, the better way to deal with bonanza gains is probably via an excess profits tax superimposed on the income tax.

INTERNATIONAL TRADE PROBLEMS
Getting to Free Trade

Free international trade is desirable. The idea that it is better to produce goods in higher cost places or that it is desirable to buy inferior or more expensive goods from certain people merely because of their being of the same nationality must seem odd to the observer off on Mars.

There are other, and perhaps more important, reasons for free trade. Why should consumers not be able to buy from the seller of their choice, and buy the products of their choice? A complicated, expensive, irritating, and unnecessary machinery and bureaucracy exists in the world to police unnatural frontiers. Major savings could be obtained by eliminating this cumbersome machinery. And the world would become a more pleasant place in which to live as a by-product of the elimination of these restrictions.

As Adam Smith was aware, it is probably not desirable to move to free trade in one sudden stroke. Businesspeople should have time to adjust. A decision rule that provided for lowering trade barriers each year by ten percent of whatever the initial barrier was, and for all countries to do this, should be workable. This procedure would bring free trade in ten years. (Or perhaps the process should be geared to 20 years.) But, it is important that the process move to complete free trade expeditiously.

Antidumping Tariffs

In a world of nation states, where trade barriers actually exist, what might reasonable policy be for the nation acting alone? It may just be that an appropriate, workable policy would be that the only trade restriction, apart from those based on health grounds, which the nation in question should maintain is the antidumping tariff. This tariff would allow for what is legitimate in terms of complaint about the behavior of foreigners, and do it in a way that is not prejudicial against the interest of the consumers of one's own country.

Antidumping tariffs might be automatically imposed (and immediately) on a showing that imports are coming in at prices lower than those prevailing for that particular product in the domestic market of the exporter. The law might specify that the exporter has to provide a document certifying as to the price for domestic sale in the exporting country. Understanding that prices and terms of sale are properly matters of public record is needed to facilitate this process. Once the information is in hand, the amount of the antidumping tariff is, or should be, automatically set as the amount of discount the importer received by comparison with the foreign domestic price. As matters stand, obtaining antidumping relief is a long and uncertain process, which takes much of the merit away from one of the few legitimate international trade restrictions. Trying to tie antidumping measures to foreign production costs is not a desirable procedure. Those costs are virtually impossible to obtain and *average*.

There is an alternative with some appeal to the type of antidumping tariff suggested above. It might provide that, for goods to be imported into the United States, the minimum wage in the company or plant producing the goods must be higher than some level, perhaps one-half or three-fourths of the minimum wage in the United States.[9] Otherwise the goods are simply excluded. That proposal has many interesting implications.

Foreign Exchange Rates (Leaning against the Wind)

An international legal tender currency is the really desirable development in this area. But, so long as the world actually insists on having innumerable national currencies and foreign exchange markets where they are bought and sold for each other, a system of freely fluctuating rates is the desirable approach. But one should grant that, if there are no controls at all, the markets *may* fluctuate with undesirable violence. Almost any international crisis will be made worse by gyrations on the foreign exchange markets. Monetary authorities like to try to deal with such situations in secret negotiations and secret operations on the foreign

exchange markets. A highly uncertain situation is created and destabilizing speculation is likely to occur and make matters worse. Why monetary authorities have
the attitude that secrecy and discretionary buying and selling on their part is the
indicated procedure is difficult to understand until one recalls that people like to
play God.

A desirable decision rule might well be one that mandates open, free foreign
exchange operations. On this market, governmental monetary authorities would
make purchases of one's own currency with one's foreign exchange reserves if
the value of one's own currency is falling, but carefully avoid going to the extent
of trying to turn around the direction of movement of the rate. Underreacting
rather than overreacting is appropriate. The operations should be modest operations, aimed at slowing down rapid swings. And once the monetary authorities
have exhausted their foreign exchange reserves, that is the end of the "leaning
against the wind" support effort. For better or worse, the currency will, to put
it brutally, be allowed to fall. This is the price paid for the power of nation states
to print or create money and sometimes to do so in irresponsible amounts.

There are those that feel that the system of fluctuating rates existing since the
early 1970s has not worked well. But it is worth noting that there has not been
a foreign exchange market disaster such as occurred in 1931. The record has
been pretty good for a fledgling system that came into existence in most troubled
times.

INTERNATIONAL PEACEKEEPING AND
UNITED NATIONS REFORM

The world needs an effective United Nations. Name-calling and flexing of mus-
cles by the great powers and vituperation by the underdeveloped countries of the
great powers and of each other does not create a very salubrious international
climate, especially when the brew is agitated frequently with a little international
terrorism and there is no respected arbiter. The United States should understand
that it is not a respected arbiter.

The United Nations desperately needs reform. It needs a police force strong
enough summarily to prevent war. It also needs responsible decision-making
machinery in control of that police force and its other activities. The Security
Council with its veto power is a monstrosity. The General Assembly of some 150
nations with equal votes in a setting where four nations have half of the world's
population can scarcely be a responsible decision-making body. And the type of
bargaining involved in selecting the secretary general is calculated to throw up
an ineffective figurehead.

Why is there not a major effort afoot to restructure the United Nations? The
underdeveloped and small countries would be well advised to forget their nationalistic egos and lead in this effort. If the United States really desires world peace it
would be well advised also to lead in this effort; the same goes for the Soviet Union.

Neither the Security Council, with its big power veto, nor the General Assembly,
where one-nation-one-vote applies, regardless of the size of the country, is a

satisfactory institution. What are the possible changes? Countries might be required to have a certain size or population to be entitled to vote. This might encourage some highly desirable fusions of some very small countries. It might also be reasonable to require that, to be entitled to vote, the government of the country should have obtained power by procedures that the United Nations recognizes as legitimate. The initial establishment of the criteria for legitimacy should generate an interesting discussion. But such discussion should be worthwhile and might be helpful to the cause of democracy.

The United Nations needs to have a permanent and strong armed force of its own. And, in a setting where technology has been overworked to improve the killing power of military hardware, the United Nations peace-keeping force must also command the best technology. A procedure for financing this might well stipulate that each nation must turn over to the United Nations a sum equal to some percentage such as 25 or 30 percent of its military budget. The implications of this policy are worth a second thought. Such a procedure might both provide a reasonably strong United Nations force and also stimulate arms reduction at the same time, as the nations come to realize that arms races automatically increase the military power of the United Nations.

The United States' stake in a workable, responsible, and impartial United Nations is greater than constant critics of the United Nations seem to realize. *The United States is seriously overextended in the world,* busily telling other countries how to run their business. And it is vociferously and self-righteously engaged in this activity while it is not doing a particularly good job of running its business at home.

We are trying to enforce a three-mile limit off the Crimea on the Soviet Union. We are patrolling the Mediterranean, blustering in Lebanon, having trouble keeping our Israeli protegés in line, policing the Persian Gulf and escorting Kuwaiti tankers, lecturing South Africa, licking the wounds we received in Vietnam, encouraging revolutions in the Philippines and Panama, invading Grenada, trying to straighten out El Salvador, sporadically supporting rebels in Nicaragua, freely denouncing miscellaneous governments as evil empires and foreign rulers as cowards. Supplement the everchanging list for yourself.

We have too many irons in the fire. And the rest of the world is not particularly appreciative of our frequently clumsy efforts to run everybody's business.

It may be a bitter pill to swallow—the realization that we cannot do it all and cut taxes at the same time, while protecting ourselves behind a Chinese-SDI-INS-drug interdiction wall. We would do well to co-opt the rest of the world into helping with the thankless job of running the world. A reformed United Nations is the only feasible vehicle for this purpose.

ECONOMIC DEVELOPMENT IN THE THIRD WORLD

The First World is more or less the "Western" developed market countries, the Second World is the Soviet Bloc countries, and the Third World is the underdeveloped countries. The development of the latter has been an object of considerable concern since World War II. Economists from the First World have offered a lot of advice on the subject, using the analytical tools with which they are familiar: price theory, national income theory (Harrod-Domar growth models), and so on. The results have not been outstandingly successful. If the truth be told, evolutionary economics has a good deal more to offer that is useful in fostering economic development.

In this setting, the crux of the matter is the adaptation of the institutional order in the underdeveloped countries in ways that permit the appropriate modification and effective use of the technology that can be obtained from the developed countries. By and large the technology that is most relevant is freely available. (The military and computer secrets that the United States is unsuccessfully trying to keep from the Russians and others are not the crux of the matter for this purpose.) The difficult step is the adjustment of the institutional arrangements in the underdeveloped countries to permit the effective use of the available knowledge.

The United States is currently pressuring the underdeveloped countries to adopt the market or free private enterprise system. The Soviet Union pressures them to adopt some form of socialism. The truth of the matter is that both the United States and the Soviet Union would do well to keep out of the ideology peddling business. For the new institutional arrangements in the underdeveloped countries to be acceptable and viable in those countries, the patterns need to be indigenously molded, although specific ingredients may be imported.[10] This means that in the context of their own background these countries may select features of the United States system, features of the Soviet system, or features of the Japanese system, that seem appropriate to them. (The apparently successful Japanese development has not involved carbon copying some other institutional system. It has involved selective adaptation, with the crucial decisions being made by the Japanese.)

At all events, the crux of the development story involves the decisions of the underdeveloped country itself in the institutional adaptation area. Assorted policies, some imported, are going to need to be adjusted and assimilated to take particular and local circumstances into account. Depending on those circumstances, a progressive income tax, or a major reduction in the size of the armed forces, or land reform, or a better educational system, or thoughtful interpretation of market price signals may any and all be useful institutional changes. But the most important institutional change of them all is the change in attitude that permits thoughtful consideration of and implementation of institutional changes as the society deems such changes to be desirable.

EVALUATION

The policy proposals made in this chapter are not to be thought of as having their validity proven by some logical magic hidden away in the black box of institutional model building. There is no such black box, no logical model capable of grinding out unique and definitive solutions to most problems.

On the basis of our currently held values we make judgments about policy proposals. We endorse policies publicly, give reasons, and perhaps gain supporters. We and others test our proposals. Do they seem to work to our satisfaction, or to society's satisfaction? We back and fill in a process of self-correcting value judgments, as does society, as we reappraise our position in the light of results and in the context of our, perhaps changing, valuations. And society, influenced by all this, is the ongoing arbiter of the process, working through the institutions which make it up and which are themselves being changed in the process.

Meanwhile a bit of advice to the novice reformer may not be amiss. Learn well how the institution with which you are concerned actually works before you vigorously advocate a proposal for change.

NOTES

[1]*Fortune,* April 29, 1985, p. 284, and April 27, 1987; *Statistical Abstract of the United States, 1987.*

[2]Adolf A. Berle, Jr. and Gardiner C. Means, *The Modern Corporation and Private Property* (New York: Macmillan, 1933), p. 94.

[3]Wendell Gordon, *Institutional Economics* (Austin: University of Texas Press, 1980), ch. 13.

[4]Ibid., ch. 17.

[5]Ibid., p. 329.

[6]Wendell Gordon, *Economics from an Institutional Viewpoint* (Austin, Texas: University Stores, Inc., 1974), ch. 12, "The Handicapped. . . ."

[7]*The New York Times,* Sept. 23, 1986, National Edition, p. 31.

[8]Wendell Gordon, "International Price Relations," *Inter-American Economic Affairs* 29 (Spring, 1976), pp. 59-84.

[9]For a similar proposal see: Fred Schmidt, "Workers of the World . . . ," *The Texas Observer,* June 12, 1987, pp. 11-13.

[10]Wendell C. Gordon, *The Political Economy of Latin America* (New York: Columbia University Press, 1965), esp. ch. 1; Wendell Gordon, "The Implementation of Economic Development," *Journal of Economic Issues* XVIII (March 1984), pp. 295-313.

Part IV

The Larger Picture

Chapter XVI

The Larger Picture

Let us suppose the universe expands and contracts and then again expands and contracts.[1] In one phase it contracts into a super black hole which is fantastically concentrated and this black hole has such powerful attractive force that, while it is forming, light and everything else flows in but not out. Then, at some stage in the process of concentration, the universe has had enough and explodes far and fast. The concentrated mass of the black hole expands and disintegrates in the process, essentially evolving into nebulae and stars and planets circumnavigating the stars and vacationing tourists. Meanwhile everything, except possibly the center, whatever or wherever that is, is flying outward. When the universe has dispersed as far as it can or wants to, it may proceed to contract again back into the fantastically concentrated black hole. (As a by-product of this process, some minor black holes, such as seem to have been observed, may come and go along the way.)

It is well not to lose any sleep worrying about the question as to how or when this process got started. Or, if the process got started in the infinitely long ago, how did it ever find the time to get down to date?

At any rate, since here we are, the possibility exists that occasionally (maybe thousands of times in the course of one of the expansion phases) some one or another of the planets ellipsing around some one or another of the stars may generate life. In some of these instances the life thus generated may evolve into something capable of thinking and acting. And that planet is then participating in a process involving the evolution of the biology of the beings, the accumulation of knowledge by the beings, the institutionalization of behavior patterns, and the use of the available natural resources (neutral stuff), stuff that will be more or less useful depending on the current state of technical knowledge. The style of the culture at any given time is dependent on how these ingredients have interacted up to then, a healthy dosage of chance likely being involved in the process.

245

Such a society evolves from simple beginnings up to some level of competence in appreciating the nature of this (sociological) process, and its members may acquire some degree of awareness as to what is happening to them and to the universe. The beings' appreciation of all this evolves through a process of self-correcting value judgments. And they acquire some degree of ability to influence the process itself. They may even acquire the capability for traveling some distance through space to other planets where they may not be fried or frozen or, indeed, where they may be. They may even be able to tune in on societies even farther away.

Nevertheless, they are at the mercy of the great overriding physical phenomenon that is the expansion and contraction of the universe. At some point in the process the society is wiped out. Or it might wipe itself out before its time with some injudicious use of the technical knowledge it possesses. Some sorehead or some hero may outdo herself or himself or itself.

There is no Garden of Eden, no paradise, no utopia into which the beings of this society can settle in eternal bliss. (Or maybe there is, and what a bore that would be.) They perform upon the stage, make much or little of themselves along the way, and pass on back into the black hole from which they came. Yet along the way they exercise certain options, and they may themselves influence whether being is a more or less pleasant experience.

Or this may not be the way things are at all. Perhaps there is some supergod standing on a solid chunk of concrete somewhere, operating this expansion-contraction process like a yo-yo. The god may or may not care particularly about the beings that, along with their societies, appear and disappear in the process. The god may be an entity that exists in some meaningful sense or may merely be an intangible influence. It may have one hip pocket that it calls paradise where it can put the nice people and another one called hell, farmed out to the devil, to look after the other people. Or it may just let the beings disintegrate into dust which later collapses into the great primal black hole, which is where the yo-yo is on the extreme of the downswing. (In this case, one might ask, where did the supergod come from and where is it going, if anywhere.)

Reading Matthew Arnold's "Dover Beach" may or may not give one much comfort as one tries to think one's way through these cosmic possibilities.

In any event, the decision still rests with any one of these groups of beings, after it gets squared away with itself, to decide as to how it wants to exploit its allotted time, cussing each other out or trying to make the process a reasonably satisfactory experience while it lasts.

NOTE

[1]Owen Gringerich ed., *Cosmology + 1: Readings from "Scientific American"* (San Francisco: W. H. Freeman, 1977); Steven Weinberg, *The First Three Minutes* (New York: Basic Books, 1976).

Bibliography

Adams, John, ed. *Institutional Economics*. Boston: Martinus Nijhoff, 1980.

Allen, Francis R. *Social-Cultural Dynamics*. New York: Macmillan, 1971.

Averitt, Robert T. *The Dual Economy: The Dynamics of American Industry Structure*. New York: Norton, 1968.

Ayres, C. E. *The Industrial Economy*. Boston: Houghton-Mifflin, 1952.

Ayres, C. E. *The Theory of Economic Progress*. Chapel Hill: University of North Carolina Press, 1944.

Ayres, C. E. *Toward a Reasonable Society*. Austin: University of Texas Press, 1961.

Benedict, Ruth. *Patterns of Culture*. Boston: Houghton-Mifflin, 1934.

Boulding, Kenneth E. "Toward the Development of Cultural Economics," *Social Science Quarterly* 53 (September 1972), pp. 267-84.

Breit, William, and William Patton Culbertson, Jr. *Science and Ceremony: The Institutional Economics of C. E. Ayres*. Austin: University of Texas Press, 1976.

Brinkman, Richard L. *Cultural Economics*. Portland, Oregon: Hapi Press, 1981.

Chapin, F. Stuart. *Cultural Change*. New York: Century, 1928.

Commons, John R. *Institutional Economics*. 2 vols. Madison: University of Wisconsin Press, 1934.

Commons, John R. *Legal Foundations of Capitalism*. New York: Macmillan, 1924.

Copeland, Morris. *Fact and Theory in Economics: The Testament of an Institutionalist*. Ithaca: Cornell, 1958.

DeGregori, Thomas. *A Theory of Technology: Continuity and Change in Human Development*. Ames, Iowa: Iowa State University Press, 1985.

Dewey, John. *Intelligence in the Modern World: John Dewey's Philosophy*. New York: Modern Library, 1939.

Dewey, John. *The Quest for Certainty*. New York: Minton, Balch, 1929.

Dewey, John. *Reconstruction in Philosophy*. New York: Holt, 1920.

Dewey, John. *Studies in Logical Thinking.* Chicago: University of Chicago Press, 1903.

Dewey, John. *Theory of Valuation.* Chicago: University of Chicago Press, 1939.

Dorfman, Joseph, et al. *Institutional Economics.* Berkeley: University of California Press, 1963.

Dorfman, Joseph, *Thorstein Veblen and His America.* New York: Viking, 1934.

Dowd, Douglas F., ed. *Thorstein Veblen.* Ithaca: Cornell University Press, 1958.

Dugger, William. *An Alternative to Economic Retrenchment.* New York: Petrocelli Books, 1984.

Foster, J. Fagg. *The Papers of J. Fagg Foster.* A special issue of the *Journal of Economic Issues* XV (December 1981).

Galbraith, John Kenneth. *The Affluent Society.* Boston: Houghton Mifflin, 1958.

Galbraith, John Kenneth. *American Capitalism: The Concept of Countervailing Power.* Boston: Houghton Mifflin, 1952.

Gambs, John S. *Economics and Man.* Homewood, Ill.: Irwin, 1968.

Geiger, George R. *Philosophy and the Social Order.* Boston: Houghton Mifflin, 1947.

Gruchy, Allan G. *Contemporary Economic Thought.* Clifton, N.J.: Kelley, 1972.

Gruchy, Allan G. *Modern Economic Thought.* New York: Prentice-Hall, 1947.

Gruchy, Allan G. *The Reconstruction of Economics.* Westport, Conn.: Greenwood Press, 1987.

Hamilton, David. *Evolutionary Economics.* Albuquerque: University of New Mexico Press, 1970.

Hamilton, Walton H. *Industrial Policy and Institutionalism.* Edited by Joseph Dorfman. Clifton, N.J.: Kelley, 1974.

Hayden, F. Gregory. "Social Fabric Matrix," *Journal of Economic Issues* XVI (September 1982), pp. 637-62.

Journal of Economic Issues, Department of Economics, University of Nebraska, Lincoln.

Junker, Louis. "The Social and Economic Thought of Clarence Edwin Ayres." Unpublished Ph.D. dissertation, University of Wisconsin, 1962.

Klein, Philip A. *The Management of Market-Oriented Economies.* Belmont, Cal.: Wadsworth, 1973.

Mills, C. Wright. *The Sociological Imagination.* New York: Oxford, 1959.

Mitchell, Wesley C. *Lecture Notes on Types of Economic Theory from Mercantilism to Institutionalism.* 2 vols. New York: Kelley, 1949.

Munkirs, John R. *The Transformation of American Capitalism.* Armonk, New York: M.E. Sharpe, 1985.

Myrdal, Gunnar. *Against the Stream.* New York: Pantheon, 1973.

Ogburn, William T. *On Cultural and Social Change.* Chicago: University of Chicago Press, 1964.

Ogburn, William T. *Social Change with Respect to Culture and Original Nature.* New York: Huebsch, 1922.

Peterson, Wallace C. *Our Overloaded Economy.* Armonk, New York: M.E. Sharpe, 1982.

Polanyi, Karl. *The Great Transformation.* Boston: Beacon, 1957 (1944).

Robinson, Joan. *Economic Philosophy.* Chicago: Aldine, 1962.

Samuels, Warren J. *The Classical Theory of Economic Policy.* Cleveland: World Publishing, 1966.

Stanfield, J. Ron. *Economic Thought and Social Change.* Carbondale and Edwardsville, Ill.: Southern Illinois University Press, 1979.

Sumner, William Graham. *Folkways.* Boston: Ginn, 1906.

Tawney, Richard H. *Religion and the Rise of Capitalism.* London: Murray, 1926.

Thompson, Carey C., ed. *Institutional Adjustment.* Austin: University of Texas Press, 1967.

Tool, Marc R. *The Discretionary Economy.* Santa Monica: Goodyear, 1979.

Veblen, Thorstein. *Imperial Germany and the Industrial Revolution.* New York: Kelley, 1964[1915]).

Veblen, Thorstein. *Instinct of Workmanship.* New York: Kelley, 1964 [1914]).

Veblen, Thorstein. *Theory of Business Enterprise.* New York: Kelley, 1965 [1904]).

Veblen, Thorstein. *Theory of the Leisure Class.* New York: B. W. Huebsch, 1899.

Wallas, Graham. *Our Social Heritage.* London: Allen & Unwin, 1921.

Weber, Max. *The Protestant Ethic and the Spirit of Capitalism.* New York: Scribner, 1930 [1904]).

Wilber, Charles K., and K. P. Jameson. *An Inquiry into the Poverty of Economics.* Notre Dame, Ind.: University of Notre Dame Press, 1983.

Index

Abortion, 91
Accounting, 56
Advertising, ii, 5, 105-06, 108, 202
Aggression, 103-04
Agriculture, 10; and price supports, 17, 36, 197, 225, 235-36; sedentary, 42; and production controls, 221-22
Alienation, 21, 111
Alliance for Progress, 221
American Economic Association, 123
American Indians: and slavery, 42; and Christianity, 96
American Petroleum Institute, 212
American South: and slavery, 42; and desegregation, 48
American Sugar Refining Company, 43
American Telephone and Telegraph Company, Bell Laboratories, 64
American Tobacco Company, 43
Animal rights, 91
Aquinas, Thomas, 94
Argentina, and currency devaluation, 165
Aristotle, 167
Arms race, 239
Arnold, Matthew, 246
Arnold, Thurman, 5
Aronson, Elliot, 103
Arrow, Kenneth, 59-60, 63, 123, 132-33, 209-11, 222
Automobile industry, U.S., 18, 24, 45, 50
Ayres, Clarence, ii, 4-7, 9, 13, 72-75, 86, 89, 92-93, 95, 113, 158

Bacon, Francis, 69, 78
Bakewell, Robert, 10
Balance of trade, see International trade
Banking: and bankers, 198, 216; international, 200-01; and deregulation, 232
Barlett, Bruce, 169
Barnes, Harry Elmer, 60
Baumol, William, 123
Behavior modification, 105-08
Behavior norms, institutionalized, 17-20, 51-52
Behavior reinforcement, 153-56
Bell, Alexander Graham, 10
Benedict, Ruth, 96
Bentham, Jeremy, 122
Bergson, Abram, 123
Berkeley, Bishop, 75
Berkeley, George, 70
Berle, Adolf, 5
Bessemer, Henry, 12
Best-practice technique, 128
Bimetallism, 155
Biology: and psychology, 29-34; sociobiology, 32-33; biotechnology (or human engineering), 33-34, 49
Blaug, Mark, 123
Boas, Franz, 96
Bohr, Niels, 9-10
Boland, Lawrence, 77
Bolivia, and law of the sea, 205
Boole, George, 80

Boorstin, Daniel, 19
Boulding, Kenneth, 5, 136, 189, 198
Branson, William, 131
Braudel, Fernand, 64
Brazil, and currency devaluation, 165
Bridgman, P. W., 75
Brookings Institution, 5, 199
Budget, cyclically balanced, 235
Business, regulation of, 229-32
Business cycle: and Keynesian theory, 161; and the constancy assumption, 174-75; and Marxism, 177, 181, 190
Byzantium, 203

Cambridge, Mass., 123
Cantor, Georg, 80
Capitalism, 229; and resistance of institutions, 46; and the Industrial Revolution, 51; and the profit motive, 58, 230; and Marxism, 178-91, 213
Capital, 15, 56-57, 62-63, 129-31, 135, 162, 169, 176-86, 201, 215
Carnap, Rudolf, 73-74
Chamberlin, Edward H., 10, 150
Change, theory of, 3-4
Chapin, Francis Stuart, 47
Chernobyl, 45
Chicago Bureau of Trade, 236
Chicago economists, 75, 123, 155, 224
Chile: and currency devaluation, 165; and law of the sea, 205
China, 45, 63, 203
Choice, social, 209-20
Cicero, 94
Civilization, 24-27; and aggression, 103-04; and rebellion, 219
Clark, John Maurice, 5
Classical economics, 84-85, 177
Clements, 49
Club of Rome, 35-36
Cobweb theorem, 154-55
Coffee and Sugar Exchange, 236
Columbus, 42
Commons, John R., 5-6, 17
Communism, 22, 181, 188-89
Computer, effect on institutions, 42; and process, 91; programmer alienation, 111
Comte, Auguste, 71
Condorcet, 209-10
Congress, U.S., 51, 224; seniority system of, 210; and pressure groups, 235
Constructive self-expression, 109-112, 115, 138
Consumption, 135-36, 143, 161-64, 170-72, 174; conspicuous, 185
Copeland, Morris, 5
Copernicus, 9-10, 13
Corn Laws, 187, 204
Corporate executives: and the profit motive, 58-59; and inflation, 155; and leverage, 216; and white-collar crime, 231
Corporate takeover, 215, 230
Cost curves, 148-50

Crane, Stephen, 113
Creationism, 31-32
Crick, Francis Harry Compton, 10, 33, 105
Crime, 92, 106, 157
Cross-cultural values, 96-97
Cuba, revolutionary leaders in, 51
Cultural relativism, 96-97
Currency devaluation, 164-66

Danzinger, James N., 42
Darby, Abraham, 34
Darwin, 10, 32
David, Paul A., 62
Davy, Humphrey, 10
Day care, 233
DDT, 91, 156
Decent minimum standard of living, 102, 112-13, 115, 138
Decentralization, 217-18
Declaration of Independence, 94-95
Deductivism, see Popper
Democracy, 209-11, 218-20, 223, 239
Depression, 223
Descartes, 70, 78
Dewey, John, ii, 4-6, 49, 62, 72-75, 77, 83-84, 89, 108, 111, 219
Dictatorship, 215, 219-20, 223
Discretionary authority, 223-24
DNA, 10, 29, 33-34, 49, 105
Drug abuse, 90-91, 107, 156
Dynamism, 11-12

Econometric methods, 14, 35, 46-48, 137, 145, 159, 164, 168-76, 199-200, 217, 222, 233
Economic development, 59, 107, 133, 217-19, 225, 238-40
Edison, Thomas Alva, 10, 60
Education, 59, 106
Efficiency, 128
Einstein, Albert, 7, 9-11, 14, 74-75, 79
Eisenhower, Dwight, 48
El Salvador, 239
Elasticity: of supply and demand, 147-48, 156-57, 197-98; of demand for imports, 173-74
Eldridge, Niles, 32
Empiricism, 70-71
Enclosure movement, 203-04
Energy, 35-37
England: and the Luddite movement, 46; and Marxism, 183, 187; and the Industrial Revolution, 202-04
Enlightenment, 93
Entrepreneur, 35, 56-61, 90, 154
Equilibrium, i-ii, 64, 90-91, 136, 148-50, 153-56, 197; static, 3, 20, 159; punctuated, 32; general, 60-61, 121-139, 158, 210, 213
Eron, Leonard D., 104
Ervin Committee of the United States Senate, 196
Establishment, The, 24, 27, 104, 188, 213, 219
Europe: and the Holy Inquisition, 45; and labor-saving inventions, 63; imposing Christianity, 96; and the Industrial Revolution, 202-03
Evolutionary processes, 31-32
Export dumping, 187

Falsification, see Verification-falsification
Family: nuclear, 17; friction within, 26; and adjustment to technological change, 41-42; and the Industrial Revolution, 204
Farnsworth, 30
Federal Reserve, 223
Feigl, Herbert, 73-74
Fleming, Alexander, 12
Food and Drug Administration, 45
Ford Foundation, 64, 170
Forecasting, 46-51, 170
Foreign exchange markets, 237-38; and rational expectations, 168; and planning, 225
France, 203; and development, 48
Franklin, Benjamin, 11
Fraternities, college, 25
Freedom, 25-27, 158; of choice, 23; and the middle class, 43; and the role of government, 214
Freeman, Christopher, 60-61
Frenkel, Jacob, 168
Freud, Sigmund, 31, 103, 152
Friedmann, Wolfgang, 88-89
Friedman, Milton and Rose, 25; Milton, 75-77, 155, 167, 170, 175, 214, 224-25
Fromm, Erich, 103, 109-110
Full employment assumption, 124, 126, 144, 153

Galbraith, John Kenneth, 5, 150
Galileo, 9-10, 13, 78
General Electric, 56, 60
General Motors, 18
Genetic engineering, 10
Germany, 230
Gilder, George, 169
Goethe, 110
Goldsmith, Oliver, 204
Goodyear, Charles, 12
Gorbachev, Mikhail, 45
Gordon, R.A., 5
Gould, Stephen Jay, 32, 78
Government: role of, 102, 113, 128, 131, 158, 163, 167, 197, 204, 214, 217-26, 230, 232; spending, 161-64
Gray, Elisha, 10
Great Depression, 50, 161, 164, 238
Greek Stoics, 94
Grenada, 239
Grotius, Hugo, 94
Gruchy, Allan, 5-6
Guild system, 51, 204
Gutenberg, 9
Guttentag, Jack M., 200

Habakkuk, H. J., 62, 64
Hahn, Frank, 136
Hahn, Hans, 73-74
Hamilton, Walton, 5, 196
Harrod-Domar growth model, 240
Harvey, William, 9
Hayek, Friedrich von, 19-20, 60
Hegel, 110
Hero of Alexandria, 13
Herodotus, 19
Heroult, Paul Louis Toussaint, 34
Herring, Richard, 200
Herskovits, Melville, 96-97
Hicks, J. R., 62-63
Hierarchy, 216
Hitler, Adolf, 106
Hobbes, Thomas, 70, 122
Hobson, John, 185
Holy Inquisition, 45
Homeostasis, 153-56
Hudson Institute, 35
Human engineering, see biology
Hume, David, 70-71
Humphrey-Hawkins Act of 1978, 220

Iacocca, Lee, 50, 217
Imperialism, 185-87
Income distribution and redistribution, 49, 124, 126-31, 137, 163
India, 203
Indirect adaptation, 52
Industrial Revolution, 9, 13, 19, 35, 46, 51-52, 60, 63, 114, 202-05
Inflation, 21, 155, 163-64, 167, 185, 223, 225
Information, market for, 59
Innovation possibility frontier, 62-63
Innovation, 61-64, 215
Inquisition, 203-04
Instrumental value judgment, see Self-correcting value judgment
Instrumentalism, 72-77, 83
Insurance companies, 215-16
Interest rates, 56-57, 155, 183, 186
International trade, 164-66, 187, 197, 236-38
Invention, 12; process, 60-64; modifying institutions, 201-02
Investment, 49, 56, 161-64, 169-70, 186, 215, 217
Iran: revolutionary leaders in, 51; and hostages, 223; and Iran-Contra scandal, 223
Iron and Steel Institute, 212
Israel, 239
Italy, 203
Izmailvo, K., 186

Jaguaribe, Helio, 43-44
James, William, ii, 4-5, 72-73, 75, 90, 93, 96
Japan: and the automobile industry, 24; and the Meiji Restoration, 44; and sewing machine competition, 50; and capital-intensive industry, 51; and long-run perspective, 56; and capital accumulation, 185; and business, 230
Jenner, Edward, 9
Jevons, Stanley, 122
Jewkes, John, 49, 65
Jones, Reginald H., 56

Kaldor, 64
Kant, Immanuel, 94
Kay's flying shuttle, 64, 203
Kelvin, Lord, 78
Kemp, Jack, 169
Kennedy, Charles, 62-63
Kennedy, John, and the Alliance for Progress, 221
Keynesian economics, i, 161-67, 169, 174-75
Keynes, John Maynard, 19, 153, 175
Keynes, John Neville, 75
Klevorick, Alvin, 131
Knight, Frank, 57
Knowledge, cumulative, 3-4, 8-12, 78, 245
Koran, 203
Korman, Abraham, 111
Ku Klux Klan, 21-22, 24
Kuhn, Thomas, 14, 170

Labor, 14, 57, 62-63, 129-31, 176-191, 203-04; labor unions, 17, 21, 43, 52, 155, 181; theory of value, 85, 122, 179-185
Laffer, Arthur, 169
Laissez faire, 41, 77, 143, 150, 181, 204, 224
Lamb, Charles, 8, 12
Landes, David S., 48, 62
LaPiere, 30
Latin America, 44; and positivism, 71; and capital accumulation, 185
Law: Locke's three types, 22-23; natural, 93-95; and behavior norms, 114-16; and Marxism, 178
Lebanon, 239
Leibniz, Baron, 10, 70
Lenin, V. I., 50, 185-86
Leontief, Wassily, 199
Leverage, 214-17
Libertarians, 25
Libya, revolutionary leaders in, 51
Lichty, 12
Liebhafsky, H. H., 159
Liebig, Justus, 10
Ligachev, Yegor K., 45-46
Litigation: and innovation, 45; and medical malpractice, 91
Locke, John, 21-23, 70, 94, 122
Lohr, Steve, 56
Lorenz, Konrad, 31
Lucas, Robert E., 168
Luther, Martin, 45

Maccoby, Michael, 58-59
Mach, Ernst, 75
Macroeconomics, 3, 161-76
Magna Carta, 203
Malpighi, Marcello, 9
Malthus, Thomas, 32
Marshall, Alfred, 122, 153, 159
Marxism, i, ii, 3, 56, 61, 84-85, 131, 177-91, 213, 215, 218
Marx, Karl, 25-26, 31, 110-11, 122
Maslow, Abraham H., 31, 103, 109, 112-13
Mathematics, see Econometric methods
McClelland, David, 107
McDougall, William, 30-31
Meade, J. E., 154
Mead, Margaret, 96, 198
Means, Gardiner C., 5
Mercantilism, 122
Metric system, 23, 45
Mexico, and middlemen, 216
Mexico City, 156
Microeconomics, 3, 137-39, 143-59
Middle class, 43, 185, 188
Middlemen, 216
Military expenditure, 109-10, 156, 182, 239
Mills, C. Wright, 5, 23, 43
Mill, John Stuart, 122
Milward, Alan, 63
Mises, Ludwig von, 19-20, 60, 136-37
Mitchell, Wesley C., 5
Monetarism, 167, 174
Monopolistic competition, 57, 150-51, 214
Monopoly, 57, 143, 150-51
Moral Majority, 21, 25
Morality, 95-96; of price theory, 157
More, Thomas, 3
Morgan, J. Pierpont, 60
Muller, Herman, 33, 105
Mussa, Michael, 168
Muth, John F., 167-68
Myrdal, Gunnar, 5, 50

NASA, 64
National Association for the Advancement of Colored People, 219
National Association of Manufacturers, 212
National Bureau of Economic Research, 199, 224
National Institute of Occupational Safety and Health, 111
National Science Foundation, 64, 170
Nationalism, 218-19
Neoclassical economics, 61, 122-23, 138, 144, 201
Neoinstitutionalism, 5
Neutral stuff, 34-37, 88, 203
Newton, Isaac, 9-11, 14, 70, 74-75, 78, 203
Nicaragua: revolutionary leaders in, 51; U.S. intervention in, 239
Nixon, Richard, 21
Normative economics, 4-5, 87, 95
Northern Ireland, revolutionary leaders in, 51
Nourse, Edwin G., 5

Ogburn, William, 41-42, 52
Oil industry, 18, 196-97, 221
Oligopoly, 57, 143, 150-51, 212, 214
OPEC, 196
Orthodox economics, i, ii, 3-5, 7, 12, 20, 46-47, 55, 77, 123, 143, 157, 177, 213
Osmosis, as decision-making process, 211-12

Paine, Tom, 94
Paley Report, 35
Panama, 239
Pareto optimality, 130, 136, 138
Pareto, Vilfredo, 122-23, 128
Pasteur, Louis, 9
Patent and Trademark Office, U.S., 10
Patriotism, 58
Peace Corps, 110
Peirce, Charles Sanders, ii, 4-5, 72-73, 75
Perkins, William Henry, 12
Persian Gulf, 239
Phelps, Edmund, 136
Philippines, 239
Planning, 34, 37, 46, 106, 170, 220-26
Platt, John, 155
Poincare, 75
Policy and policymaking, 131, 133, 161, 163-64, 167, 190, 196, 209-26
Pollution, 97
Pope, Alexander, 48
Popper, Karl, 74-77, 83
Population, control, 37; adjustment to growth, 41-42; and homeostasis, 154
Positive economics, ii, 4-5, 75-77
Positivism, 71; logical, 73-74
Power, 214-17
Pragmatism, 72-73
Prakken, Joel L., 128
President's Council of Economic Advisers, 164, 220
Pressure groups, 212-13, 235
Price theory, 157-59
Private property, and Marxism, 178-179, 187
Profit motive, ii, 6-8, 10-12, 27, 55-61, 151-53, 196, 204, 211, 230
Prohibition, 88
Protestant Reformation, 203
Psychology: defensibility, 20-21; and biology, 29-34; and aggression, 103-04; and behavior modification, 105-08; and needs, 112-13; versus orthodox economics, 138-39; and homeostasis, 154
Public finance, 233-35
Pure competition, 57, 59, 76, 95, 121-128, 143-50, 154, 158-59, 161, 177, 213-14, 224

Quantity theory of money, 155, 167

Racism: and E. O. Wilson, 33; and segregation, 47-48; modifying, 108
Railroads, 63, 155
Ramsey, Frank, 133, 136
Rand, Ayn, 50, 177, 217
Rational expectations, 167-69, 174
Rationality, 27, 60-61, 93-94, 137, 153-54, 156
Rawls, John, 94
Reaganomics, 169
Reagan, Ronald: and taxes, 49; and conservative attitudes, 101-102; and law of the sea, 205
Reference groups, 28
Reformation, 45
Religion: as source of values, 93; and freedom of worship, 94; imposition of, 96; and Marxism, 178
Research, 13, 60, 195-206; planned, 64-65; cancer, 64-65, 70

Resistance of institutions, 45-51
Resources, 4, 34-37, 245; allocation of, 124-26; and consumer and producer surplus, 131; and the Industrial Revolution, 203; and sea mining, 205; and decision making, 211-12
Revealed preference, 23, 123
Revolution, 46, 51, 181-82, 189-90, 218-20, 239
Ricardo, David, 122, 177, 179, 204
Richta, Radovan, 180-81
Right to Life groups, 25
Risk, 57
Roberts, Paul Craig, 169
Robert's Rules of Order, 210
Robinson, Joan, 10, 150
Roman Empire: Eastern, 45; and labor-saving inventions, 63; and England, 203
Roosevelt, Franklin, 161
Rosenberg, Nathan, 62
Rotary Club, 23
Rothbarth, 64
Rousseau, 94

Sabin, Albert Bruce, 9
Salam, Abdus, 79
Salk, Jonas, 9
Sampson, Anthony, 196
Samuelson, Paul, 61, 63, 123
Sargent, Thomas J., 168
Saving, 135, 143, 161-64, 169, 215; and the Industrial Revolution, 204
Schlick, Moritz, 73-74
Schrodinger, 75
Schumpeter, Joseph, 15, 57, 61-62, 215
Science: versus technology, 7; chemistry, 12; philosophy of 69-82; methodology of, 77-79; and behavior modification, 105
Scotland: and capital accumulation, 185; and the Industrial Revolution, 202-03
Security, 111-12, 115, 138
Selfishness: in the Reagan-Thatcher era, 101; and orthodox price theory, 157; and social choice, 213
Self-correcting value judgments, 86-92, 96-98, 101-02, 106-08, 139, 209, 211-12, 214, 222, 224, 226, 241, 246
Service, 110
Sherif, Muzafer and Carolyn, 28; Muzafer, 30, 108
Sierra Club, 202
Singer Sewing Machine Company, 50
Skinner, B. F., 31, 105-07
Slavery, 42
Smith, Adam, 95, 122, 236
Socialism, 51, 181, 189, 216, 240
Sociobiology, see Biology
South Africa, 239
Southern Christian Leadership Council, 219
Soviet Union: and glasnost, 45-46; and Lenin, 50; and capital-intensive industry, 51; and Marxism, 182; and planning, 222; and U.S. intervention, 239
Spain, 203
Spencer, Herbert, 122
Spinoza, 70, 110
Statistics, see Econometric methods
Steel industry, U.S., 18, 45-46, 59, 198
Steffens, Lincoln, 196
Stockholders, 58, 230-31
Stocking, George, 196
Stress, 111
Suburbs, and the suburban shopping center, 42, 202
Sumner, William Graham, 18
Supply-side economics, 169, 174
Surplus, producer and consumer, 131-33, 158
Sutton, Robert, 9
Swift and Company, 43
Switzerland, and law of the sea, 205

Tarbell, Ida, 196
Tariffs, 225; and international dumping, 237
Taxation, 49, 94, 102, 109, 112, 233-36; and supply-side economics, 169
Technicians, see Technocrats
Technocrats, 43-44
Technological determinism, 51
Technology: versus science, 7; accumulation of, 8-13, 32, 88, 180; classification of 14-15; and ceremonialism, 25; Marx's technology-institutions dichotomy, 179; Interrelation with institutions, 201-05; and economic development, 240
Terrorism, 104-05, 215
Tesla, Nikola, 60
Texas Railroad Commission, 221
Textiles, 63-64, 203
Thatcher, Margaret, 101
Tinbergen, Jan, 222
Tool, Marc, 5, 92
Townshend, Charles, 10
Tugwell, Rexford Guy, 5
Tull, Jethro, 10

Uncertainty, see Risk
Unemployment: worker fear of, 63; insurance, 70; and job guarantee, 50, 70, 102, 111, 223, 232-33; and Keynesian theory, 163-64; natural rate of, 168; and Marxism, 181-82, 185, 190; and planning, 220
United Nations, 109, 217-19, 231, 238-39
University of Texas Board of Regents, 23
Usher, Abbott Payson, 9
Utilitarianism, 122

Vaccination, 9, 62
Valuation, theory of, 3-4
Values, currently held, 101-16, 138
Veblen, Thorstein, 5-6, 11-12, 24-25, 30-31, 44, 103-04, 109, 112, 158, 179
Verification-falsification, 73-75, 77, 79
Vienna Circle, 73-74, 76
Vietnam War, 90, 108, 239
Violence, 46, 219
Voting, inconsistent choices in, 209-211; who can, 211

Wages, 57, 63-64, 129-31, 155, 181, 186, 213; and international dumping, 237
Wallace, Alfred, Russel, 10, 32
Wallace, George, 47
War of the Pacific, 205
Washington, George, 218
Watergate scandals, 21, 90, 196
Watkins, Myron, 196
Watson, James D., 10, 33, 105
Watson, J. B., 31
Watt, James, 9, 203
Wealth, 122-23, 166, 234
Weinberg, Steven, 79
Welch, Louie, 217
Welfare economics, 121-39, 158, 167, 214
Weydemeyer, 182
White, Lynn, Jr., 43
White-collar workers, 43, 111; and crime, 231
Whitney, Eli, 42
Wilderness Society, 202
Williamson, Oliver, 5
Williams, Harvey, 152
Wilson, Edward O., 32-33
Wittgenstein, Ludwig, 73-74
Women: adaptation to technological change, 52; and the women's liberation movement, 104; and day care, 233
Wordsworth, William, 108
Workmanship, 30-31, 109, 112

Zimmermann, Erich, 34